Darwin, and After Darwin

Volume II

Post-Darwinian Questions: Heredity and Utility

George John Romanes

Alpha Editions

This edition published in 2021

ISBN : 9789354547577

Design and Setting By
Alpha Editions
www.alphaedis.com
Email - info@alphaedis.com

Contents

PREFACE   - 1 -

NOTE   - 2 -

CHAPTER   - 3 -

SECTION I HEREDITY   - 24 -

CHAPTER II   - 25 -

CHAPTER III   - 36 -

(A.) Indirect Evidence in favour of the
Inheritance of Acquired Characters.   - 36 -

(B.) Inherited Effects of Use and of Disuse.   - 55 -

CHAPTER IV   - 59 -

(C.) Experimental Evidence in favour of
the Inheritance of Acquired Characters.   - 59 -

CHAPTER V   - 77 -

(A. and B.) Direct and Indirect Evidence in favour
of the Non-inheritance of Acquired Characters[81].   - 77 -

(C.) Experimental Evidence as to the
Non-inheritance of Acquired Characters.   - 82 -

CHAPTER VI   - 87 -

SECTION II UTILITY   - 91 -

CHAPTER VII.   - 93 -

CHAPTER VIII   - 116 -

I. Climate.   - 117 -

II. Food.   - 127 -

III. Sexual Selection.   - 129 -

IV. Isolation.   - 132 -

V. Laws of Growth.   - 133 -

CHAPTER IX   - 134 -

(A.)   - 140 -

(B.)   - 142 -

(C.)   - 147 -

CHAPTER X   - 149 -

Summary.   - 163 -

APPENDICES AND NOTES   - 171 -

APPENDIX I ON PANMIXIA.   - 172 -

PREFACE

As its sub-title announces, the present volume is mainly devoted to a consideration of those Post-Darwinian Theories which involve fundamental questions of Heredity and Utility.

As regards Heredity, I have restricted the discussion almost exclusively to Professor Weismann's views, partly because he is at present by far the most important writer upon this subject, and partly because his views with regard to it raise with most distinctness the issue which lies at the base of all Post-Darwinian speculation touching this subject—the issue as to the inheritance or non-inheritance of acquired characters.

My examination of the Utility question may well seem to the general reader needlessly elaborate; for to such a reader it can scarcely fail to appear that the doctrine which I am assailing has been broken to fragments long before the criticism has drawn to a close. But from my previous experience of the hardness with which this fallacious doctrine dies, I do not deem it safe to allow even one fragment of it to remain, lest, hydra-like, it should re-develop into[Pg vi] its former proportions. And I can scarcely think that naturalists who know the growing prevalence of the doctrine, and who may have followed the issues of previous discussions with regard to it, will accuse me of being more over-zealous in my attempt to make a full end thereof.

One more remark. It is a misfortune attending the aim and scope of Part II that they bring me into frequent discord with one or other of the most eminent of Post-Darwinian writers—especially with Mr. Wallace. But such is the case only because the subject-matter of this volume is avowedly restricted to debateable topics, and because I choose those naturalists who are deservedly held in most esteem to act spokesmen on behalf of such Post-Darwinian views as appear to me doubtful or erroneous. Obviously, however, differences of opinion on particular points ought not to be taken as implying any failure on my part to recognize the general scientific authority of these men, or any inability to appreciate their labours in the varied fields of Biology.

G. J. R.

NOTE

Some time before his death Mr. Romanes decided to publish those sections of his work which deal with Heredity and Utility, as a separate volume, leaving Isolation and Physiological Selection for the third and concluding part of *Darwin, and after Darwin.*

Most of the matter contained in this part was already in type, but was not finally corrected for the press. The alterations made therein are for the most part verbal.

Chapter IV was type-written; in it, too, no alterations of any moment have been made.

For Chapters V and VI there were notes and isolated paragraphs not yet arranged. I had promised during his life to write for Mr. Romanes Chapter V on the basis of these notes, extending it in such ways as seemed to be desirable. In that case it would have been revised and amended by the author and received his final sanction. Death annulled this friendly compact; and since, had I written the chapter myself, it could not receive that imprimatur which would have given its chief value, I have decided[Pg viii] to arrange the material that passed into my hands without adding anything of importance thereto. The substance of Chapters V and VI is therefore entirely the author's: even the phraseology is his; the arrangement only is by another hand.

Such parts of the Preface as more particularly refer to Isolation and Physiological Selection are reserved for publication in Part III. A year or more must elapse before that part will be ready for publication.

Mr. F. Howard Collins has, as a kindly tribute to the memory of the author, read through the proofs. Messrs. F. Darwin, F. Galton, H. Seebohm, and others, have rendered incidental assistance. After much search I am unable to give the references to one or two passages.

I have allowed a too flattering reference to myself to stand, in accordance with a particular injunction of Mr. Romanes given shortly before that sad day on which he died, leaving many to mourn the loss of a personal friend most bright, lovable, and generous-hearted, and thousands to regret that the hand which had written so much for them would write for them no more.

C. Ll M.

University College, Bristo

CHAPTER I

Introductory: The Darwinism of Darwin, and of the Post-Darwinian Schools.

It is desirable to open this volume of the treatise on *Darwin and after Darwin* by taking a brief survey of the general theory of descent, first, as this was held by Darwin himself, and next, as it is now held by the several divergent schools of thought which have arisen since Darwin's death.

The most important of the questions in debate is one which I have already had occasion to mention, while dealing, in historical order, with the objections that were brought against the theory of natural selection during the life-time of Darwin[1]. Here, however, we must consider it somewhat more in detail, and justify by quotation what was previously said regarding the very definite nature of his utterances upon the matter. This question is whether natural selection has been the sole, or but the main, cause of organic evolution.

Must we regard survival of the fittest as the one and only principle which has been concerned in the progressive modification of living forms, or are we to suppose that this great and leading principle has been assisted by other and subordinate principles, without the co-operation of which the results, as presented in the animal and vegetable kingdoms, could not have been effected? Now Darwin's answer to this question was distinct and unequivocal. He stoutly resisted the doctrine that natural selection was to be regarded as the only cause of organic evolution. On the other hand, this opinion was—and still continues to be—persistently maintained by Mr. Wallace; and it constitutes the source of all the differences between his views and those of Darwin. Moreover, up to the time of Darwin's death, Mr. Wallace was absolutely alone in maintaining this opinion: the whole body of scientific thought throughout the world being against him; for it was deemed improbable that, in the enormously complex and endlessly varied processes of organic evolution, only a single principle should be everywhere and exclusively concerned[2]. But since Darwin's death there has been a great revolution of biological thought in favour of Mr. Wallace's opinion. And the reason for this revolution has been, that his doctrine of natural selection as the sole cause of organic evolution has received the corroborative support of Professor Weismann's theory of heredity—which has been more or less cordially embraced by a certain section of evolutionists, and which appears to carry the doctrine in question as a logical corollary, so far, at all events, as adaptive structures are concerned.

Now in this opening chapter we shall have to do merely with a setting forth of Darwin's opinion: we are not considering how far that opinion ought to be regarded as having been in any measure displaced by the results of more recent progress. Such, then, being the only matter which here concerns us, I will supply a few brief quotations, to show how unequivocally Darwin has stated his views. First, we may take what he says upon the "Lamarckian factors[3];" and next we may consider what he says with regard to other factors, or, in general, upon natural selection not being the sole cause of organic evolution.

> "Changed habits produce an inherited effect, as in the period of the flowering of plants when transported from one climate to another. With animals the increased use or disuse of parts has had a more marked influence[4]."

> "There can be no doubt, from the facts given in this chapter, that extremely slight changes in the conditions of life sometimes, probably often, act in a definite manner on our domesticated productions; and, as the action of changed conditions in causing indefinite variability is accumulative, so it may be with their definite action. Hence considerable and definite modifications of structure probably follow from altered conditions acting during long series of generations[5]."

> "How, again, can we explain the inherited effects of the use and disuse of particular organs? The domesticated duck flies less and walks more than the wild duck, and its limb bones have become diminished and increased in a corresponding manner in comparison with those of the wild duck. A horse is trained to certain paces, and the colt inherits similar consensual movements. The domesticated rabbit becomes tame from close confinement; the dog, intelligent from associating with man; the retriever is taught to fetch and carry; and these mental endowments and bodily powers are all inherited. Nothing in the whole circuit of physiology is more wonderful. How can the use or disuse of a particular limb or of the brain affect a small aggregate of reproductive cells, seated in a distant part of the body, in such a manner that the being developed from these cells inherits the characters of either one or both parents?... In the chapters devoted to inheritance, it was shown that a multitude of newly acquired characters, whether injurious or beneficial, whether of the lowest or

highest vital importance, are often faithfully transmitted[6]."

"When discussing special cases, Mr. Mivart passes over the effects of the increased use and disuse of parts, which I have always maintained to be highly important, and have treated in my 'Variation under Domestication' at greater length than, as I believe, any other writer[7]."

So much for the matured opinion of Darwin touching the validity of the theory of use-inheritance. Turning now to his opinion on the question whether or not there are yet any further factors concerned in the process of organic evolution, I think it will be sufficient to quote a single passage from the *Origin of Species*. The first paragraph of the "Conclusion" is devoted to a *résumé* of his views upon this matter, and consists of the following most emphatic words.

"I have now recapitulated the facts and considerations which have thoroughly convinced me that species have been modified, during a long course of descent. This has been effected chiefly through the natural selection of numerous successive, slight, favourable variations; aided in an important manner by the inherited effects of the use and disuse of parts; and in an unimportant manner, that is in relation to adaptive structures, whether past or present, by the direct action of external conditions, and by variations which seem to us in our ignorance to arise spontaneously. It appears that I formerly underrated the frequency and value of these latter forms of variation, as leading to permanent modifications of structure independently of natural selection. But as my conclusions have lately been much misrepresented, and it has been stated that I attribute the modification of species exclusively to natural selection, I may be permitted to remark that in the first edition of this work, and subsequently, I placed in a most conspicuous position— namely, at the close of the Introduction—the following words: 'I am convinced that natural selection has been the main, but not the exclusive means of modification.' This has been of no avail. Great is the power of steady misrepresentation; but the history of science shows that fortunately this power does not long endure."

In the whole range of Darwin's writings there cannot be found a passage so strongly worded as this: it presents the only note of bitterness in all the thousands of pages which he has published. Therefore I do not think it is necessary to supply any further quotations for the purpose of proving the state of his opinion upon the point in question. But, be it carefully noted, from this great or radical difference of opinion between the joint originators of the theory of natural selection, all their other differences of opinion arise; and seeing that since the death of Darwin a large number of naturalists have gone over to the side of Wallace, it seems desirable here to state categorically what these other or sequent points of difference are. Without at present discussing them, therefore, I will merely set them out in a tabular form, in order that a clear perception may be gained of their logical connexion with this primary point of difference.

The Theory of Natural Selection according to Darwin.	The theory of Natural Selection according to Wallace.
Natural Selection has been the main means of modification, not excepting the case of Man.	Natural Selection has been the sole means of modification, excepting in the case of Man.
(*a*) Therefore it is a question of evidence whether the Lamarckian factors have co-operated.	(*a*) Therefore it is antecedently impossible that the Lamarckian factors can have co-operated.
(*b*) Neither all species, nor, *a fortiori*, all specific characters, have been due to natural selection.	(*b*) Not only all species, but all specific characters, must necessarily have been due to natural selection.
(*c*) Thus the principle of Utility is not of universal application, even where species are concerned.	(*c*) Thus the principle of Utility must necessarily be of universal application, where species are concerned.
(*d*) Thus, also, the suggestion as to Sexual Selection, or any other supplementary cause of modification, may be entertained; and, as in the case of the Lamarckian factors, it is a question of evidence whether, or how far, they have co-operated.	(*d*) Thus, also, the suggestion as to Sexual Selection, or of any other supplementary cause of modification, must be ruled out; and, as in the case of the Lamarckian factors, their co-operation deemed impossible.
(*e*) No detriment arises to the theory of natural selection as a theory of the origin of species by entertaining the possibility, or the probability, of supplementary factors.	(*e*) The possibility—and, *a fortiori* the probability—of any supplementary factors cannot be entertained without serious detriment to the theory of natural selection, as a theory of the origin of species.
(*f*) Cross-sterility in species cannot possibly be due to natural selection.	(*f*) Cross-sterility in species is probably due to natural selection[8].

As it will be my endeavour in the ensuing chapters to consider the rights and the wrongs of these antithetical propositions, I may reserve further quotations from Darwin's works, which will show that the above is a correct epitome of his views as contrasted with those of Wallace and the Neo-Darwinian school of Weismann. But here, where the object is merely a statement of Darwin's theory touching the points in which it differs from those of Wallace and Weismann, it will be sufficient to set forth these points of difference in another and somewhat fuller form. So far then as we are at present concerned, the following are the matters of doctrine which have been clearly, emphatically, repeatedly, and uniformly expressed throughout the whole range of Darwin's writings.

1. That natural selection has been the main means of modification.

2. That, nevertheless, it has not been the only means; but has been supplemented or assisted by the co-operation of other causes.

3. That the most "important" of these other causes has been the inheritance of functionally-produced modifications (use-inheritance); but this only because the transmission of such modifications to progeny must always have had immediate reference to *adaptive* ends, as distinguished from merely useless change.

4. That there are sundry other causes which lead to merely useless change—in particular, "the direct action of external conditions, and variations which seem to us in our ignorance to arise spontaneously."

5. Hence, that the "principle of utility," far from being of universal occurrence in the sphere of animate nature, is only of what may be termed highly general occurrence; and, therefore, that certain other advocates of the theory of natural selection were mistaken in representing the universality of this principle as following by way of necessary consequence from that theory.

6. Cross-sterility in species cannot possibly be due to natural selection; but everywhere arises as a result of some physiological change having exclusive reference to the sexual system—a change which is probably everywhere due to the same cause, although what this cause could be Darwin was confessedly unable to suggest.

Such, then, was the theory of evolution as held by Darwin, so far as the points at present before us are concerned. And, it may now be added, that the longer he lived, and the more he pondered these points, the less exclusive was the *rôle* which he assigned to natural selection, and the more importance did he attribute to the supplementary factors above named. This admits of being easily demonstrated by comparing successive editions of his works; a method adopted by Mr. Herbert Spencer in his essay on the *Factors of Organic Evolution.*

My object in thus clearly defining Darwin's attitude regarding these sundry points is twofold.

In the first place, with regard to merely historical accuracy, it appears to me undesirable that naturalists should endeavour to hide certain parts of Darwin's teaching, and give undue prominence to others. In the second place, it appears to me still more undesirable that this should be done—as it usually is done—for the purpose of making it appear that Darwin's teaching did not really differ very much from that of Wallace and Weismann on the important points in question. I myself believe that Darwin's judgement with regard to all these points will eventually prove more sound and accurate than that of any of the recent would-be improvers upon his system; but even apart from this opinion of my own it is undesirable that Darwin's views should be misrepresented, whether the misrepresentation be due to any unfavourable bias against one side of his teaching, or to sheer carelessness in the reading of his books. Yet the new school of evolutionists, to which allusion has now so frequently been made, speak of their own modifications of Darwin's teaching as "pure Darwinism," in contradistinction to what they call "Lamarckism." In other words, they represent the principles of "Darwinism" as standing in some kind of opposition to those of "Lamarckism": the Darwinian principle of natural selection, they think, is in itself enough to account for all the facts of adaptation in organic nature. Therefore they are eager to dispense with the Lamarckian principle of the inherited effects of use and disuse, together with the direct influence of external conditions of life, and all or any other causes of modification which either have been, or in the future may possibly be, suggested. Now, of course, there is no reason why any one should not hold these or any other opinions to which his own independent study of natural science may lead him; but it appears to me that there is the very strongest reason why any one who deviates from the carefully formed opinions of such a man as Darwin, should above all things be careful to be absolutely fair in his representations of them; he should be scrupulously jealous, so to speak, of not letting it appear that he is unjustifiably throwing over his own opinions the authority of Darwin's name.

But in the present case, as we have seen, not only do the Neo-Darwinians strain the teachings of Darwin; they positively reverse those teachings—representing as anti-Darwinian the whole of one side of Darwin's system, and calling those who continue to accept that system in its entirety by the name "Lamarckians." I know it is sometimes said by members of this school, that in his utilization of Lamarckian principles as accessory to his own, Darwin was actuated by motives of "generosity." But a more preposterous suggestion could not well be made. We may fearlessly challenge any one who speaks or writes in such a way, to show any other instance where Darwin's great generosity of disposition had the effect of influencing by one hair's breadth his still greater loyalty to truth. Moreover, and with special regard to this particular case, I would point out that in no one of his many allusions to, and often lengthy discussions of, these so-called Lamarckian principles, does he ever once introduce the name of Lamarck; while, on the other hand, in the only places where he does so—whether in his books or in his now published letters—he does so in order to express an almost contemptuous dissatisfaction, and a total absence of obligation. Hence, having regard to the "generosity" with which he always acknowledged obligations, there can be no reasonable doubt that Darwin was not in the smallest degree influenced by the speculative writings of Lamarck; or that, even if Lamarck had never lived, the *Origin of Species* would have differed in any single particular from the form in which it now stands. Finally, it must not be forgotten that Darwin's acceptance of the theory of use-inheritance was vitally essential to his theory of Pangenesis—that "beloved child" over which he had "thought so much as to have lost all power of judging it[9]."

What has just been said touching the relations between Darwin's theory and that of Lamarck, applies with equal force to the relations between Darwin's theory and any other theory appertaining to evolution which has already been, or may hereafter be propounded. Yet so greatly have some of the Neo-Darwinians misunderstood the teachings of Darwin, that they represent as "Darwinian heresy" any suggestions in the way of factors "supplementary to," or "co-operative with" natural selection. Of course, if these naturalists were to avow themselves followers of Wallace, instead of followers of Darwin, they would be perfectly justified in repudiating any such suggestions as, *ipso facto* heretical. But, as we have now seen, through all his life Darwin differed from Wallace with regard to this very point; and therefore, unlike Wallace, he was always ready to entertain "additional suggestions" regarding the causes of organic evolution—several of which, indeed, he himself supplied. Hence we arrive at this curious state of matters. Those biologists who of late years have been led by Weismann to adopt the opinions of Wallace, represent as anti-Darwinian the opinions of other biologists who still adhere to the unadulterated doctrines of Darwin. Weismann's *Essays on Heredity* (which argue that natural selection is the only possible cause of adaptive modification) and Wallace's work on *Darwinism* (which in all the respects where any charge of "heresy" is concerned directly contradicts the doctrine of Darwin)—these are the writings which are now habitually represented by the Neo-Darwinians as setting forth the views of Darwin in their "pure" form. The result is that, both in conversation and in the press, we habitually meet with complete inversions of the truth, which show the state of confusion into which a very simple matter has been wrought by the eagerness of certain naturalists to identify the views of Darwin with those of Wallace and Weismann. But we may easily escape this confusion, if we remember that wherever in the writings of these naturalists there occur such phrases as "pure Darwinism" we are to understand pure *Wallaceism*, or the pure theory of natural selection to the exclusion of any supplementary theory. Therefore it is that for the sake of clearness I coined, several years ago, the terms "Neo-Darwinian" and "Ultra-Darwinian" whereby to designate the school in question.

So much, then, for the Darwinism of Darwin, as contrasted with the Darwinism of Wallace, or, what is the same thing, of the Neo-Darwinian school of Weismann. Next we may turn, by way of antithesis, to the so-called "Neo-Lamarckian" school of the United States. For, by a curious irony of fate, while the Neo-Darwinian school is in Europe seeking to out-Darwin Darwin by assigning an exclusive prerogative to natural selection in both kingdoms of animate nature, the Neo-Lamarckian school is in America endeavouring to reform Darwinism in precisely the opposite direction—viz. by transferring the sovereignty from natural selection to the principles of Lamarck. Without denying to natural selection a more or less important part in the process of organic evolution, members of this school believe that much greater importance ought to be assigned to the inherited effects of use and disuse than was assigned to these agencies by Darwin. Perhaps this noteworthy state of affairs, within a decade of Darwin's death, may lead us to anticipate that his judgement—standing, as it does, between these two extremes—will eventually prove the most accurate of all, with respect to the relative importance of these factors of evolution. But, be this as it may, I must now offer a few remarks upon the present position of the matter.

In the first place, to any one who (with Darwin and against Weismann) admits not only the abstract possibility, but an actual working, of the Lamarckian factors, it becomes difficult to determine, even approximately, the degrees of value which ought to be ascribed to them and to natural selection respectively. For, since the results are in both cases identical in kind (as, adaptive changes of organic types), where both sets of causes are supposed to be in operation together, we have no means of estimating the relative shares which they have had in bringing about these results. Of course there are large numbers of cases where it cannot possibly be supposed that the Lamarckian factors have taken any part at all in producing the observed effects; and therefore in such cases there is almost full agreement among evolutionists in theoretically ascribing such effects to the exclusive agency of natural selection. Of such, for instance, are the facts of protective colouring, of mimicry, of the growth of parts which, although *useful*, are never *active* (e.g. shells of mollusks, hard coverings of seeds), and so on. But in the majority of cases where adaptive structures are concerned, there is no means of discriminating between the influences of the Lamarckian and the Darwinian factors. Consequently, if by the Neo-Lamarckian school we understand all those naturalists who assign any higher importance to the Lamarckian factors than was assigned to them by Darwin, we may observe that members of this school differ very greatly among themselves as to the degree of importance that ought to be assigned. On the one hand we have, in Europe, Giard, Perrier, and Eimer, who stand nearer to Darwin than do a number of the American representatives—of whom the most prominent are Cope, Osborn, Packard, Hyatt, Brooks, Ryder, and Dall. The most extreme of these is Professor Cope, whose collection of essays entitled *The Origin of the Fittest*, as well as his more recent and elaborate monograph on *The Development of the Hard Parts of the Mammalia*, represent what appears even to some other members of his school an extravagant estimate of the importance of Lamarckian principles.

But the most novel, and in many respects the most remarkable school of what may be termed Anti-selectionists is one which is now (1894) rapidly increasing both in numbers and in weight, not only in the New World, but also in Germany, and to a lesser extent, in Great Britain.

This school, without being either Lamarckian or Darwinian (for its individual members differ widely from one another in these respects) maintains a principle which it deems of more importance than either use-inheritance or natural selection. This principle it calls Self-adaptation. It is chiefly botanists who constitute this school, and its principal representatives, in regard to authority, are Sachs, Pfeffer and Henslow.

Apart from topics which are to be dealt with in subsequent chapters, the only matters of much importance which have been raised in the Post-Darwinian period are those presented by the theories of Geddes, Cope, Hyatt, and others, and certain more or less novel ideas set forth in Wallace's *Darwinism*.

Mr. Geddes has propounded a new theory of the origin of species, which in his judgement supersedes to a large extent the theory of natural selection. He has also, in conjunction with Mr. Thomson, propounded a theory of the origin of sex. For my own part, I cannot see that these views embody any principles or suggestions of a sufficiently definite kind to constitute them theories at all. In this respect the views of Mr. Geddes resemble those of Professors Cope, Hyatt, and others, on what they term "the law of acceleration and retardation." In all these cases, so far as I can see, the so-called explanations are not in fact any explanations; but either a mere re-statement of the facts, or else an enunciation of more or less meaningless propositions. Thus, when it is said that the evolution of any given type has been due to the "acceleration of growth-force" with respect to some structures, and the "retardation of growth-force" with respect to others, it appears evident that we have not any real explanation in terms of causality; we have only the form of an explanation in the terms of a proposition. All that has been done is to express the fact of evolution in somewhat obscure phraseology, since the very thing we want to know about this fact is—What are the causes of it as a fact, or the reasons which have led to the increase of some of the parts of any given type, and the concomitant decrease of others? It is merely the facts themselves that are again presented by saying that the development has been in the one case accelerated, while in the other it has been retarded[10].

So much for what may be termed this New World theory of the origin of species: it is a mere re-statement of the facts. Mr. Geddes' theory, on the other hand, although more than a mere re-statement of the facts, appears to me too vague to be of any explanatory service. His view is that organic evolution has everywhere depended upon an antagonism, within the limits of the same organism, between the processes of nutrition and those of reproduction. But although he is thus able hypothetically to explain certain facts—such as the shortening of a flower-spike into a composite flower— the suggestion is obviously inadequate to meet, even hypothetically, most of the facts of organic evolution, and especially the development of *adaptive* structures. Therefore, it seems to me, we may dismiss it even as regards the comparatively few facts which it might conceivably explain—seeing that these same facts may be equally well explained by the causes which are already known to operate in other cases. For it is the business of natural selection to ensure that there shall nowhere be any needless expenditure of vital energy, and, consequently, that everywhere the balance between nutrition and reproduction shall be most profitably adjusted.

Similarly with respect to the theory of the *Origin of Sex*, I am unable to perceive even this much of scientific relevancy. As stated by its authors the theory is, that the female is everywhere "anabolic," as compared with the male, which is "katabolic." By anabolic is meant comparative inactivity of protoplasmic change due to a nutritive winding up of molecular constitution, while by katabolic is meant the opposite condition of comparative activity due to a dynamic running down of molecular constitution. How, then, can the *origin* of sex be explained, or the *causes* which led to the differentiation of the sexes be shown by saying that the one sex is anabolic and the other katabolic? In so far as these verbal statements serve to express what is said to be a general fact—namely, that the female sexual elements are less mobile than the male—they merely

- 13 -

serve to re-state this general fact in terminology which, as the authors themselves observe, is "unquestionably ugly." But in so far as any question of *origin* or *causality* is concerned, it appears to me that there is absolutely no meaning in such statements. They belong to the order of merely formal explanations, as when it is said that the toxic qualities of morphia are due to this drug possessing a soporific character.

Much the same, in my opinion, has to be said of the Rev. G. Henslow's theory of the origin of species by what he terms "self-adaptation." Stated briefly his view is that there is no sufficient evidence of natural selection as a *vera causa*, while there is very abundant evidence of adjustments occurring without it, first in individual organisms, and next, by inheritance of acquired characters, in species. Now, much that he says in criticism of the selection theory is of considerable interest as such; but when we pass from the critical to the constructive portions of his books and papers, we again meet with the want of clearness in thought between a statement of facts in terms of a proposition, and an explanation of them in those of causality. Indeed, I understand from private correspondence, that Mr. Henslow himself admits the validity of this criticism; for in answer to my questions,—"How does Self-adaptation work in each case, and why should protoplasm be able to *adapt itself* into the millions of diverse mechanisms in nature?"—he writes. "Self-adaptation does not profess to be a *vera causa* at all; for the true causes of variation can only be found in the answer to your [above] questions, and I must say at once, *these questions cannot be answered.*" That is, they cannot be answered on the hypothesis of self-adaptation, which is therefore a statement of the facts of adaptation as distinguished from an explanation of them. Nevertheless, two things have here to be noted. In the first place, the statement of facts which Mr. Henslow has collected is of considerable theoretical importance as tending to show that there are probably causes of an internal kind (i. e. other than natural selection) which have been largely concerned in the adaptive modification of plants. And, in the second place, it is not quite true that the theory of self-adaptation is, as its author says in the sentences above quoted, a mere statement of the facts of adaptation, without any attempt at explaining their causes. For in his published words he does attempt to do so[11]. And, although I think his attempt is a conspicuous failure, I ought in fairness to give examples of it. His books are almost exclusively concerned in an application of his theory to the mechanisms of flowers for securing their own fertilization. These mechanisms he ascribes, in the case of entomophylous flowers, to the "thrusts," "strains," and other "irritations" supplied to the flowers by their insect visitors, and consequent "reactions" of the vegetable "protoplasm." But no attempt is made to show why these "reactions" should be of an *adaptive* kind, so as to build up the millions of diverse and often elaborate mechanisms in question—including not only forms and movements, but also colours, odours, and secretions. For my own part I confess that, even granting to an ultra-Lamarckian extent the inheritance of acquired characters, I could conceive of "self-adaptation" alone producing all such innumerable and diversified adjustments only after seeing, with Cardinal Newman, an angel in every flower. Yet Mr. Henslow somewhat vehemently repudiates any association between his theory and that of teleology.

On the whole, then, I regard all the works which are here classed together (those by Cope, Geddes, and Henslow), as resembling one another both in their merits and defects. Their common merits lie in their erudition and much of their criticism, while their common defects consist on the one hand in not sufficiently distinguishing between mere statements and real explanations of facts, and, on the other, in not perceiving that the theories severally suggested as substitutes for that of natural selection, even if they be granted true, could be accepted only as co-operative factors, and by no stretch of logic as substitutes.

Turning now to Mr. Wallace's work on *Darwinism*, we have to notice, in the first place, that its doctrine differs from "Darwinism" in regard to the important dogma which it is the leading purpose of that work to sustain— namely, that "the law of utility" is, to all intents and purposes, universal, with the result that natural selection is virtually the only cause of organic evolution. I say "to all intents and purposes," or "virtually," because Mr. Wallace does not expressly maintain the abstract impossibility of laws and causes other than those of utility and natural selection; indeed, at the end of his treatise, he quotes with approval Darwin's judgement, that "natural selection has been the most important, but not the exclusive means of modification." Nevertheless, as he nowhere recognizes any other law or cause of adaptive evolution[12], he practically concludes that, on inductive or empirical grounds, there *is* no such other law or cause to be entertained— until we come to the particular case of the human mind. But even in making this one particular exception—or in representing that some other law than that of utility, and some other cause than that of natural selection, must have been concerned in evolving the mind of man—he is not approximating his system to that of Darwin. On the contrary, he is but increasing the divergence, for, of course, it was Darwin's view that no such exception could be legitimately drawn with respect to this particular instance. And if, as I understand must be the case, his expressed agreement with Darwin touching natural selection not being the only cause of adaptive evolution has reference to this point, the quotation is singularly inapt.

Looking, then, to these serious differences between his own doctrine of evolution—both organic and mental—and that of Darwin, I cannot think that Mr. Wallace has chosen a suitable title for his book; because, in view of the points just mentioned, it is unquestionable that *Darwinism* differs more widely from the *Origin of Species* than does the *Origin of Species* from the writings of the Neo-Lamarckians. But, passing over this merely nominal matter, a few words ought to be added on the very material question regarding the human mind. In subsequent chapters the more general question, or that which relates to the range of utility and natural selection elsewhere will be fully considered.

Mr. Wallace says,—

> "The immense interest that attaches to the origin of the human race, and the amount of misconception which prevails regarding the essential teachings of Darwin's theory on the question, as well as regarding my own special views upon it, induce me to devote a final chapter to its discussion."

Now I am not aware that there is any misconception in any quarter as to the essential teachings of Darwin's theory on this question. Surely it is rather the case that there is a very general and very complete understanding on this point, both by the friends and the foes of Darwin's theory—so much so, indeed, that it is about the only point of similar import in all Darwin's writings of which this can be said. Mr. Wallace's "special views" on the other hand are, briefly stated, that certain features, both of the morphology and the psychology of man, are inexplicable by natural selection—or indeed by any other cause of the kind ordinarily understood by the term natural: they can be explained only by supposing "the intervention of some distinct individual intelligence," which, however, need not necessarily be "one Supreme Intelligence," but some other order of Personality standing anywhere in "an infinite chasm between man and the Great Mind of the universe[13]." Let us consider separately the corporeal and the mental peculiarities which are given as justifying this important conclusion.

The bodily peculiarities are the feet, the hands, the brain, the voice, and the naked skin.

As regards the feet Mr. Wallace writes, "It is difficult to see why the prehensile power [of the great toe] should have been taken away," because, although "it may not be compatible with perfectly easy erect locomotion," "how can we conceive that early man, *as an animal*, gained anything by purely erect locomotion[14]?" But surely it is not difficult to conceive this. In the proportion that our simian progenitors ceased to be arboreal in their habits (and there may well have been very good utilitarian reasons for such a change of habitat, analogous to those which are known to have occurred in the phylogenesis of countless other animals), it would clearly have been of advantage to them that their already semi-erect attitude should have been rendered more and more erect. To name one among several probabilities, the more erect the attitude, and the more habitually it was assumed, the more would the hands have been liberated for all the important purposes of manipulation. The principle of the physiological division of labour would thus have come more and more into play: natural selection would therefore have rendered the upper extremities more and more suited to the execution of these purposes, while at the same time it would have more and more adapted the lower ones to discharging the sole function of locomotion. For my own part, I cannot perceive any difficulty about this: in fact, there is an admirable repetition of the process in the ontogeny of our own children[15].

Next, with regard to the hand, Mr. Wallace says, that it "contains latent capacities which are unused by savages, and must have been even less used by palaeolithic man and his still ruder predecessors." Thus, "it has all the appearance of an organ prepared for the use of civilized man[16]." Even if this be true, however, it would surely be a dangerous argument to rely upon, seeing that we cannot say of how much importance it may have been for early man—or even apes—to have had their power of manipulation progressively improved. But is the statement true? It appears to me that if Mr. Wallace had endeavoured to imitate the manufactures that were practised by "palaeolithic man," he would have found the very best of reasons for cancelling his statement. For it is an extremely difficult thing to chip a flint into the form of an arrow-head: when made, the suitable attachment of it to a previously prepared arrow is no easy matter: neither a bow nor a bow-string could have been constructed by hands of much less perfection than our own: and the slaying of game with the whole apparatus, when it has been constructed, requires a manual dexterity which we may be perfectly certain that Mr. Wallace—unless he has practised the art from boyhood—does not possess.

So it is with his similar argument that the human voice is more "powerful," more "flexible," and presents a greater "range" and "sweetness" than the needs of savage life can be held to require. The futility of this argument is self-evident as regards "power." And although its weakness is not so obvious with respect to the other three qualities which are named, need we go further than the closely analogous case of certain birds to show the precariousness of arguing from such facts of organic nature to the special operation of "a superior intelligence"? I can hardly suppose that Mr. Wallace will invoke any such agency for the purpose of explaining the "latent capacities" of the voice of a parrot. Yet, in many respects, these are even more wonderful than those of the human voice, albeit in a wild state they are "never required or used[17]."

Once more, with regard to the naked skin, it seems sufficient to quote the following passage from the first edition of the *Descent of Man*.

"The Rev. T. R. Stebbing, in commenting on this view, remarks, that had Mr. Wallace 'employed his usual ingenuity on the question of man's hairless skin, he might have seen the possibility of its selection through its superior beauty, or the health attaching to superior cleanliness. At any rate it is surprising that he should picture to himself a superior intelligence plucking the hair from the backs of savage men (to whom, according to his own account, it would have been useful and beneficial), in order that the descendants of the poor shorn wretches might, after many deaths from cold and damp in the course of many generations,' have been forced to raise themselves in the scale of civilization through the practice of various arts, in the manner indicated by Mr. Wallace[18]."

To this it may be added that the Chimpanzee "Sally" was largely denuded of hair, especially on the back, or the part of "man's organization" on which Mr. Wallace lays special stress, as being in this respect out of analogy with other mammalia[19].

Lastly, touching his statement that the brain of savage man is both quantitatively and qualitatively in advance of his requirements, it is here also sufficient to refer to Darwin's answer, as given in the *Descent of Man*. Mr. Wallace, indeed, ignores this answer in his recent re-publication of the argument; but it is impossible to understand why he should have done so. To me, at all events, it seems that one out of several considerations which Darwin advances is alone sufficient to show the futility of this argument. I allude to the consideration that the power of forming abstract ideas with the complex machinery of language as the vehicle of their expression, is probably of itself enough to account for both the mass and the structure of a savage's brain. But this leads us to the second division of Mr. Wallace's argument, or that derived from the mental endowments of mankind.

Here the peculiarities called into evidence are, "the Mathematical Faculty," "the Artistic Faculties," and "the Moral Sense." With regard to the latter, he avows himself a member of the intuitional school of ethics; but does not prove a very powerful advocate as against the utilitarian[20].

It comes, then, to this. According to Mr. Wallace's eventual conclusion, man is to be separated from the rest of organic nature, and the steady progress of evolution by natural causes is to be regarded as stopped at its final stage, because the human mind presents the faculties of mathematical calculation and aesthetic perception. Surely, on antecedent grounds alone, it must be apparent that there is here no kind of proportion between the conclusion and the *data* from which it is drawn. That we are not confined to any such grounds, I will now try to show.

Let it be remembered, however, that in the following brief criticism I am not concerned with the issue as to whether, or how far, the "faculties" in question have owed their origin or their development to *natural selection*. I am concerned only with the doctrine that in order to account for such and such particular "faculty" of the human mind, some order of causation must be supposed other than what we call natural. I am not a Neo-Darwinist, and so have no desire to make "natural selection" synonymous with "natural causation" throughout the whole domain of life and of mind. And I quite agree with Mr. Wallace that, at any rate, the "aesthetic faculty" cannot conceivably have been produced by natural selection—seeing that it is of no conceivable life-serving value in any of the stages of its growth. Moreover, it appears to me that the same thing has to be said of the play instincts, sense of the ludicrous, and sundry other "faculties" of mind among the lower animals. It being thus understood that I am not differing from Mr. Wallace where he imposes "limits" on the powers of natural selection, but only where he seems to take for granted that this is the same thing as imposing limits on the powers of natural causation, my criticism is as follows.

In the first place, it is a psychological fallacy to regard the so-called "faculties" of mind as analogous to "organs" of the body. To classify the latter with reference to the functions which they severally perform is to follow a natural method of classification. But it is an artificial method which seeks to partition mental *faculty* into this, that, and the other mental *faculties*. Like all other purely artificial classifications, this one has its practical uses; but, also like them, it is destitute of philosophical meaning. This statement is so well recognized by psychologists, that there is no occasion to justify it. But I must remark that any cogency which Mr. Wallace's argument may appear to present, arises from his not having recognized the fact which the statement conveys. For, had he considered the mind as a whole, instead of having contemplated it under the artificial categories of constituent "faculties," he would probably not have laid any such special stress upon some of the latter. In other words, he would have seen that the general development of the human mind as a whole has presumably involved the growth of those conventionally abstracted parts, which he regards as really separate endowments. Or, if he should find it easier to retain the terms of his metaphor, we may answer him by saying that the "faculties" of mind are "correlated," like "organs" of the body; and, therefore, that any general development of the various other "faculties" have presumably entailed a collateral development of the two in question.

Again, in the second place, it would seem that Mr. Wallace has not sufficiently considered the co-operation of either well-known natural causes, which must have materially assisted the survival of the fittest where these two "faculties" are concerned. For, even if we disregard the inherited effects of use—which, however, if entertained as possible in any degree at all, must have here constituted an important factor,—there remain on the one hand, the unquestionable influences of individual education and, on the other hand, of the selection principle operating in the mind itself.

Taking these two points separately, it is surely sufficiently well known that individual education—or special training, whether of mind or body— usually raises congenital powers of any kind to a more or less considerable level above those of the normal type. In other words, whatever doubt there may be touching the *inherited* effects of use, there can be no question touching the immense *developmental* effects thereof in the individual life-time. Now, the conditions of savage life are not such as lead to any deliberate cultivation of the "faculties" either of the mathematical or aesthetic order. Consequently, as might be expected, we find both of them in what Mr. Wallace regards as but a "latent" stage of development. But in just the same way do we find that the marvellous powers of an acrobat when specially trained from childhood—say to curve his spine backwards until his teeth can bite his heels—are "latent" in all men. Or, more correctly, they are *potential in every child*. So it is with the prodigious muscular development of a trained athlete, and with any number of other cases where either the body or the mind is concerned. Why then should Mr. Wallace select the particular instances of the mathematical and aesthetic powers in savages as in any special sense "prophetic" of future development in trained members of civilized races? Although it is true that these "latent capacities and powers are unused by savages," is it not equally true that savages fail to use their latent capacities and powers as tumblers and athletes? Moreover, is it not likewise true that *as* used by savages, or as occurring normally in man, such capacities and powers are no less poorly developed than are those of the "faculties" on which Mr. Wallace lays so much stress? In other words, are not "latent capacities and powers" of all kinds more or less equally in excess of anything that is ever required of them by man in a state of nature? Therefore, if we say that where mathematics and the fine arts are concerned the potential capacities of savage man are in some mystical sense "prophetic" of a Newton or a Beethoven, so in consistency ought we to say that in these same capacities we discern a similar prophecy of those other uses of civilized life which we have in a rope-dancer or a clown.

Again, and in addition to this, it should be remembered that, even if we do suppose any prophecy of this kind where the particular capacities in question are concerned, we must clearly extend the reference to the lower animals. Not a few birds display aesthetic feelings in a measure fairly comparable with those of savages; while we know that some animals present the germs of a "faculty" of computation[21]. But, it is needless to add, this fact is fatal to Mr. Wallace's argument as I understand it——viz. that the "faculties" in question have been in some special manner communicated by some superior intelligence to *man*.

Once more, it is obviously unfair to select such men as a "Newton, a La Place, a Gauss, or a Cayley" for the purpose of estimating the difference between savages and civilized man in regard to the latter "faculty." These men are the picked mathematicians of centuries. Therefore they are men who not only enjoyed all the highest possible benefits of individual culture, but likewise those who have been most endowed with mathematical power congenitally. So to speak, they are the best variations in this particular direction which our race is known to have produced. But had such variations arisen among savages it is sufficiently obvious that they could have come to nothing. Therefore, it is the *normal average* of "mathematical faculty" in civilized man that should be contrasted with that of savage man; and, when due regard is paid to the all-important consideration which immediately follows, I cannot feel that the contrast presents any difficulty to the theory of human evolution by natural causation.

Lastly, the consideration just alluded to is, that civilized man enjoys an advantage over savage man far in advance even of those which arise from a settled state of society, incentives to intellectual training, and so on. This inestimable advantage consists in the art of writing, *and the consequent transmission of the effects of culture from generation to generation*. Quite apart from any question as to the hereditary transmission of acquired characters, we have in this *intellectual* transmission of acquired *experience* a means of accumulative cultivation quite beyond our powers to estimate. For, unlike all other cases where we recognize the great influence of individual use or practice in augmenting congenital "faculties" (such as in the athlete, pianist, &c.), in this case the effects of special cultivation do not end with the individual life, but are carried on and on through successive generations *ad infinitum*. Hence, a civilized man inherits mentally, if not physically, the effects of culture for ages past, and this in whatever direction he may choose to profit therefrom. Moreover—and I deem this an immensely important addition—in this unique department of purely intellectual transmission, a kind of non-physical natural selection is perpetually engaged in producing the best results. For here a struggle for existence is constantly taking place among "ideas," "methods," and so forth, in what may be termed a psychological environment. The less fit are superseded by the more fit, and this not only in the mind of the individual, but, through language and literature, still more in the mind of the race. "A Newton, a La Place, a Gauss, or a Cayley," would all alike have been impossible, but for a previously prolonged course of mental evolution due to the selection principle operating in the region of mathematics, by means of continuous survivals of the best products in successive generations. And, of course, the same remark applies to art in all its branches[22].

Quitting then the last, and in my opinion the weakest chapter of *Darwinism*, the most important points presented by other portions of this work are—to quote its author's own enumeration of them—an attempted "proof that all specific characters are (or once have been) either useful in themselves or correlated with useful characters": an attempted "proof that natural selection can, in certain cases, increase the sterility of crosses": an attempted "proof that the effects of use and disuse, even if inherited, must be overpowered by natural selection": an attempted proof that the facts of variation in nature are in themselves sufficient to meet the difficulty which arises against the theory of natural selection, as held by him, from the swamping effects of free intercrossing: and, lastly, "a fuller discussion on the colour relations of animals, with additional facts and arguments on the origin of sexual differences of colour." As I intend to deal with all these points hereafter, excepting the last, it will be sufficient in this opening chapter to remark, that in as far as I disagree with Mr. Wallace (and agree with Darwin), on the subject of "sexual differences of colour," my reasons for doing so have been already sufficiently stated in Part I. But there is much else in his treatment of this subject which appears to me highly valuable, and therefore presenting an admirable contribution to the literature of Darwinism. In particular, it appears to me that the most important of his views in this connexion probably represents the truth— namely, that, among the higher animals, more or less conspicuous peculiarities of colour have often been acquired for the purpose of enabling members of the same species quickly and certainly to recognize one another. This theory was first published by Mr. J. E. Todd, in 1888, and therefore but a short time before its re-publication by Mr. Wallace. As his part in the matter has not been sufficiently recognized, I should like to conclude this introductory chapter by drawing prominent attention to the merits of Mr. Todd's paper. For not only has it the merit of priority, but it deals with the whole subject of "recognition colours"—or, as he calls them, "directive colours"—in a more comprehensive manner than has been done by any of his successors. In particular, he shows that the principle of recognition-marking is not restricted to facilitating sexual intercourse, but extends also to several other matters of importance in the economy of animal life[23].

Having thus briefly sketched the doctrines of the sundry Post-Darwinian Schools from a general point of view, I shall endeavour throughout the rest of this treatise to discuss in appropriate detail the questions which have more specially come to the front in the post-Darwinian period. It can scarcely be said that any one of these questions has arisen altogether *de novo* during this period; for glimmerings, more or less conspicuous, of all are to be met with in the writings of Darwin himself. Nevertheless it is no less true that only after his death have they been lighted up to the full blaze of active discussion[24]. By far the most important of them are those to which the rest of this treatise will be confined. They are four in number, and it is noteworthy that they are all intimately connected with the great question which Darwin spent the best years of his life in contemplating, and which has therefore, in one form or another, occupied the whole of the present chapter—the question as to whether natural selection has been the sole cause, or but the chief cause of modification.

The four questions above alluded to appertain respectively to Heredity, Utility, Isolation, and Physiological Selection. Of these the first two will form the subject-matter of the present volume, while the last two will be dealt with in the final instalment of *Darwin, and after Darwin.*

SECTION I
HEREDITY

CHAPTER II
Characters As Hereditary and Acquired
(Preliminary).

We will proceed to consider, throughout Section I of the present work, the most important among those sundry questions which have come to the front since the death of Darwin. For it was in the year after this event that Weismann published the first of his numerous essays on the subject of Heredity, and, unquestionably, it has been these essays which have given such prominence to this subject during the last decade.

At the outset it is desirable to be clear upon certain points touching the history of the subject; the limits within which our discussion is to be confined; the relation in which the present essay stands to the one that I published last year under the title *An Examination of Weismannism*; and several other matters of a preliminary kind.

The problems presented by the phenomena of heredity are manifold; but chief among them is the hitherto unanswered question as to the transmission or non-transmission of acquired characters. This is the question to which the present Section will be confined.

Although it is usually supposed that this question was first raised by Weismann, such was not the case. Any attentive reader of the successive editions of Darwin's works may perceive that at least from the year 1859 he had the question clearly before his mind; and that during the rest of his life his opinion with regard to it underwent considerable modifications— becoming more and more Lamarckian the longer that he pondered it. But it was not till 1875 that the question was clearly presented to the general public by the independent thought of Mr. Galton, who was led to challenge the Lamarckian factors *in toto* by way of deduction from his theory of Stirp—the close resemblance of which to Professor Weismann's theory of Germ-plasm has been shown in my *Examination of Weismannism*. Lastly, I was myself led to doubt the Lamarckian factors still further back in the seventies, by having found a reason for questioning the main evidence which Mr. Darwin had adduced in their favour. This doubt was greatly strengthened on reading, in the following year, Mr. Galton's *Theory of Heredity* just alluded to; and thereupon I commenced a prolonged course of experiments upon the subject, the general nature of which will be stated in future chapters. Presumably many other persons must have entertained similar misgivings touching the inheritance of acquired characters long before the publication of Weismann's first essay upon the subject in 1883.

The question as to the inheritance of acquired characters was therefore certainly not first raised by Weismann—although, of course, there is no doubt that it was conceived by him independently, and that he had the great merit of calling general attention to its existence and importance. On the other hand, it cannot be said that he has succeeded in doing very much towards its solution. It is for these reasons that any attempt at dealing with Weismann's fundamental postulate—i.e. that of the non-inheritance of acquired characters—was excluded from my *Examination of Weismannism*. As there stated, he is justified in assuming, for the purposes of his discussion, a negative answer to the question of such inheritance; but evidently the question itself ought not to be included within what we may properly understand by "Weismannism." Weismannism, properly so called, is an elaborate system of theories based on the fundamental postulate just mentioned—theories having reference to the mechanism of heredity on the one hand, and to the course of organic evolution on the other. Now it was the object of the foregoing *Examination* to deal with this system of theories *per se*; and therefore we have here to take a new point of departure and to consider separately the question of fact as to the inheritance or non-inheritance of acquired characters. At first sight, no doubt, it will appear that in adopting this method I am putting the cart before the horse. For it may well appear that I ought first to have dealt with the validity of Weismann's postulate, and not till then to have considered the system of theories which he has raised upon it. But this criticism is not likely to be urged by any one who is well acquainted with the questions at issue. For, in the first place, it is notorious that the question of fact is still open to question; and therefore it ought to be considered separately, or apart from any theories which may have been formed with regard to it. In the second place, our judgement upon this question of fact must be largely influenced by the validity of general reasonings, such as those put forward in the interests of rival theories of heredity; and, as the theory of germ-plasm has been so thoughtfully elaborated by Professor Weismann, I have sought to give it the attention which it deserves as preliminary to our discussion of the question of fact which now lies before us. Thirdly and lastly, even if this question could be definitely answered by proving either that acquired characters are inherited or that they are not, it would by no means follow that Weismann's theory of heredity would be proved wholly false in the one case, or wholly true in the other. That it need not be wholly true, even were its fundamental postulate to be proved so, is evident, because, although the fact might be taken to prove the theory of Continuity, the theory of Germ-plasm is, as above stated, very much more than this. That the theory of Germ-plasm need not be wholly false, even if acquired characters should ever be proved heritable, a little thought may easily show, because, in this event, the further question would immediately arise as to the degrees and the comparative frequency of such inheritance. For my own part, as stated in the *Examination*, I have always been disposed to accept Mr. Galton's theory of Stirp in preference to that of Germ-plasm on this very ground—i. e. that it does not dogmatically exclude the possibility of an occasional inheritance of acquired characters in faint though cumulative degrees. And whatever our individual opinions may be touching the admissibility of such a *via media* between the theories of Pangenesis and Germ-plasm, at least we may all agree on the desirability of fully considering the matter as a preliminary to the discussion of the question of fact.

As it is not to be expected that even those who may have read my previous essay can now carry all these points in their memories, I will here re-state them in a somewhat fuller form.

The following diagram will serve to give a clearer view of the sundry parts of Professor Weismann's system of theories, as well as of their relations to one another.

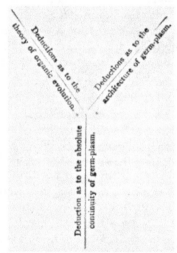

Postulate as to the absolute non-inheritance of acquired characters.

Now, as just explained, the parts of this system which may be properly and distinctively called "Weismannism" are those which go to form the Y-like structure of deductions from the fundamental postulate. Therefore, it was the Y-like system of deductions which were dealt with in the *Examination of Weismannism*, while it is only his basal postulate which has to be dealt with in the following chapters.

So much, then, for the relations of Weismann's system of theories to one another. It is, however, of even more importance that we should gain a clear view of the relations between his theory of *heredity* to those of Darwin and of Galton, as preliminary to considering the fundamental question of fact.

As we have already seen, the theory of germ-plasm is not only a theory of heredity: it is also, and more distinctively, a theory of evolution, &c. As a theory of heredity it is grounded on its author's fundamental postulate—the *continuity* of germ-plasm. But as a theory of evolution, it requires for its support this additional postulate, that the continuity of germ-plasm has been *absolute* "since the first origin of life." It is clear that this additional postulate is not needed for his theory of heredity, but only for his additional theory of evolution, &c. There have been one or two other theories of heredity, prior to this one, which, like it, have been founded on the postulate of Continuity of the substance of heredity; but it has not been needful for any of these theories to postulate further that this substance has been *always* thus isolated, or even that it is now *invariably* so. For even though the isolation be frequently invaded by influences of body-changes on the congenital characters of this substance, it does not follow that this principle of Continuity may not still be true *in the main*, even although it is supplemented in some degree by that of use-inheritance. Indeed, so far as the phenomena of heredity are concerned, it is conceivable that all congenital characters were originally acquired, and afterwards became congenital on account of their long inheritance. I do not myself advocate this view as biologically probable, but merely state it as logically possible, and in order to show that, so far as the phenomena of heredity are concerned, there appears to be no reason for Weismann's deduction that the principle of Continuity, if true at all, must be *absolute*. And it would further appear, the only reason why he makes this deduction (stem of the Y) is in order to provide a foundation for his further theories of evolution, &c. (arms of the Y). It is indeed necessary for these further theories that body-changes should never exercise any hereditary influence on the hereditary endowments of germ-plasm, and therefore it is that he posits the substance of heredity as, not only continuous, but uninterruptably so "since the first origin of life."

Now, this may be made more clear by briefly comparing Weismann's theory with those of Darwin and of Galton. Weismann's theory of heredity, then, agrees with its predecessors which we are considering in all the following respects. The substance of heredity is particulate; is mainly lodged in highly specialized cells; is nevertheless also distributed throughout the general cellular tissues, where it is concerned in all processes of regeneration, repair, and a-sexual reproduction; presents an enormously complex structure, in that every constituent part of a potentially future organism is represented in a fertilized ovum by corresponding particles; is everywhere capable of virtually unlimited multiplication, without ever losing its hereditary endowments; is often capable of carrying these endowments in a dormant state through a long series of generations until at last they reappear in what we recognize as recursions. Thus far all three theories are in agreement. In fact, the only matter of any great importance wherein they disagree has reference to the doctrine of Continuity[25]. For while Darwin's theory supposes the substance of heredity to be mainly formed anew in each ontogeny, and therefore that the continuity of this substance is for the most part interrupted in every generation[26], Weismann's theory supposes this substance to be formed only during the phylogeny of each species, and therefore to have been absolutely uninterrupted since the first origin of life.

But now, Galton's theory of heredity stands much nearer to Weismann's in this matter of Continuity; for it is, as he says, a theory of "modified pangenesis," and the modification consists in allowing very much more for the principle of Continuity than is allowed by Darwin's theory; in fact he expresses himself as quite willing to adopt (on adequate grounds being shown) the doctrine of Continuity as absolute, and therefore propounded, as logically possible, the identical theory which was afterwards and independently announced by Weismann. Or, to quote his own words—

> "We might almost reserve our belief that the structural [i. e. somatic] cells can react on the sexual elements at all, and we may be confident that at most they do so in a very faint degree; in other words, that acquired modifications are barely, if at all, *inherited*, in the correct sense of that word[27]."

So far Mr. Galton; but for Weismann's further theory of evolution, &c., it is necessary to postulate the additional doctrine in question; and it makes a literally immeasurable difference to any theory of evolution whether or not we entertain this additional postulate. For no matter how faintly or how fitfully the substance of heredity may be modified by somatic tissues, the Lamarckian principles are hypothetically allowed some degree of play. And although this is a lower degree than Darwin supposed, their influence in determining the course of organic evolution may still have been enormous; seeing that their action in any degree must always have been *directive* of variation on the one hand, and *cumulative* on the other.

Thus, by merely laying this theory side by side with Weismann's we can perceive at a glance how a *pure* theory of *heredity* admits of being based on the postulate of Continuity alone, without cumbering itself by any further postulate as to this Continuity being *absolute*. And this, in my opinion is the truly scientific attitude of mind for us to adopt as preliminary to the following investigation. For the whole investigation will be concerned— and concerned only—with this question of Continuity as absolute, or as admitting of degrees. There is, without any question, abundant evidence to prove that the substance of heredity is at least partly continuous (Gemmules). It may be that there is also abundant evidence to prove this substance much more *largely* continuous than Darwin supposed (Stirp); but be this as it may, it is certain that any such question as to the *degree* of continuity differs, *toto caelo*, from that as to whether there can ever be any continuity at all.

How, then, we may well ask, is it that so able a naturalist and so clear a thinker as Weismann can have so far departed from the inductive methods as to have not merely propounded the question touching Continuity and its degrees, or even of Continuity as absolute; but to have straightway assumed the latter possibility as a basis on which to run a system of branching and ever-changing speculations concerning evolution, variation, the ultimate structure of living material, the intimate mechanism of heredity, or, in short, such a system of deductive conjectures as has never been approached in the history of science? The answer to this question is surely not far to seek. Must it not be the answer already given? Must it not have been for the sake of rearing this enormous structure of speculation that Weismann has adopted the assumption of Continuity as absolute? As we have just seen, Galton had well shown how a theory of heredity could be founded on the general doctrine of Continuity, without anywhere departing from the inductive methods—even while fully recognizing the possibility of such continuity as absolute. But Galton's theory was a "*Theory of Heredity*," and nothing more. Therefore, while clearly perceiving that the Continuity in question *may* be absolute, he saw no reason, either in fact or in theory, for concluding that it *must* be. On the contrary, he saw that this question is, for the present, necessarily unripe for profitable discussion—and, *a fortiori*, for the shedding of clouds of seed in all the directions of "Weismannism."

Hence, what I desire to be borne in mind throughout the following discussion is, that it will have exclusive reference to the question of fact already stated, without regard to any superjacent theories; and, still more, that there is a vast distinction between any question touching the degrees in which acquired characters are transmitted to progeny, and the question as to whether they are ever transmitted in any degree at all. Now, the latter question, being of much greater importance than the former, is the one which will mainly occupy our attention throughout the rest of this Section.

We have already seen that before the subject was taken up by Weismann the difference between acquired and congenital characters in respect to transmissibility was generally taken to be one of degree; not one of kind. It was usually supposed that acquired characters, although not so fully and not so certainly inherited as congenital characters, nevertheless were inherited in some lesser degree; so that if the same acquired character continued to be successively acquired in a number of sequent generations, what was at first only a slight tendency to be inherited would become by summation a more and more pronounced tendency, till eventually the acquired character might become as strongly inherited as a congenital one. Or, more precisely, it was supposed that an acquired character, in virtue of such a summation of hereditary influence, would in time become congenital. Now, if this supposition be true, it is evident that more or less assistance must be lent to natural selection in its work of evolving adaptive modifications[28]. And inasmuch as we know to what a wonderful extent adaptive modifications are secured during individual life-times—by the direct action of the environment on the one hand, and by increased or diminished use of special organs and mental faculties on the other—it becomes obvious of what importance even a small measure of transmissibility on their part would be in furnishing to natural selection ready-made variations in required directions, as distinguished from promiscuous variations in all directions. Contrariwise, if functionally-produced adaptations and adaptations produced by the direct action of the environment are never transmitted in any degree, not only would there be an incalculable waste, so to speak, of adaptive modifications—these being all laboriously and often most delicately built up during life-times of individuals only to be thrown down again as regards the interest of species—but so large an additional burden would be thrown upon the shoulders of natural selection that it becomes difficult to conceive how even this gigantic principle could sustain it, as I shall endeavour to show more fully in future chapters. On the other hand, however, Weismann and his followers not only feel no difficulty in throwing overboard all this ready-made machinery for turning out adaptive modifications when and as required; but they even represent that by so doing they are following the logical maxim, *Entia non sunt multiplicanda praeter necessitatem*—which means, in its relation to causality, that we must not needlessly multiply hypothetical principles to explain given results. But when appeal is here made to this logical principle—the so-called Law of Parsimony—two things are forgotten.

In the first place, it is forgotten that the very question in debate is whether causes of the Lamarckian order *are* unnecessary to explain all the phenomena of organic nature. Of course if it could be proved that the theory of natural selection alone is competent to explain all these phenomena, appeal to the logical principle in question would be justifiable. But this is precisely the point which the followers of Darwin refuse to accept; and so long as it remains the very point at issue, it is a mere begging the question to represent that a class of causes which have hitherto been regarded as necessary are, in fact, unnecessary. Or, in other words, when Darwin himself so decidedly held that these causes are necessary as supplements to natural selection, the burden of proof is quite as much on the side of Weismann and his followers to show that Darwin's opinion was wrong, as it is on the side of Darwin's followers to show that it was right. Yet, notwithstanding the elaborate structure of theory which Weismann has raised, there is nowhere one single fact or one single consideration of much importance to the question in debate which was not perfectly well known to Darwin. Therefore I say that all this challenging of Darwinists to justify their "Lamarckian assumptions" really amounts to nothing more than a pitting of opinion against opinion, where there is at least as much call for justification on the one side as on the other.

Again, when these challenges are thrown down by Weismann and his followers, it appears to be forgotten that the conditions of their own theory are such as to render acceptance of the gauge a matter of great difficulty. The case is very much like that of a doughty knight pitching his glove into the sea, and then defying any antagonist to take it up. That this is the case a very little explanation will suffice to show.

The question to be settled is whether acquired characters are ever transmitted by heredity. Now suppose, for the sake of argument, that acquired characters are transmitted by heredity—though not so fully and not so certainly as congenital characters—how is this fact to be proved to the satisfaction of Weismann and his followers? First of all they answer,— Assuredly by adducing experimental proof of the inheritance of injuries, or mutilations. But in making this answer they appear to forget that Darwin has already shown its inefficiency. That the self-styled Neo-Lamarckians have been much more unguarded in this respect, I fully admit; but it is obviously unfair to identify Darwin's views with those of a small section of evolutionists, who are really as much opposed to Darwin's teaching on one side as is the school of Weismann on the other. Yet, on reading the essays of Weismann himself—and still more those of his followers—one would almost be led to gather that it is claimed by him to have enunciated the distinction between congenital and acquired characters in respect of transmissibility; and therefore also to have first raised the objection which lies against the theory of Pangenesis in respect of the non-transmissibility of mutilations. In point of fact, however, Darwin is as clear and decided on these points as Weismann. And his answer to the obvious difficulty touching the non-transmissibility of mutilations is, to quote his own words, "the long-continued inheritance of a part which has been removed during many generations is no real anomaly, for gemmules formerly derived from the part are multiplied and transmitted from generation to generation[29]." Therefore, so far as Darwin's theory is concerned, the challenge to produce evidence of the transmission of injuries is irrelevant: it is no more a part of

Darwin's theory than it is of Weismann's to maintain that injuries *are* transmitted.

There is, however, one point in this connexion to which allusion must here be made. Although Darwin did not believe in the transmissibility of mutilations when these consist merely in the amputation of parts of an organism, he did believe in a probable tendency to transmission when removal of the part is followed by gangrene. For, as he says, in that case, all the gemmules of the mutilated or amputated part, as they are gradually attracted to that part (in accordance with the law of affinity which the theory assumes), will be successively destroyed by the morbid process. Now it is of importance to note that Darwin made this exception to the general rule of the non-transmissibility of mutilations, not because his theory of pangenesis required it, but because there appeared to be certain very definite observations and experiments—which will be mentioned later on—proving that when mutilations are followed by gangrene they are apt to be inherited: his object, therefore, was to reconcile these alleged facts with his theory, quite as much as to sustain his theory by such facts.

So much, then, for the challenge to produce direct evidence of the transmissibility of acquired characters, so far as mutilations are concerned: believers in Darwin's theory, as distinguished from Weismann's, are under no obligation to take up such a challenge. But the challenge does not end here. Show us, say the school of Weismann, a single instance where an acquired character *of any kind* (be it a mutilation or otherwise) has been inherited: this is all that we require: this is all that we wait for: and surely, unless it be acknowledged that the Lamarckian doctrine reposes on mere assumption, at least one such case ought to be forthcoming. Well, nothing can sound more reasonable than this in the first instance; but as soon as we begin to cast about for cases which will satisfy the Neo-Darwinians, we find that the structure of their theory is such as to preclude, in almost every conceivable instance, the possibility of meeting their demand. For their theory begins by assuming that natural selection is the one and only cause of organic evolution. Consequently, what their demand amounts to is throwing upon the other side the burden of disproving this assumption— or, in other words, of proving the negative that in any given case of transmitted adaptation natural selection has *not* been the sole agent at work. Now, it must obviously be in almost all cases impossible to prove this negative among species in a state of nature. For, even supposing that among such species Lamarckian principles have had a large share in the formation of hereditary and adaptive characters, how would Weismann himself propose that we should set about the proof of such a fact, where the proof demanded by his assumption is, that the *abstract possibility* of natural selection having had anything to do with the matter must be excluded? Obviously this is impossible in the case of inherited characters which are also *adaptive* characters. How then does it fare with the case of inherited characters which are not also adaptive? Merely that this case is met by another and sequent assumption, which constitutes an integral part of the Neo-Darwinian creed—namely, that in nature there *can be no such characters*. Seeing that natural selection is taken to be the only possible cause of change in species, it follows that all changes occurring in species must necessarily be adaptive, whether or not we are able to perceive the adaptations. In this way apparently useless characters, as well as obviously useful ones, are ruled out of the question: that is to say, *all* hereditary characters of species in a state of nature are *assumed* to be due to natural selection, and then it is demanded that the validity of this assumption should be disproved by anybody who doubts it. Yet Weismann himself would be unable to suggest any conceivable method by which it can be disproved among species in a state of nature—and this even supposing that the assumption is entirely false[30].

Consequently, the only way in which these speciously-sounding challenges can be adequately met is by removing some individuals of a species from a state of nature, and so from all known influences of natural selection; then, while carefully avoiding artificial selection, causing these individuals and their progeny through many generations unduly to exercise some parts of their bodies, or unduly to fail in the exercise of others. But, clearly, such an experiment is one that must take years to perform, and therefore it is now too early in the day to reproach the followers of Darwin with not having met the challenges which are thrown down by the followers of Weismann[31].

Probably enough has now been said to show that the Neo-Darwinian assumption precludes the possibility of its own disproof from any of the facts of nature (as distinguished from domestication)—and this even supposing that the assumption be false. On the other hand, of course, it equally precludes the possibility of its own proof; and therefore it is as idle in Darwinists to challenge Weismann for proof of his negative (i. e. that acquired characters are not transmitted), as it is in Weismann to challenge Darwinists for proof of the opposite negative (i. e. that all seeming cases of such transmission are not due to natural selection). This dead-lock arises from the fact that in nature it is beyond the power of the followers of Darwin to exclude the abstract possibility of natural selection in any given case, while it is equally beyond the power of the followers of Weismann to exclude the abstract possibility of Lamarckian principles. Therefore at present the question must remain for the most part a matter of opinion, based upon general reasoning as distinguished from special facts or crucial experiments. The evidence available on either side is presumptive, not demonstrative[32]. But it is to be hoped that in the future, when time shall have been allowed for the performance of definite experiments on a number of generations of domesticated plants or animals, intentionally shielded from the influences of natural selection while exposed to those of the Lamarckian principles, results will be gained which will finally settle the question one way or the other.

Meanwhile, however, we must be content with the evidence as it stands; and this will lead us to the second division of our subject. That is to say, having now dealt with the antecedent, or merely logical, state of the question, we have next to consider what actual, or biological, evidence there is at present available on either side of it. Thus far, neither side in the debate has any advantage over the other. On grounds of general reasoning alone they both have to rely on more or less dogmatic assumptions. For it is equally an unreasoned statement of opinion whether we allege that all the phenomena of organic evolution can be, or can not be, explained by the theory of natural selection alone. We are at present much too ignorant touching the causes of organic evolution to indulge in dogmatism of this kind; and if the question is to be referred for its answer to authority, it would appear that, both in respect of number and weight, opinions on the side of having provisionally to retain the Lamarckian factors are more authoritative than those *per contra*[33].

Turning then to the question of fact, with which the following chapters are concerned, I will conclude this preliminary one with a few words on the method of discussion to be adopted.

First I will give the evidence in favour of Lamarckianism; this will occupy the next two chapters. Then, in Chapter V, I will similarly give the evidence *per contra*, or in favour of Continuity as absolute. Lastly, I will sum up the evidence on both sides, and give my own judgement on the whole case. But on whichever side I am thus acting as special pleader for the time being, I will adduce only such arguments as seem to me valid—excluding alike from both the many irrelevant or otherwise invalid reasonings which have been but too abundantly published. Moreover, I think it will be convenient to consider all that has been said—or may be said—in the way of criticism to each argument by the opposite side while such argument is under discussion—i. e. not to wait till all the special pleading on one side shall have been exhausted before considering the exceptions which have been (or admit of being) taken to the arguments adduced, but to deal with such exceptions at the time when each of these arguments shall have been severally stated. Again, and lastly, I will arrange the evidence in each case— i. e. on both sides—under three headings, viz. (A) Indirect, (B) Direct, and (C) Experimental[34].]

CHAPTER III
CHARACTERS AS HEREDITARY AND ACQUIRED
(*continued*).

(A.)
Indirect Evidence in favour of the Inheritance of Acquired Characters.

Starting with the evidence in favour of the so-called Lamarckian factors, we have to begin with the Indirect—and this without any special reference to the theories, either of Weismann or of others.

It has already been shown, while setting forth in the preceding chapter the antecedent standing of the issue, that in this respect the *prima facie* presumption is wholly on the side of the transmission, in greater degree or less, of acquired characters. Even Weismann allows that all "*appearances*" point in this direction, while there is no inductive evidence of the action of natural selection in any one case, either as regards germs or somas, and therefore, *a fortiori*, of the "all-sufficiency" of this cause[35]. It is true that in some of his earlier essays he has argued that there is no small weight of *prima facie* evidence in favour of his own views as to the non-inheritance of acquired characters. This, however, will have to be considered in its proper place further on. Meanwhile I shall say merely in general terms that it arises almost entirely from a confusion of the doctrine of Continuity as absolute with that of Continuity as partial, and therefore, as admitting of degrees in different cases—which, as already explained, are doctrines wide as the poles asunder. But, leaving aside for the present such *prima facie* evidence as Weismann has adduced on his side of the issue, I may quote him as a hostile witness to the weight of this kind of evidence *per contra*, in so far as it has already been presented in the foregoing chapter. Indeed, Weismann is much too logical a thinker not to perceive the cogency of the "appearances" which lie against his view of Continuity as absolute—although he has not been sufficiently careful in distinguishing between such Continuity and that which admits of degrees.

We may take it, then, as agreed on all hands that whatever weight merely *prima facie* evidence may in this matter be entitled to, is on the side of what I have termed moderated Lamarckianism: first sight "appearances" are against the Neo-Darwinian doctrine of the absolute non-inheritance of acquired characters.

Let us now turn to another and much more important line of indirect evidence in favour of moderated Lamarckianism.

The difficulty of *excluding the possibility* of natural selection having been at work in the case of wild plants and animals has already been noticed. Therefore we may now appreciate the importance of all facts or arguments which *attenuate the probability* of natural selection having been at work. This may be done by searching for cases in nature where a congenital structure, although unquestionably adaptive, nevertheless presents so small an amount of adaptation, that we can scarcely suppose it to have been arrived at by natural selection in the struggle for existence, as distinguished from the inheritance of functionally-produced modifications. For if functionally-produced modifications are ever transmitted at all, there is no limit to the minuteness of adaptive values which may thus become congenital; whereas, in order that any adaptive structure or instinct should be seized upon and accumulated by natural selection, it must from the very first have had an adaptive value sufficiently great to have constituted its presence a matter of life and death in the struggle for existence. Such structures or instincts must not only have always presented some measure of adaptive value, but this must always have been sufficiently great to reach what I have elsewhere called a selection-value. Hence, if we meet with cases in nature where adaptive structures or instincts present so low a degree of adaptive value that it is difficult to conceive how they could ever have exercised any appreciable influence in the battle for life, such cases may fairly be adduced in favour of the Lamarckian theory. For example, the Neo-Lamarckian school of the United States is chiefly composed of palaeontologists; and the reason of this seems to be that the study of fossil forms—or of species in process of formation—reveals so many instances of adaptations which in their nascent condition present such exceedingly minute degrees of adaptive value, that it seems unreasonable to attribute their development to a survival of the fittest in the complex struggle for existence. But as this argument is in my opinion of greatest force when it is applied to certain facts of physiology with which I am about to deal, I will not occupy space by considering any of the numberless cases to which the Neo-Lamarckians apply it within the region of palaeontology[36].

Turning then to inherited actions, it is here that we might antecedently expect to find our best evidence of the Lamarckian principles, if these principles have really had any share in the process of adaptive evolution. For we know that in the life-time of individuals it is action, and the cessation of action, which produce nearly all the phenomena of acquired adaptation—use and disuse in animals being merely other names for action and the cessation of action. Again, we know that it is where neuro-muscular machinery is concerned that we meet with the most conclusive evidence of the remarkable extent to which action is capable of co-ordinating structures for the ready performance of particular functions; so that even during the years of childhood "practice makes perfect" to the extent of organizing neuro-muscular adjustments, so elaborate and complete as to be indistinguishable from those which in natural species we recognized as reflex actions on the one hand, and instinctive actions on the other. Hence, if there be any such thing as "use-inheritance" at all, it is in the domain of reflex actions and instinctive actions that we may expect to find our best evidence of the fact. Therefore I will restrict the present line of evidence—(A)—to these two classes of phenomena, as together yielding the best evidence obtainable within this line of argument.

The evidence in favour of the Lamarckian factors which may be derived from the phenomena of reflex action has never, I believe, been pointed out before; but it appears to me of a more cogent nature than perhaps any other. In order to do it justice, I will begin by re-stating an argument in favour of these factors which has already been adduced by previous writers, and discussed by myself in published correspondence with several leaders of the ultra-Darwinian school.

Long ago Professor Broca and Mr. Herbert Spencer pointed to the facts of co-adaptation, or co-ordination within the limits of the same organism, as presenting good evidence of Lamarckian principles, working in association with natural selection. Thus, taking one of Lamarck's own illustrations, Mr. Spencer argued that there must be numberless changes— extending to all the organs, and even to all the tissues, of the animal— which in the course of many generations have conspired to convert an antelope into a giraffe. Now the point is, that throughout the entire history of these changes their utility must always have been dependent on their association. It would be useless that an incipient giraffe should present the peculiar form of the hind-quarters which we now perceive, unless at the same time it presented the correspondingly peculiar form of the fore-quarters; and as each of these great modifications entails innumerable subordinate modifications throughout both halves of the creature concerned, the chances must have been infinitely great against the required association of so many changes happening to have arisen congenitally in the same individuals by way of merely fortuitous variation. Yet, if we exclude the Lamarckian interpretation, which gives an intelligible *cause* of co-ordination, we are required to suppose that such a happy concurrence of innumerable independent variations must have occurred by mere accident—and this on innumerable different occasions in the bodies of as many successive ancestors of the existing species. For at each successive stage of the improvement natural selection (if working alone) must have needed all, or at any rate most, of the co-ordinated parts to occur in the same individual organisms[37].

In alluding to what I have already published upon the difficulty which thus appears to be presented to his theory, Weismann says, "At no distant time I hope to be able to consider this objection, and to show that the apparent support given to the old idea [i. e. of the transmission of functionally-produced modifications] is really insecure, and breaks down as soon as it is critically examined[38]."

So much for what Weismann has said touching this matter. But the matter has also been dealt with both by Darwin and by Wallace. Darwin very properly distinguishes between the fallacy that "with animals such as the giraffe, of which the whole structure is admirably co-ordinated for certain purposes, it has been supposed that all the parts must have been simultaneously modified[39]," and the sound argument that the co-ordination itself cannot have been due to natural selection alone. This important distinction may be rendered more clear as follows.

The facts of artificial selection prove that immense modifications of structure may be caused by a cumulative blending in the same individuals of characters which were originally distributed among different individuals. Now, in the parallel case of natural selection the characters thus blended will usually—if not invariably—be of an adaptive kind; and their eventual blending together in the same individuals will be due to free intercrossing of the most fit. But this *blending of adaptations* is quite a different matter from the *occurrence of co-ordination*. For it belongs to the essence of co-ordination that each of the co-ordinated parts should be destitute of adaptive value *per se*: the adaptation only begins to arise if all the parts in question occur associated together in the same individuals *from the very first*. In this case it is obvious that the analogy of artificial selection can be of no avail in explaining the facts, since the difficulty presented has nothing to do with the blending in single individuals of adaptations previously distributed among different individuals; it has to do with the simultaneous appearance in single individuals of a co-adaptation of parts, none of which could ever have been of any adaptive value had it been previously distributed among different individuals. Consequently, where Darwin comes to consider this particular case (or the case of co-adaptation as distinguished from the blending of adaptations), he freely invokes the aid of the Lamarckian principles[40].

Wallace, on the other hand, refuses to do this, and says that "the best answer to the difficulty" of supposing natural selection to have been the only cause of co-adaptation may be "found in the fact that the very thing said to be impossible by variation and natural selection, has been again and again affected by variation and artificial selection[41]." This analogy (which Darwin had already and very properly adduced with regard to the *blending of adaptations*) he enforces by special illustrations; but he does not appear to perceive that it misses the whole and only point of the "difficulty" against which it is brought. For the case which his analogy sustains is not that which Darwin, Spencer, Broca and others, mean by *co-adaptation*: it is the case of a blending of *adaptations*. It is not the case where adaptation is *first initiated in spite of intercrossing*, by a fortuitous concurrence of variations each in itself being without adaptive value: it is the case where adaptation is *afterwards increased by means of intercrossing*, through the blending of variations each of which has always been in itself of adaptive value.

From this I hope it will be apparent that the only way in which the "difficulty" from co-adaptation can be logically met by the ultra-Darwinian school, is by denying that the phenomenon of co-adaptation (as distinguished from the blending of adaptations) is ever to be really met with in organic nature. It may be argued that in all cases where co-adaptation *appears* to occur, closer examination will show that the facts are really due to a blending of adaptations. The characters A + B + C + D, which are now found united in the same organism, and, as thus united, all conspiring to a common end, may originally have been distributed among different organisms, where they *severally* subserved some other ends—or possibly the same end, though in a less efficient manner. Obviously, however, in this case their subsequent combination in the same organism would not be an instance of co-adaptation, but merely of an advantageous blending together of already existing adaptations. This argument, or rejoinder, has in point of fact been adopted by Professor Meldola, he believes that all cases of seeming co-adaptation are thus due to a mere blending of adaptations[42]. Of course, if this position can be maintained, the whole difficulty from co-adaptation would lapse. But even then it would lapse on the ground of *fact*. It would not have been overturned, or in any way affected, by Wallace's *argument* from artificial selection. For, in that event, no such argument would be required, and, if adduced, would be irrelevant, since no one has ever alleged that there is any difficulty in understanding the mere confluence of adaptations by free-intercrossing of the best adapted.

Now, if we are agreed that the only question in debate is the question of fact whether or not co-adaptation ever occurs in nature, it appears to me that the best field for debating the question is furnished by the phenomena of reflex action. I can well perceive that the instances adduced by Broca and Spencer in support of their common argument—such as the giraffe, the elk, &c.—are equivocal. But I think that many instances which may be adduced of reflex action are much more to the point. *For it belongs to the very nature of reflex action that it cannot work unless all parts of the machinery concerned are already present, and already co-ordinated, in the same organism.* It would be useless, in so far as such action is concerned if the afferent and efferent nerves, the nerve-centre, and the muscles organically grouped together, were not all present from the very first in the same individuals, and from the very first were not co-ordinated as a definite piece of organic machinery.

With respect to reflex actions, therefore, it is desirable to begin by pointing out how widely the adaptations which they involve differ from those where no manufacture, so to speak, of special machinery is required. Thus, it is easy to understand how natural selection alone is capable of gradually accumulating congenital variations in the direction of protective colouring; of mimicry; of general size, form, mutual correlation of parts as connected with superior strength, fleetness, agility, &c.; of greater or less development of particular parts, such as legs, wings, tails, &c. For in all such cases the adaptation which is in process of accumulation is from its very commencement and throughout each of its subsequent stages, of *use* in the struggle for existence. And inasmuch as all the individuals of each successive generation vary round the specific mean which characterized the preceding generation, there will always be a sufficient number of individuals which present congenital variations of the kind required for natural selection to seize upon, without danger of their being swamped by free intercrossing—as Mr. Wallace has very ably shown in his *Darwinism*. But this law of averages can apply only to cases where single structures—or a single group of correlated structures—are already present, and already varying round a specific mean. The case is quite different where a *co-ordination* of structures is required for the performance of a *previously non-existent* reflex action. For some, at least, of these structures must be *new*, as must also be the function which all of them first conspire to perform. Therefore, neither the new elements of structure, nor the new combination of structures, can have been previously given as varying round a specific mean. On the contrary, a very definite piece of machinery, consisting of many co-ordinated parts, must somehow or other be originated in a high degree of working efficiency, before it can be capable of answering its purpose in the prompt performance of a particular action under particular circumstances of stimulation. Lastly, such pieces of machinery are always of a highly delicate character, and usually involve so immensely complex a co-ordination of mutually dependent parts, that it is only a physiologist who can fully appreciate the magnitude of the distinction between "adaptations" of this kind, and "adaptations" of the kind which arise through natural selection seizing upon congenital variations as these oscillate round a specific mean.

Or the whole argument may be presented in another form, under three different headings, thus:—

In the first place, it will be evident from what has just been said, that such a piece of machinery as is concerned in even the simplest reflex action cannot have occurred in any considerable number of individuals of a species, *when it first began to be constructed.* On the contrary, if its *origin* were dependent on congenital variations alone, the needful co-adaptation of parts which it requires can scarcely have happened to occur in more than a very small percentage of cases—even if it be held conceivable that by such means alone it should ever have occurred at all. Hence, instead of preservation and subsequent improvement having taken place *in consequence of* free intercrossing among all individuals of the species (as in the cases of protective colouring, &c., where adaptation has no reference to any mechanical co-adaptation of parts), they must have taken place *in spite of* such intercrossing.

In the second place, adaptations due to organic machineries of this kind differ in another all-important respect from those due to a summation of adaptive characters which are already present and already varying round a specific mean. The latter depend for their summation upon the fact—not merely, as just stated, that they are already present, already varying round a specific mean, and therefore owe their progressive evolution to free intercrossing, but also—*that they admit of very different degrees of adaptation.* It is only because the degree of adaptation in generation B is superior to that in generation A that *gradual improvement* in respect of adaptation is here possible. In the case of protective resemblance, for example, a very imperfect and merely accidental resemblance to a leaf, to another insect, &c., may at the first start have conferred a sufficient degree of adaptive imitation to count for something in the struggle for life; and, if so, the basis would be given for a progressive building up by natural selection of structures and colours in ever-advancing degrees of adaptive resemblance. There is here no necessity to suppose—nor in point of fact is it ever supposed, since the supposition would involve nothing short of a miracle— that such extreme perfection in this respect as we now so frequently admire has originated suddenly in a single generation, as a collective variation of a congenital kind affecting simultaneously a large proportional number of individuals. But in the case of a reflex mechanism—which may involve even greater marvels of adaptive adjustment, and *all* the parts of which must occur in the same *individuals* to be of any use—it *is* necessary to suppose some such sudden and collective origin in some very high degree of efficiency, if natural selection has been the only principle concerned in afterwards perfecting the mechanism. For it is self-evident that a reflex action, from its very nature, cannot admit of any great differences in its degrees of adaptation: if it is to work at all, so as to count for anything in the struggle for life, it must already be given in a state of working efficiency. So that, unless we invoke either the doctrine of "prophetic types" or the theory of sudden creations, I confess I do not see how we are to explain either the origin, or the development, of a reflex mechanism by means of natural selection alone.

Lastly, in the third place, *even when reflex mechanisms have been fully formed*, it is often beyond the power of sober credence to believe that they now are, or ever can have been, of selective value in the struggle for existence, as I will show further on. And such cases go to fortify the preceding argument. For if not conceivably of selective value even when completely evolved, much less can they conceivably have been so through all the stages of their complex evolution back to their very origin. Therefore, supposing for the present that there are such cases of reflex action in nature, neither their origin nor their development can conceivably have been due to natural selection alone. The Lamarckian factors, however, have no reference to degrees of adaptation, any more than they have to degrees of complexity. No question of value, as selective or otherwise, can obtain in their case: neither in their case does any difficulty obtain as regards the co-adaptation of severally useless parts.

Now, if all these distinctions between the Darwinian and Lamarckian principles are valid—and I cannot see any possibility of doubt upon this point—strong evidence in favour of the latter would be furnished by cases (if any occur) where structures, actions, instincts, &c., although of some adaptive value, are nevertheless plainly not of selective value. According to the ultra-Darwinian theory, no such cases ought ever to occur: according to the theory of Darwin himself, they ought frequently to occur. Therefore a good test, or criterion, as between these different theories of organic evolution is furnished by putting the simple question of fact—Can we, or can we not, show that there are cases of adaptation where the degree of adaptation is so small as to be incompatible with the supposition of its presenting a selective value? And if we put the wider question—Are there any cases where the co-adaptation of severally useless parts has been brought about, when even the resulting whole does not present a selective value?—then, of course, we impose a still more rigid test.

Well, notwithstanding the difficulty of proving such a negative as the absence of natural selection where adaptive development is concerned, I believe that there are cases which conform to both these tests simultaneously; and, moreover, that they are to be found in most abundance where the theory of use-inheritance would most expect them to occur—namely, in the province of reflex action. For the very essence of this theory is the doctrine, that constantly associated use of the same parts for the performance of the same action will progressively organize those parts into a reflex mechanism—no matter how high a degree of co-adaptation may thus be reached on the one hand, or how low a degree of utilitarian value on the other.

Having now stated the general or abstract principles which I regard as constituting a defence of the Lamarckian factors, so far as this admits of being raised on grounds of physiology, we will now consider a few concrete cases by way of illustration. It is needless to multiply such cases for the mere purpose of illustration. For, on reading those here given, every physiologist will at once perceive that they might be added to indefinitely. The point to observe is, the relation in which these samples of reflex action stand to the general principles in question; for there is nothing unusual in the samples themselves. On the contrary, they are chosen because they are fairly typical of the phenomena of reflex action in general.

In our own organization there is a reflex mechanism which ensures the prompt withdrawal of the legs from any source of irritation supplied to the feet. For instance, even after a man has broken his spine in such a manner as totally to interrupt the functional continuity of his spinal cord and brain, the reflex mechanism in question will continue to retract his legs when his feet are stimulated by a touch, a burn, &c. This responsive action is clearly an adaptive action, and, as the man neither feels the stimulation nor the resulting movement, it is as clearly a reflex action. The question now is as to the mode of its origin and development.

I will not here dwell upon the argument from co-adaptation, because this may be done more effectually in the case of more complicated reflex actions, but will ask whether we can reasonably hold that this particular reflex action—comparatively simple though it is—has ever been of selective value to the human species, or to the ancestors thereof? Even in its present fully-formed condition it is fairly questionable whether it is of any adaptive *value* at all. The movement performed is no doubt an adaptive *movement*; but is there any occasion upon which the reflex mechanism concerned therein can ever have been of adaptive *use*? Until a man's legs have been paralyzed as to their voluntary motion, he will always promptly withdraw his feet from any injurious source of irritation by means of his conscious intelligence. True, the reflex mechanism secures an almost inappreciable saving in the time of response to a stimulus, as compared with the time required for response by an act of will; but the difference is so exceedingly small, that we can hardly suppose the saving of it in this particular case to be a matter of any adaptive—much less selective—importance. Nor is it more easy to suppose that the reflex mechanism has been developed by natural selection for the purpose of replacing voluntary action when the latter has been destroyed or suspended by grave spinal injury, paralysis, coma, or even ordinary sleep. In short, even if for the sake of argument we allow it to be conceivable that any single human being, ape, or still more distant ancestor, has ever owed its life to the possession of this mechanism, we may still be certain that not one in a million can have done so. And, if this is the case with regard to the mechanism as now fully constructed, still more must it have been the case with regard to all the previous stages of construction. For here, without elaborating the point, it would appear that a process of construction by survival of the fittest alone is incomprehensible.

On the other hand, of course, the theory of use-inheritance furnishes a fully intelligible—whether or not a true—explanation. For those nerve-centres in the spinal cord which co-ordinate the muscles required for retracting the feet are the centres used by the will for this purpose. And, by hypothesis, the frequent use of them for this purpose under circumstances of stimulation which render the muscular response appropriate, will eventually establish an organic connexion between such response and the kind of stimulation to which it is appropriate—even though there be no utilitarian reason for its establishment[43]. To invert a phrase of Aristotle, we do not frequently use this mechanism because we have it (seeing that in our normal condition there is no necessity for such use); but, by hypothesis, we have it because we have frequently used its several elements in appropriate combination.

I will adduce but one further example in illustration of these general principles—passing at once from the foregoing case of comparative simplicity to one of extreme complexity.

There is a well-known experiment on a brainless frog, which reveals a beautiful reflex mechanism in the animal, whereby the whole body is enabled continually to readjust its balance on a book (or any other plane surface), as this is slowly rotated on a horizontal axis. So long as the book is lying flat, the frog remains motionless; but as soon as the book is tilted a little, so that the frog is in danger of slipping off, all the four feet begin to crawl up the hill; and the steeper the hill becomes, the faster they crawl. When the book is vertical, the frog has reached the now horizontal back, and so on. Such being the facts, the question is—How can the complicated piece of machinery thus implied have been developed by natural selection? Obviously it cannot have been so by any of the parts concerned having been originally distributed among different individuals, and afterwards united in single individuals by survival (i.e. free intercrossing) of the fittest. In other words, the case is obviously one of co-adaptation, and not one of the blending of adaptations. Again, and no less obviously, it is impossible that the co-adaptation can have been *gradually developed* by natural selection, because, in order to have been so, it must by hypothesis have been of some degree of use in every one of its stages; yet it plainly cannot have been until it had been fully perfected in all its astonishing complexity[44].

Lastly, not only does it thus appear impossible that during all stages of its development—or while as yet incapable of performing its intricate function—this nascent mechanism can have had any adaptive value; but even as now fully developed, who will venture to maintain that it presents any selective value? As long as the animal preserves its brain, it will likewise preserve its balance, by the exercise of its intelligent volition. And, if the brain were in some way destroyed, the animal would be unable to breed, or even to feed; so that natural selection can never have had any *opportunity*, so to speak, of developing this reflex mechanism in brainless frogs. On the other hand, as we have just seen, we cannot perceive how there can ever have been any *raison d'être* for its development in normal frogs—even if its development were conceivably possible by means of this agency. But if practice makes perfect in the race, as it does in the individual, we can immediately perceive that the constant habit of correctly adjusting its balance may have gradually developed, in the batrachian organization, this non-necessary reflex[45].

And, of course, this example—like that of withdrawing the feet from a source of stimulation, which a frog will do as well as a man—does not stand alone. Without going further a-field than this same animal, any one who reads, from our present point of view, Goltz's work on the reflex actions of the frog, will find that the great majority of them—complex and refined though most of them are—cannot conceivably have ever been of any use to any frog that was in undisturbed possession of its brain.

Hence, not to occupy space with a reiteration of facts all more or less of the same general kind, and therefore all presenting identical difficulties to ultra-Darwinian theory, I shall proceed to give two others which appear to me of particular interest in the present connexion, because they furnish illustrations of reflex actions in a state of only partial development, and are therefore at the present moment demonstrably useless to the animal which displays them.

Many of our domesticated dogs, when we gently scratch their sides and certain other parts of the body, will themselves perform scratching movements with the hind leg of the same side as that upon which the irritation is being supplied. According to Goltz[46], this action is a true reflex; for he found that it is performed equally well in a dog which has been deprived of its cerebral hemispheres, and therefore of its normal volition. Again, according to Haycraft[47], this reflex is congenital, or not acquired during the life-time of each individual dog. Now, although the action of scratching is doubtless adaptive, it appears to me incredible that it could ever have become organized into a congenital reflex by natural selection. For, in order that it should, the scratching away fleas would require to have been a function of selective value. Yet, even if the irritation caused by fleas were supposed to be so far fatal in the struggle for existence, it is certain that they would always be scratched away by the conscious intelligence of each individual dog; and, therefore, that no advantage could be gained by organizing the action into a reflex. On the other hand, if acquired characters are ever in any degree transmitted, it is easy to understand how so frequently repeated an action should have become, in numberless generations of dogs, congenitally automatic.

So much for the general principle of selective value as applied to this particular case. And similarly, of course, we might here repeat the application of all the other general principles, which have just been applied in the two preceding cases. But it is only one of these other general principles which I desire in the present case specially to consider, for the purpose of considering more closely than hitherto the difficulty which this principle presents to ultra-Darwinian theory.

The difficulty to which I allude is that of understanding how all the stages in the *development* of a reflex action can have been due to natural selection, seeing that, before the reflex mechanism has been sufficiently elaborated to perform its function, it cannot have presented any degree of utility. Now the particular force of the present example, the action of scratching—as also of the one to follow—consists in the fact that it is a case where a reflex action is not yet completely organized. It appears to be only in course of construction, so that it is neither invariably present, nor, when it is present, is it ever fully adapted to the performance of its function.

That it is not invariably present (when the brain is so) may be proved by trying the simple experiment on a number of puppies—and also of full-grown dogs. Again, that even when it is present it is far from being fully adapted to the performance of its function, may be proved by observing that only in rare instances does the scratching leg succeed in scratching the place which is being irritated. The movements are made more or less at random, and as often as not the foot fails to touch the body at any place at all. Hence, although we have a "prophecy" of a reflex action well designed for the discharge of a particular function, at present the machinery is not sufficiently perfected for the adequate discharge of that function. In this important respect it differs from the otherwise closely analogous reflex action of the frog, whereby the foot of the hind leg is enabled to localize with precision a seat of irritation on the side of the body. But this beautiful mechanism in the frog cannot have sprung into existence ready formed at any historical moment in the past history of the phyla. It must have been the subject of a more or less prolonged evolution, in some stage of which it must presumably have resembled the now nascent scratching reflex of the dog, in making merely abortive attempts at localizing the seat of irritation— supposing, of course, that some physiologist had been there to try the experiment by first removing the brain. Now, even if one could imagine it to be, either in the frog or in the dog, a matter of selective importance that so exceedingly refined a mechanism should have been developed for the sole purpose of inhibiting the bites of parasites—which in every normal animal would certainly be discharged by an *intentional* performance of the movements in question,—even if, in order to save an hypothesis at all costs, we make so violent a supposition as this, still we should do so in vain. For it would still remain undeniably certain that the reflex mechanism is *not* of any selective value. Even now the mechanism in the dog is not sufficiently precise to subserve the only function which occasionally and abortively it attempts to perform. Thus it has all the appearance of being but an imitating shadow of certain neuro-muscular adjustments, which have been habitually performed in the canine phyla by a volitional response to cutaneous irritation. Were it necessary, this argument might be strengthened by observing that the reflex action is positively *improved* by removal of the brain.

The second example of a nascent reflex in dogs which I have to mention is as follows.

Goltz found that his brainless dogs, when wetted with water, would shake themselves as dry as possible, in just the same way as normal dogs will do under similar circumstances. This, of course, proves that the shaking movements may be performed by a reflex mechanism, which can have no other function to perform in the organization of a dog, and which, besides being of a highly elaborate character, will respond only to a very special kind of stimulation. Now, here also I find that the mechanism is congenital, or not acquired by individual experience. For the puppies on which I experimented were kept indoors from the time of their birth—so as never to have had any experience of being wetted by rain, &c.—till they were old enough to run about with a full power of co-ordinating their general movements. If these young animals were suddenly plunged into water, the shock proved too great: they would merely lie and shiver. But if their feet alone were wetted, by being dipped in a basin of water, the puppies would soon afterwards shake their heads in the peculiar manner which is required for shaking water off the ears, and which in adult dogs constitutes the first phase of a general shaking of the whole body.

Here, then, we seem to have good evidence of all the same facts which were presented in the case of the scratching reflex. In the first place, co-adaptation is present in a very high degree, because this shaking reflex in the dog, unlike the skin-twitching reflex in the horse, does not involve only a single muscle, or even a single group of muscles; it involves more or less the co-ordinated activity of many voluntary muscles all over the body. Such, at any rate, is the case when the action is performed by the intelligent volition of an adult dog; and if a brainless dog, or a young puppy, does not perform it so extensively or so vigorously, this only goes to prove that the reflex has not yet been sufficiently developed to serve as a substitute for intelligent volition—i.e. that it is *useless*, or a mere organic shadow of the really adaptive substance. Again, even if this nascent reflex had been so far developed as to have been capable of superseding voluntary action, still we may fairly doubt whether it could have proved of selective value. For it is questionable whether the immediate riddance of water after a wetting is a matter of life and death to dogs in a state of nature. Moreover, even if it were, every individual dog would always have got rid of the irritation, and so of the danger, by means of a *voluntary* shake—with the double result that natural selection has never had any opportunity of gradually building up a special reflex mechanism for the purpose of securing a shake, and that the canine race have not had to wait for any such unnecessary process. Lastly, such a process, besides being unnecessary, must surely have been, under any circumstances, impossible. For even if we were to suppose—again for the sake of saving an hypothesis at any cost—that the presence of a fully-formed shaking reflex is of selective value in the struggle for existence, it is perfectly certain that all the stages through which the construction of so elaborate a mechanism must have passed could not have been, under any circumstances, of any such value.

But, it is needless to repeat, according to the hypothesis of use-inheritance, there is no necessity to suppose that these incipient reflex mechanisms *are* of any value. If function produces structure in the race as it does in the individual, the voluntary and frequently repeated actions of scratching and shaking may very well have led to an organic integration of the neuro-muscular mechanisms concerned. Their various parts having been always co-ordinated for the performance of these actions by the intelligence of innumerable dogs in the past, their co-adapted activity in their now automatic responses to appropriate stimuli presents no difficulty. And the consideration that neither in their prospectively more fully developed condition, nor, *a fortiori*, in their present and all previous stages of evolution, can these reflex mechanisms be regarded as presenting any selective—or even so much as any adaptive—value, is neither more nor less than the theory of use-inheritance would expect.

Thus, with regard to the phenomena of reflex action in general, all the facts are such as this theory requires, while many of the facts are such as the theory of natural selection alone cannot conceivably explain. Indeed, it is scarcely too much to say, that most of the facts are such as directly contradict the latter theory in its application to them. But, be this as it may, at present there are only two hypotheses in the field whereby to account for the facts of adaptive evolution. One of these hypotheses is universally accepted, and the only question is whether we are to regard it as *alone* sufficient to explain *all* the facts. The other hypothesis having been questioned, we can test its validity only by finding cases which it is fully capable of explaining, and which do not admit of being explained by its companion hypothesis. I have endeavoured to show that we have a large class of such cases in the domain of reflex action, and shall next endeavour to show that there is another large class in the domain of instinct.

If instinct be, as Professor Hering, Mr. Samuel Butler, and others have argued, "hereditary habit"—i. e. if it comprises an element of transmitted experience—we at once find a complete explanation of many cases of the display of instinct which otherwise remain inexplicable. For although a large number—or even, as I believe, a large majority—of instincts are explicable by the theory of natural selection alone, or by supposing that they were gradually developed by the survival of fortuitous variations in the way of advantageous psychological peculiarities, this only applies to comparatively simple instincts, such as that of a protectively coloured animal exhibiting a preference for the surroundings which it resembles, or even adopting attitudes in imitation of objects which occur in such surroundings. But in all cases where instincts become complex and refined, we seem almost compelled to accept Darwin's view that their origin is to be sought in consciously intelligent adjustments on the part of ancestors.

Thus, to give only one example, a species of Sphex preys upon caterpillars, which it stings in their nerve-centres for the purpose of paralyzing, without killing them. The victims, when thus rendered motionless, are then buried with the eggs of the Sphex, in order to serve as food for her larvae which subsequently develop from these eggs. Now, in order thus to paralyze a caterpillar, the Sphex has to sting it successively in nine minute and particular points along the ventral surface of the animal— and this the Sphex unerringly does, to the exclusion of all other points of the caterpillar's anatomy. Well, such being the facts—according to M. Fabre, who appears to have observed them carefully—it is conceivable enough, as Darwin supposed[48], that the ancestors of the Sphex, being like many other hymenopterous insects highly intelligent, should have observed that on stinging caterpillars in these particular spots a greater amount of effect was produced than could be produced by stinging them anywhere else; and, therefore, that they habitually stung the caterpillars in these places only, till, in course of time, this originally intelligent habit became by heredity instinctive. But now, on the other hand, if we exclude the possibility of this explanation, it appears to me incredible that such an instinct should ever have been evolved at all; for it appears to me incredible that natural selection, unaided by originally intelligent action, could ever have developed such an instinct out of merely fortuitous variations—there being, by hypothesis, nothing to *determine* variations of an insect's mind in the direction of stinging caterpillars only in these nine intensely localized spots[49].

Again, there are not a few instincts which appear to be wholly useless to their possessors, and others again which appear to be even deleterious. The dusting over of their excrement by certain freely-roaming carnivora; the choice by certain herbivora of particular places on which to void their urine, or in which to die; the howling of wolves at the moon; purring of cats, &c., under pleasurable emotion; and sundry other hereditary actions of the same apparently unmeaning kind, all admit of being readily accounted for as useless habits originally acquired in various ways, and afterwards perpetuated by heredity, because not sufficiently deleterious to have been stamped out by natural selection[50]. But it does not seem possible to explain them by survival of the fittest in the struggle for existence.

Finally, in the case of our own species, it is self-evident that the aesthetic, moral, and religious instincts admit of a natural and easy explanation on the hypothesis of use-inheritance, while such is by no means the case if that hypothesis is rejected. Our emotions of the ludicrous, of the beautiful, and of the sublime, appear to be of the nature of hereditary instincts; and be this as it may, it would further appear that, whatever else they may be, they are certainly not of a life-preserving character. And although this cannot be said of the moral sense when the theory of natural selection is extended from the individual to the tribe, still, when we remember the extraordinary complexity and refinement to which they have attained in civilized man, we may well doubt whether they can have been due to natural selection alone. But space forbids discussion of this large and important question on the present occasion. Suffice it therefore to say, that I doubt not Weismann himself would be the first to allow that his theory of heredity encounters greater difficulties in the domain of ethics than in any other—unless, indeed, it be that of religion[51].

I have now given a brief sketch of the indirect evidence in favour of the so-called Lamarckian factors, in so far as this appears fairly deducible from the facts of reflex action and of instinct. It will now be my endeavour to present as briefly what has to be said against this evidence.

As previously observed, the facts of reflex action have not been hitherto adduced in the present connexion. This has led me to occupy considerably more space in the treatment of them than those of instinct. On this account, also, there is here nothing to quote, or to consider, *per contra*. On the other hand, however, Weismann has himself dealt with the phenomena of instinct in animals, though not, I think, in man—if we except his brilliant essay on music. Therefore let us now begin this division of our subject by briefly stating, and considering, what he has said upon the subject.

The answer of Weismann to difficulties which arise against the ultra-Darwinian theory in the domain of instinct, is as follows:—

> "The necessity for extreme caution in appealing to the supposed hereditary effects of use, is well shown in the case of those numerous instincts which only come into play once in a life-time, and which do not therefore admit of improvement by practice. The queen-bee takes her nuptial flight only once, and yet how many and complex are the instincts and the reflex mechanisms which come into play on that occasion. Again, in many insects the deposition of eggs occurs but once in a life-time, and yet such insects always fulfil the necessary conditions with unfailing accuracy[52]."

But in this rejoinder the possibility is forgotten, that although such actions are *now* performed only once in the individual life-time, *originally*— i.e. when the instincts were being developed in a remote ancestry—they may have been performed on many frequent and successive occasions during the individual life-time. In all the cases quoted by Weismann, instincts of the kind in question bear independent evidence of high antiquity, by occurring in whole genera (or even families), by being associated with peculiar and often highly evolved structures required for their performance, and so on. Consequently, in these cases ample time has been allowed for subsequent changes of habit, and of seasonal alterations with respect to propagation—both these things being of frequent and facile occurrence among animals of all kinds, even within periods which fall under actual observation. Nevertheless, I do not question that there are instinctive activities which, as far as we are able to see, can never have been performed more than once in each individual life-time[53]. The fact, however, only goes to show what is fully admitted—that some instincts (and even highly complex instincts) have apparently been developed by natural selection alone. Which, of course, is not equivalent to showing that all instincts must have been developed by natural selection alone. The issue is not to be debated on general grounds like this, but on those of particular cases. Even if it were satisfactorily proved that the instincts of a queen-bee have been developed by natural selection, it would not thereby be proved that such has been the case with the instincts of a Sphex wasp. One can very well understand how the nuptial flight of the former, with all its associated actions, may have been brought about by natural selection alone; but this does not help us to understand how the peculiar instincts of the latter can have been thus caused.

Strong evidence in favour of Weismann's views does, however, at first sight seem to be furnished by social hymenoptera in other respects. For not only does the queen present highly specialized and altogether remarkable instincts; but the neuters present totally different and even still more remarkable instincts—which, moreover, are often divided into two or more classes, corresponding with the different "castes." Yet the neuters, being barren females, never have an opportunity of bequeathing their instincts to progeny. Thus it appears necessary to suppose that the instincts of all the different castes of neuters are latent in the queen and drones, together with the other instincts which are patent in both. Lastly, it seems necessary to suppose that all this wonderful organization of complex and segregated instincts must have been built up by natural selection acting exclusively on the queens and drones—seeing that these exercise their own instincts only once in a life-time, while, as just observed, the neuters cannot possibly bequeath their individual experience to progeny. Obviously, however, natural selection must here be supposed to be operating at an immense disadvantage; for it must have built up the often diverse and always complex instincts of neuters, not directly, but indirectly through the queens and drones, which never manifest any of these instincts themselves.

Now Darwin fully acknowledged the difficulty of attributing these results to the unaided influence of natural selection; but the fact of neuter insects being unable to propagate seemed to him to leave no alternative. And so it seems to Weismann, who accordingly quotes these instincts in support of his views. And so it seemed to me, until my work on *Animal Intelligence* was translated into French, and an able Preface was supplied to that translation by M. Perrier. In this Preface it is argued that we are not necessarily obliged to exclude the possibility of Lamarckian principles having operated in the original formation of these instincts. On the contrary, if such principles ever operate at all, Perrier shows that here we have a case where it is virtually certain that they must have operated. For although neuter insects are now unable to propagate, their organization indicates—if it does not actually prove—that they are descended from working insects which were able to propagate. Thus, in all probability, what we now call a "hive" was originally a society of sexually mature insects, all presenting the same instincts, both as to propagation and to co-operation. When these instincts, thus common to all individuals composing the hive, had been highly perfected, it became of advantage in the struggle for existence (between different hives or communities) that the functions of reproduction should devolve more upon some individuals, while those of co-operation should devolve more upon others. Consequently, this division of labour began, and gradually became complete, as we now find it in bees and ants. Perrier sustains the hypothesis thus briefly sketched by pointing to certain species of social hymenoptera where we may actually observe different stages of the process—from cases where all the females of the hive are at the same time workers and breeders, up to the cases where the severance between these functions has become complete. Therefore, it seems to me, it is no longer necessary to suppose that in these latter cases all the instincts of the (now) barren females can only have been due to the unaided influence of natural selection.

Nevertheless, although I think that Perrier has made good his position thus far, that his hypothesis fails to account for some of the instincts which are manifested by neuter insects, such as those which, so far as I can see, must necessarily be supposed to have originated after the breeding and working functions had become separated—seeing that they appear to have exclusive reference to this peculiar state of matters. Possibly, however, Perrier might be able to meet each of these particular instincts, by showing how they could have arisen out of simpler beginnings, prior to the separation of the two functions in question. There is no space to consider such possibilities in detail; but, until this shall have been done, I do not think we are entitled to conclude that the phenomena of instinct as presented by neuter insects are demonstrably incompatible with the doctrines of Lamarck—or, that these phenomena are available as a logical proof of the unassisted agency of natural selection in the case of instincts in general[54].

(B.)
Inherited Effects of Use and of Disuse.

There is no doubt that Darwin everywhere attaches great weight to this line of evidence. Nevertheless, in my opinion, there is equally little doubt that, taken by itself, it is of immeasurably less weight than Darwin supposed. Indeed, I quite agree with Weismann that the whole of this line of evidence is practically worthless; and for the following reasons.

The evidence on which Darwin relied to prove the inherited effects of use and disuse was derived from his careful measurements of the increase or decrease which certain bones of our domesticated animals have undergone, as compared with the corresponding bones of ancestral stocks in a state of nature. He chose domesticated animals for these investigations, because, while yielding unquestionable cases of increased or diminished use of certain organs over a large number of sequent generations, the results were not complicated by the possible interference of natural selection on the one hand, or by that of the economy of nutrition on the other. For "with highly-fed domesticated animals there seems to be no economy of growth, or any tendency to the elimination of superfluous details[55];" seeing that, among other considerations pointing in the same direction, "structures which are rudimentary in the parent species, sometimes become partially re-developed in our domesticated productions[56]."

The method of Darwin's researches in this connexion was as follows. Taking, for example, the case of ducks, he carefully weighed and measured the wing-bones and leg-bones of wild and tame ducks; and he found that the wing-bones were smaller, while the leg-bones were larger, in the tame than in the wild specimens. These facts he attributed to many generations of tame ducks using their wings less, and their legs more, than was the case with their wild ancestry. Similarly he compared the leg-bones of wild rabbits with those of tame ones, and so forth—in all cases finding that where domestication had led to increased use of a part, that part was larger than in the wild parent stock; while the reverse was the case with parts less used. Now, although at first sight these facts certainly do seem to yield good evidence of the inherited effects of use and disuse, they are really open to the following very weighty objections.

First of all, there is no means of knowing how far the observed effects may have been due to increased or diminished use during only the individual life-time of each domesticated animal. Again, and this is a more important point, in all Darwin's investigations the increase or decrease of a part was estimated, not by directly comparing, say the wing-bones of a domesticated duck with the wing-bones of a wild duck, but by comparing the *ratio* between the wing and leg bones of a tame duck with the *ratio* between the wing and leg bones of a wild duck. Consequently, if there be any reason to doubt the supposition that a really inherited decrease in the size of a part thus estimated is due to the inherited effects of disuse, such a doubt will also extend to the evidence of increased size being due to the inherited effects of use. Now there is the gravest possible doubt lying against the supposition that any really inherited decrease in the size of a part is due to the inherited effects of disuse. For it may be—and, at any rate to some extent, must be—due to another principle, which it is strange that Darwin should have overlooked. This is the principle which Weismann has called Panmixia, and which cannot be better expressed than in his own words:—

> "A goose or a duck must possess strong powers of flight in the natural state, but such powers are no longer necessary for obtaining food when it is brought into the poultry-yard; so that a rigid selection of individuals with well-developed wings at once ceases among its descendants. Hence, in the course of generations, a deterioration of the organs of flight must necessarily ensue[57]."

Or, to state the case in another way: if any structure which was originally built up by natural selection on account of its use, ceases any longer to be of so much use, in whatever degree it ceases to be of use, in that degree will the premium before set upon it by natural selection be withdrawn. And the consequence of this withdrawal of selection as regards that particular part will be to allow the part to degenerate in successive generations. Such is the principle which Weismann calls Panmixia, because, by the withdrawal of selection from any particular part, promiscuous breeding ensues with regard to that part. And it is easy to see that this principle must be one of very great importance in nature; because it must necessarily come into operation in all cases where any structure or any instinct has, through any change in the environment or in the habits of a species, ceased to be useful. It is likewise easy to see that its effect must be the same as that which was attributed by Darwin to the inherited effect of disuse; and, therefore, that the evidence on which he relied in proof of the inherited effects both of use and of disuse is vitiated by the fact that the idea of Panmixia did not occur to him.

Here, however, it may be said that the idea first occurred to me[58] just after the publication of the last edition of the *Origin of Species*. I called the principle the Cessation of Selection—which I still think a better, because a more descriptive, term than Panmixia; and at that time it appeared to me, as it now appears to Weismann, entirely to supersede the necessity of supposing that the effect of disuse is ever inherited in any degree at all. Thus it raised the whole question as to the admissibility of Lamarckian principles in general; or the question on which we are now engaged touching the possible inheritance of acquired, as distinguished from congenital, characters. But on discussing the matter with Mr. Darwin, he satisfied me that the larger question was not to be so easily closed. That is to say, although he fully accepted the principle of the Cessation of Selection, and as fully acknowledged its obvious importance, he convinced me that there was independent evidence for the transmission of acquired characters, sufficient in amount to leave the general structure of his previous theory unaffected by what he nevertheless recognized as a factor which must necessarily be added. All this I now mention in order to show that the issue which Weismann has raised since Darwin's death was expressly contemplated during the later years of Darwin's life. For if the idea of Panmixia—in the absence of which Weismann's entire system would be impossible—had never been present to Darwin's mind, we should have been left in uncertainty how he would have regarded this subsequent revolt against what are generally called the Lamarckian principles[59].

Moreover, in this connexion we must take particular notice that the year after I had published these articles on the Cessation of Selection, and discussed with Mr. Darwin the bearing of this principle on the question of the transmission of acquired characters, Mr. Galton followed with his highly important essay on Heredity. For in this essay Mr. Galton fully adopted the principle of the Cessation of Selection, and was in consequence the first publicly to challenge the Lamarckian principles— pointing out that, if it were thus possible to deny the transmission of acquired characters *in toto*, "we should be relieved from all further trouble"; but that, if such characters are transmitted "in however faint a degree, a complete theory of heredity must account for them." Thus the question which, in its revived condition, is now attracting so much attention, was propounded in all its parts some fifteen or sixteen years ago; and no additional facts or new considerations of any great importance bearing upon the subject have been adduced since that time. In other words, about a year after my own conversations with Mr. Darwin, the whole matter was still more effectively brought before his notice by his own cousin. And the result was that he still retained his belief in the Lamarckian factors of organic evolution, even more strongly than it was retained either by Mr. Galton or myself[60].

We have now considered the line of evidence on which Darwin chiefly relied in proof of the transmissibility of acquired characters; and it must be allowed that this line of evidence is practically worthless. What he regarded as the inherited effects of use and of disuse may be entirely due to the cessation of selection in the case of our domesticated animals, combined with an active *reversal* of selection in the case of natural species. And in accordance with this view is the fact that the degeneration of disused parts proceeds much further in the case of wild species than it does in that of domesticated varieties. For although it may be said that in the case of wild species more time has been allowed for a greater accumulation of the inherited effects of disuse than can have been the case with domesticated varieties, the alternative explanation is at least as probable—that in the case of wild species the merely negative, or passive, influence of the *cessation* of selection has been continuously and powerfully assisted by the positive, or active, influence of the *reversal* of selection, through economy of growth and the general advantage to be derived from the abolition of useless parts[61].

The absence of any good evidence of this direct kind in favour of use-inheritance will be rendered strikingly apparent to any one who reads a learned and interesting work by Professor Semper[62]. His object was to show the large part which he believed to have been played by external conditions of life in directly modifying organic types—or, in other words, of proving that side of Lamarckianism which refers to the immediate action of the environment, whether with or without the co-operation of use-inheritance and natural selection. Although Semper gathered together a great array of facts, the more carefully one reads his book the more apparent does it become that no single one of the facts is in itself conclusive evidence of the transmission to progeny of characters which are acquired through use-inheritance or through direct action of the environment. Every one of the facts is susceptible of explanation on the hypothesis that the principle of natural selection has been the only principle concerned. This, however, it must be observed, is by no means equivalent to proving that characters thus acquired are not transmitted. As already pointed out, it is impracticable with species in a state of nature to dissociate the distinctively Darwinian from the possibly Lamarckian factors; so that even if the latter are largely operative, we can only hope for direct evidence of the fact from direct experiments on varieties in a state of domestication. To this branch of our subject, therefore, we will now proceed.

CHAPTER IV
CHARACTERS AS HEREDITARY AND ACQUIRED
(*continued*).

(C.)
Experimental Evidence in favour of the Inheritance of Acquired Characters.

Notwithstanding the fact already noticed, that no experiments have hitherto been published with reference to the question of the transmission of acquired characters[63], there are several researches which, with other objects in view, have incidentally yielded seemingly good evidence of such transmission. The best-known of these researches—and therefore the one with which I shall begin—is that of Brown-Séquard touching the effects of certain injuries of the nervous system in guinea-pigs.

During a period of thirty years Brown-Séquard bred many thousands of guinea-pigs as material for his various researches; and in those whose parents had not been operated upon in the ways to be immediately mentioned, he never saw any of the peculiarities which are about to be described. Therefore the hypothesis of coincidence, at all events, must be excluded. The following is his own summary of the results with which we are concerned:—

> 1st. Appearance of epilepsy in animals born of parents which had been rendered epileptic by an injury to the spinal cord.

> 2nd. Appearance of epilepsy also in animals born of parents which had been rendered epileptic by section of the sciatic nerve.

> 3rd. A change in the shape of the ear in animals born of parents in which such a change was the effect of a division of the cervical sympathetic nerve.

> 4th. Partial closure of the eyelids in animals born of parents in which that state of the eyelids had been caused either by section of the cervical sympathetic nerve, or the removal of the superior cervical ganglion.

5th. Exophthalmia in animals born of parents in which an injury to the restiform body had produced that protrusion of the eyeball. This interesting fact I have witnessed a good many times, and seen the transmission of the morbid state of the eye continue through four generations. In these animals, modified by heredity, the two eyes generally protruded, although in the parents usually only one showed exophthalmia, the lesion having been made in most cases only on one of the corpora restiformia.

6th. Haematoma and dry gangrene of the ears in animals born of parents in which these ear-alterations had been caused by an injury to the restiform body near the nib of the calamus.

7th. Absence of two toes out of the three of the hind leg, and sometimes of the three, in animals whose parents had eaten up their hind-leg toes which had become anaesthetic from a section of the sciatic nerve alone, or of that nerve and also of the crural. Sometimes, instead of complete absence of the toes, only a part of one or two or three was missing in the young, although in the parent not only the toes but the whole foot were absent (partly eaten off, partly destroyed by inflammation, ulceration, or gangrene.)

8th. Appearance of various morbid states of the skin and hair of the neck and face in animals born of parents having had similar alterations in the same parts, as effects of an injury to the sciatic nerve.

These results[64] have been independently vouched for by two of Brown-Séquard's former assistants—Dr. Dupuy, and the late Professor Westphal. Moreover, his results with regard to epilepsy have been corroborated also by Obersteiner[65]. I may observe, in passing, that this labour of testing Brown-Séquard's statements is one which, in my opinion, ought rather to have been undertaken, if not by Weismann himself, at all events by some of his followers. Both he and they are incessant in their demand for evidence of the transmission of acquired characters; yet they have virtually ignored the foregoing very remarkable statements. However, be this as it may, all that we have now to do is to consider what the school of Weismann has had to say with regard to these experiments on the grounds of general reasoning which they have thus far been satisfied to occupy.

In view of Obersteiner's corroboration of Brown-Séquard's results touching the artificial production and subsequent transmission of epilepsy, Weismann accepts the facts, but, in order to save his theory of heredity, he argues that the transmission may be due to a traumatic introduction of "some unknown microbe" which causes the epilepsy in the parent, and, by invading the ova or spermatozoa as the case may be, also produces epilepsy in the offspring. Here, of course, there would be transmission of epilepsy, but it would not be, technically speaking, an hereditary transmission. The case would resemble that of syphilis, where the sexual elements remain unaffected as to their congenital endowments, although they have been made the vehicles for conveying an organic poison to the next generation.

Now it would seem that this suggestion is not, on the face of it, a probable one. For "some unknown microbe" it indeed must be, which is always on hand to enter a guinea-pig when certain operations are being performed on certain parts of the nervous system, but yet will never enter when operations of any kind are being effected elsewhere. Moreover, Westphal has produced the epilepsy *without any incision,* by striking the heads of the animals with a hammer[66]. This latter fact, it appears to me, entirely abolishes the intrinsically improbable suggestion touching an unknown— and strangely eclectic—microbe. However, it is but fair to state what Weismann himself has made of this fact. The following is what he says:—

> "It is obvious that the presence of microbes can have nothing to do with such an attack, but the shock alone must have caused morphological and functional changes in the centre of the pons and medulla oblongata, identical with those produced by microbes in the other cases.... Various stimuli might cause the nervous centres concerned to develop the convulsive attack which, together with its after-effects, we call epilepsy. In Westphal's case, such a stimulus would be given by a powerful mechanical shock (viz. blows on the head with a hammer); in Brown-Séquard's experiments, by the penetration of microbes[67]."

But from this passage it would seem that Weismann has failed to notice that in "Westphal's case," as in "Brown-Séquard's experiments," the epilepsy was *transmitted to progeny.* That epilepsy may be produced in guinea-pigs by a method which does not involve any cutting (i.e. possibility of inoculation) would no doubt tend to corroborate the suggestion of microbes being concerned in its transmission when it is produced by cutting, *if in the former case there were no such transmission.* But as there *is* transmission in *both* cases, the facts, so far as I can see, entirely abolish the suggestion. For they prove that even when epilepsy is produced in the parents under circumstances which render "it obvious that the presence of microbes can have nothing to do with such an attack," the epileptiform condition is notwithstanding transmitted to the progeny. What, then, is gained by retaining the intrinsically improbable hypothesis of microbes to explain the fact of transmission "in Brown-Séquard's experiments," when this very same fact is proved to occur without the possibility of microbes "in Westphal's case"?

The only other objection with regard to the seeming transmission of traumatic epilepsy which Weismann has advanced is, that such epilepsy may be produced by two or three very different operations—viz. division of the sciatic nerves (one or both), an injury to the spinal cord, and a stroke on the head. Does not this show, it is asked, that the epileptic condition of guinea-pigs is due to a generally unstable condition of the whole nervous system and is not associated with any particular part thereof? Well, supposing that such is the case, what would it amount to? I cannot see that it would in any way affect the only question in debate—viz. What is the significance of the fact that epilepsy is *transmitted*? Even if it be but "a tendency," "a disposition," or "a diathesis" that is transmitted, it is none the less a case of transmission, in fact quite as much so as if the pathological state were dependent on the impaired condition of any particular nerve-centre. For, it must be observed, there can be no question that it is always produced by an operation of *some* kind. If it were ever to originate in guinea-pigs spontaneously, there might be some room for supposing that its transmission is due to a congenital tendency running through the whole species—although even then it would remain unaccountable, on the ultra-Darwinian view, why this tendency should be congenitally *increased* by means of an operation. But epilepsy does not originate spontaneously in guinea-pigs; and therefore the criticism in question appears to me irrelevant.

Again, it may be worth while to remark that Brown-Séquard's experiments do not disprove the possibility of its being some one nerve-centre which is concerned in all cases of traumatic epilepsy. And this possibility becomes, I think, a probability in view of Luciani's recent experiments on the dog. These show that the epileptic condition can be produced in this animal by injury to the cortical substance of the hemispheres, and is then transmitted to progeny[68]. These experiments, therefore, are of great interest—first, as showing that traumatic and transmissible epilepsy is not confined to guinea-pigs; and next, as indicating that the pathological state in question is associated with the highest nerve-centres, which may therefore well be affected by injury to the lower centres, or even by section of a large nerve trunk.

So much, then, with regard to the case of transmitted epilepsy. But now it must be noted that, even if Weismann's suggestion touching microbes were fully adequate to meet this case, it would still leave unaffected those of transmitted protrusion of the eye, drooping of the eyelid, gangrene of the ear, absence of toes, &c. In all these cases the facts, as stated by Brown-Séquard, are plainly unamenable to any explanation which would suppose them due to microbes, or even to any general neurotic condition induced by the operation. They are much too definite, peculiar, and localized. Doubtless it is on this account that the school of Weismann has not seriously attempted to deal with them, but merely recommends their repetition by other physiologists[69]. Certain criticisms, however, have been urged by Weismann against the *interpretation* of Brown-Séquard's facts as evidence in favour of the transmission of acquired characters. It does not appear to me that these criticisms present much weight; but it is only fair that we should here briefly consider them[70].

First, with regard to Brown-Séquard's results other than the production of transmitted epilepsy, Weismann allows that the hypothesis of microbes can scarcely apply. In order to meet these results, therefore, he furnishes another suggestion—viz. that where the nervous system has sustained "a great shock," the animals are very likely to bear "weak descendants, and such as are readily affected by disease." Then, in answer to the obvious consideration, "that this does not explain why the offspring should suffer from the same disease" as that which has been produced in the parents, he adds—"But this does not appear to have been by any means invariably the case. For 'Brown-Séquard himself says, the changes in the eye of the offspring were of a very variable nature, and were only occasionally exactly similar to those observed in the parents.'"

Now, this does not appear to me a good commentary. In the first place, it does not apply to the other cases (such as the ears and the toes), where the changes in the offspring, when they occurred at all, *were* exactly similar to those observed in the parents, save that some of them occasionally occurred on the *opposite* side, and frequently also on *both* sides of the offspring. These subordinate facts, however, will not be regarded by any physiologist as making against the more ready interpretation of the results as due to heredity. For a physiologist well knows that homologous parts are apt to exhibit correlated variability—and this especially where variations of a congenital kind are concerned, and also where there is any reason to suppose that the nervous system is involved. Moreover, even in the case of the eye, it was always protrusion that was caused in the parent and transmitted to the offspring as a result of injuring the restiform bodies of the former; while it was always partial closure of the eyelids that was caused and transmitted by section of the sympathetic nerve, or removal of the cervical ganglia. Therefore, if we call such effects "diseases," surely it *was* "the same disease" which in each case appeared in the parents and reappeared in their offspring. Again, the "diseases" were so peculiar, definite, and localized, that I cannot see how they can be reasonably ascribed to a general nervous "shock." Why, for instance, if this were the case, should a protruding eye never result from removal of the cervical ganglia, a drooping eyelid from a puncture of the restiform body, a toeless foot from either or both of these operations, and so on? In view of such considerations I cannot deem these suggestions touching "microbes" and "diseases" as worthy of the distinguished biologist from whom they emanate.

Secondly, Weismann asks—How can we suppose these results to be instances of the transmission of acquired characters, when from Brown-Séquard's own statement of them it appears that the mutilation itself was not inherited, but only its effects? Neither in the case of the sciatic nerve, the sympathetic nerve, the cervical ganglion, nor the restiform bodies, was there ever any trace of transmitted injury in the corresponding parts of the offspring; so that, if the "diseases" from which they suffered be regarded as hereditary, we have to suppose that a consequence was in each case transmitted without the transmission of its cause, which is absurd. But I do not think that this criticism can be deemed of much weight by a physiologist as distinguished from a naturalist. For nothing is more certain to a student of physiology, in any of its branches, than that negative evidence, if yielded by the microscope alone, is most precarious. Therefore it does not need a *visible* change in the nervous system to be present, in order that the part affected should be functionally weak or incapable: pathology can show numberless cases of nerve-disorder the "structural" causes of which neither the scalpel nor the microscope can detect. So that, if any peculiar form of nerve-disorder is transmitted to progeny, and if it be certain that it has been caused by injury to some particular part of the nervous system, I cannot see that there is any reason to doubt the transmission of a nervous lesion merely on the ground that it is not visibly discernible. Of course there may be other grounds for doubting it; but I am satisfied that this ground is untenable. Besides, it must be remembered, as regards the particular cases in question, that no one has thus far investigated the histology of the matter by the greatly improved methods which are now at our disposal.

I have now considered all the criticisms which have been advanced against what may be called the Lamarckian interpretation of Brown-Séquard's results; and I think it will be seen that they present very little force—even if it can be seen that they present any force at all. But it must be remembered that this is a different thing from saying that the Lamarckian interpretation is the true one. The facts alleged are, without question, highly peculiar; and, on this account alone, Brown-Séquard's interpretation of them ought to be deemed provisional. Hence, although as yet they have not encountered any valid criticism from the side of ultra-Darwinian theory, I do not agree with Darwin that, on the supposition of their truth as facts, they furnish positive proof of the transmission of acquired characters. Rather do I agree with Weismann that further investigation is needed in order to establish such an important conclusion on the basis of so unusual a class of facts. This further investigation, therefore, I have undertaken, and will now state the results.

Although this work was begun over twenty years ago, and then yielded negative results, it was only within the last decade that I resumed it more systematically, and under the tutelage of Brown-Séquard himself. During the last two years, however, the experiments have been so much interrupted by illness that even now the research is far from complete. Therefore I will here confine myself to a tabular statement of the results as far as they have hitherto gone, on the understanding that, in so far as they are negative or doubtful, I am not yet prepared to announce them as final.

We may take Brown-Séquard's propositions in his own order, as already given on page 104.

> 1st. Appearance of epilepsy in animals born of parents which had been rendered epileptic by an injury to the spinal cord.

> 2nd. Appearance of epilepsy also in animals born of parents which had been rendered epileptic by section of the sciatic nerve.

I did not repeat these experiments with a view to producing epilepsy, because, as above stated, they had been already and sufficiently corroborated in this respect. But I repeated many times the experiments of dividing the sciatic nerve for the purpose of testing the statements made later on in paragraphs 7 and 8, and observed that it almost always had the effect of producing epilepsy in the animal thus operated upon—and this of a peculiar kind, the chief characteristics of which may here be summarized. The epileptiform habit does not supervene until some considerable time after the operation; it is then transitory, lasting only for some weeks or months. While the habit endures the fits never occur spontaneously, but only as a result of irritating a small area of skin behind the ear on the same side of the body as that on which the sciatic nerve had been divided. Effectual irritation may be either mechanical (such as gentle pinching), electrical, or, though less certainly, thermal. The area of skin in question, soon after the epileptiform habit supervenes, and during all the time that it lasts, swarms with lice of the kind which infest guinea-pigs—i.e. the lice congregate in this area, on account, I think, of the animal being there insensitive, and therefore not disturbing its parasites in that particular spot; otherwise it would presumably throw itself into fits by scratching that spot. On removing the skin from the area in question, no kind or degree of irritation supplied to the subjacent tissue has any effect in producing a fit. A fit never lasts for more than a very few minutes, during which the animal is unconscious and convulsed, though not with any great violence. The epileptiform habit is but rarely transmitted to progeny. Most of these observations are in accordance with those previously made by Brown-Séquard, and also by others who have repeated his experiments under this heading. I can have no doubt that the injury of the sciatic nerve or spinal cord produces a change in some of the cerebral centres, and that it is this change—whatever it is and in whatever part of the brain it takes place—which causes the remarkable phenomena in question.

> 3rd. A change in the shape of the ear in animals born of parents in which such a change was the effect of a division of the cervical sympathetic nerve.

> 4th. Partial closure of the eyelids in animals born of parents in which that state of the eyelids had been caused either by section of the cervical sympathetic nerve, or the removal of the superior cervical ganglion.

I have not succeeded in corroborating these results. It must be added, however, that up to the time of going to press my experiments on this, the easiest branch of the research, have been too few fairly to prove a negative.

> 5th. Exophthalmia in animals born of parents in which an injury to the restiform body had produced that protrusion of the eyeball.... In these animals, modified by heredity, the two eyes generally protruded, although in the parents usually only one showed exophthalmia, the lesion having been made in most cases only on one of the corpora restiformia.

I have fully corroborated the statement that injury to a particular spot of the restiform body is quickly followed by a marked protrusion of the eyeball on the same side. I have also had many cases in which some of the progeny of parents thus affected have shown considerable protrusion of the eyeballs on both sides, and this seemingly abnormal protrusion has been occasionally transmitted to the next generation. Nevertheless, I am far from satisfied that this latter fact is anything more than an accidental coincidence. For I have never seen the so-called exophthalmia of progeny exhibited in so high a degree as it occurs in the parents as an immediate result of the operation, while, on examining any large stock of normal guinea-pigs, there is found a considerable amount of individual variation in regard to prominence of eyeballs. Therefore, while not denying that the obviously abnormal amount of protrusion due to the operation may be inherited in lesser degrees, and thus may be the cause of the unusual degree of prominence which is sometimes seen in the eyeballs of progeny born of exophthalmic parents, I am unable to affirm so important a conclusion on the basis supplied by these experiments.

> 6th. Haematoma and dry gangrene of the ears in animals born of parents in which these ear-alterations had been caused by an injury to the restiform body.

As regards the animals operated upon (i. e. the parents), I find that the haematoma and dry gangrene may supervene either several weeks after the operation, or at any subsequent time up to many months. When it does supervene it usually affects the upper parts of both ears, and may then eat its way down until, in extreme cases, it has entirely consumed two-thirds of the tissue of both ears. As regards the progeny of animals thus affected, in some cases, but by no means in all, a similarly morbid state of the ears may arise apparently at any time in the life-history of the individual. But I have observed that in cases where two or more individuals *of the same litter* develop this diseased condition, they usually do so at about the same time—even though this be many months after birth, and therefore after the animals are fully grown. But in progeny the morbid process never goes so far as in the parents which have been operated upon, and it almost always affects the *middle* thirds of the ears. In order to illustrate these points, reproductions of two of my photographs are appended. They represent the consequences of the operation on a male and a female guinea-pig. Among the progeny of both these animals there were several in which a portion of each ear was consumed by apparently the same process, where, of course, there had been no operation.

FIG. 1.—Reproduction of photographs from life of a male and female guinea-pig, whose left restiform bodies had been injured by a scalpel six months previously. The loss of tissue in both ears was due to haematoma and dry gangrene, which, however, had ceased when the photograph was taken.

It should be observed that not only is a different *part* of the ear affected in the progeny, but also a very much less *quantity* thereof. Naturally, therefore, the hypothesis of heredity seems less probable than that of mere coincidence on the one hand, or of transmitted microbes on the other. But I hope to have fairly excluded both these alternative explanations. For, as regards merely accidental coincidence, I have never seen this very peculiar morbid process in the ears, or in any other parts, of guinea-pigs which have neither themselves had their restiform bodies injured, nor been born of parents thus mutilated. As regards the hypothesis of microbes, I have tried to inoculate the corresponding parts of the ears of normal guinea-pigs, by first scarifying those parts and then rubbing them with the diseased surfaces of the ears of mutilated guinea-pigs; but have not been able in this way to communicate the disease.

It will be seen that the above results in large measure corroborate the statements of Brown-Séquard; and it is only fair to add that he told me they are the results which he had himself obtained most frequently, but that he had also met with many cases where the diseased condition of the ears in parents affected the same parts in their progeny, and also occurred in more equal degrees. Lastly, I should like to remark, with regard to these experiments on restiform bodies, and for the benefit of any one else who may hereafter repeat them, that it will be necessary for him to obtain precise information touching the *modus operandi*. For it is only one very localized spot in each restiform body which has to be injured in order to produce any of the results in question. I myself lost two years of work on account of not knowing this exact spot before going to Paris for the purpose of seeing Brown-Séquard himself perform the operation. I had in the preceding year seen one of his assistants do so, but this gentleman had a much more careless method, and one which in my hands yielded uniformly negative results. The exact spot in question in the restiform body is as far forwards as it is possible to reach, and as far down in depth as is compatible with not producing rotatory movements.

7th. Absence of two toes out of the three of the hind leg, and sometimes of the three, in animals whose parents had eaten up their hind-leg toes which had become anaesthetic from a section of the sciatic nerve alone, or of that nerve and also of the crural. Sometimes, instead of complete absence of the toes, only a part of one or two or three was missing in the young, although in the parent not only the toes but the whole foot were absent.

As I found that the results here described were usually given by division of the sciatic nerve alone—or, more correctly, by excision of a considerable portion of the nerve, in order to prevent regeneration—I did not also divide the crural. But, although I have bred numerous litters from parents thus injured, there has been no case of any inherited deficiency of toes. My experiments in this connexion were carried on through a series of six successive generations, so as to produce, if possible, a cumulative effect. Nevertheless, no effect of any kind was produced. On the other hand, Brown-Séquard informed me that he had observed this inherited absence of toes only in about one or two per cent. of cases. Hence it is possible enough, that my experiments have not been sufficiently numerous to furnish a case. It may be added that there is here no measurable possibility of accidental coincidence (seeing that normal guinea-pigs do not seem ever to produce young with any deficiency of toes), while the only possibility of mal-observation consists in some error with regard to the isolation (or the tabulation) of parents and progeny. Such an error, however, may easily arise. For gangrene of the toes does not set in till some considerable time after division of the sciatic nerve. Hence, if the wound be healed before the gangrene begins, and if any mistake has been made with regard to the isolation (or tabulation) of the animal, it becomes possible that the latter should be recorded as an uninjured, instead of an injured, individual. On this account one would like to be assured that Brown-Séquard took the precaution of examining the state of the sciatic nerve in those comparatively few specimens which he alleges to have displayed such exceedingly definite proof of the inheritance of a mutilation. For it is needless to remark, after what has been said in the preceding chapter on the analogous case of epilepsy, that the proof would not be regarded by any physiologist as displaced by the fact that there is no observable deficiency in the sciatic nerve of the toeless young.

> 8th. Appearance of various morbid states of the skin
> and hair of the neck and face in animals born of parents
> having had similar alterations in the same parts, as effects
> of an injury to the sciatic nerve.

I have not paid any attention to this paragraph, because the facts which it alleges did not seem of a sufficiently definite character to serve as a guide to further experiment.

On the whole, then, as regards Brown-Séquard's experiments, it will be seen that I have not been able to furnish any approach to a full corroboration. But I must repeat that my own experiments have not as yet been sufficiently numerous to justify me in repudiating those of his statements which I have not been able to verify.

The only other experimental results, where animals are concerned, which seemed to tell on the side of Lamarckianism, are those of Mr. Cunningham, already alluded to. But, as the research is still in progress, the school of Weismann may fairly say that it would be premature to discuss its theoretical bearings.

Passing now from experiments on animals to experiments on plants, I must again ask it to be borne in mind, that here also no researches have been published, which have had for their object the testing of the question on which we are engaged. As in the case of animals, therefore, so in that of plants, we are dependent for any experimental results bearing upon the subject to such as have been gained incidentally during the course of investigations in quite other directions.

Allusion has already been made, in my previous essay, to De Vries' observations on the chromatophores of algae passing from the ovum of the mother to the daughter organism; and we have seen that even Weismann admits, "It appears possible that a transmission of somatogenetic variation has here occurred[71]." It will now be my object to show that such variations appear to be sometimes transmitted in the case of higher plants, and this under circumstances which carry much less equivocal evidence of the inheritance of acquired characters, than can be rendered by the much more simple organization of an alga.

I have previously mentioned Hoffmann's experiments on transplantation, the result of which was to show that variations, directly induced by changed conditions of life, were reproduced by seed[72]. Weismann, however, as we have seen, questions the *somatogenetic* origin of these variations—attributing the facts to a *blastogenetic* change produced in the plants by a direct action of the changed conditions upon the germ-plasm itself[73]. And he points out that whether he is right or wrong in this interpretation can only be settled by ascertaining whether the observable somatic changes occur in the generation which is first exposed to the changed conditions of life. If they do occur in the first generation, they are somatogenetic changes, which afterwards react on the substance of heredity, so as to transmit the acquired peculiarities to progeny. But if they do not occur till the second (or any later) generation, they are presumably blastogenetic. Unfortunately Hoffmann does not appear to have attended to this point with sufficient care, but there are other experiments of the same kind where the point has been specially observed.

For instance, M. L. A. Carrière[74] gathered seed from the wild radish (*Raphanus Raphanistrum*) in France, and sowed one lot in the light dry soil near the Museum of Natural History in Paris, while another lot was sown by him at the same time in heavy soil elsewhere. His object was to ascertain whether he could produce a good cultivated radish by methodical selection; and this he did; in a wonderfully rapid manner, during the course of a very few generations. But the point for us is, that *from the first* the plants grown in the light soil of Paris presented sundry marked differences from those grown in the heavy soil of the country; and that these points of difference had nothing to do with the variations on which his artificial selection was brought to bear. For while his artificial selection was directed to increasing the *size* of the "root," the differences in question had reference to its *form* and *colour*. In Paris an elongated form prevailed, which presented either a white or a rose colour: in the country the form was more rounded, and the colour violet, dark brown, or "almost black." Now, as these differences were strongly apparent in the first generation, and were not afterwards made the subject of selection, both in origin and development they must have been due to "climatic" influences acting on the somatic tissues. And although the author does not appear to have tested their hereditary characters by afterwards sowing the seed from the Paris variety in the country, or *vice versa*, we may fairly conclude that these changes must have been hereditary—1st, from the fact of their intensification in the course of the five sequent generations over which the experiment extended, and, 2nd, from the very analogous results which were similarly obtained in the following case with another genus, where both the somatogenetic and the hereditary characters of the change were carefully and specially observed. This case is as follows.

The late Professor James Buckman, F.R.S., saved some seed from wild parsnips (*P. sativa*) in the summer of 1847, and sowed under changed conditions of life in the spring of 1848. The plants grown from these wild seeds were for the most part like wild plants; but some of them had "already (i.e. in the autumn of 1848) the light green and smooth aspect devoid of hairs which is peculiar to the cultivated plant; and among the latter there were a few with longer leaves and broader divisions of leaf-lobes than the rest—the leaves, too, all growing systematically round one central bud. The roots of the plant when taken up were observed to be for the most part more fleshy than those of wild examples[75]."

Professor Buckman then proceeds to describe how he selected the best samples for cultivation in succeeding generations, till eventually the variety which he called "The Student" was produced, and which Messrs. Sutton still regard as the best variety in their catalogue. That is to say, it has come true to seed for the last forty years; and although such great excellence and stability are doubtless in chief part due to the subsequent process of selection by Professor Buckman in the years 1848-1850, this does not affect the point with which we are here concerned—namely, that the somatogenetic changes of the plants in the first generation were transmitted by seed to the second generation, and thus furnished Professor Buckman with the material for his subsequent process of selection. And the changes in question were not merely of a very definite character, but also of what may be termed a very *local* character—affecting only particular tissues of the soma, and therefore expressive of a high degree of *representation* on the part of the subsequently developed seed, by which they were faithfully reproduced in the next generation.

Here is another case. M. Lesage examined the tissues of a large number of plants growing both near to, and remote from, the sea. He suspected that the characteristic fleshiness, &c. of seaside plants was due to the influence of sea-salt; and proved that such was the case by causing the characters to occur in inland plants as a result of watering them with salt-water. Then he adds:—

> "J'ai réussi surtout pour le *Lepidium sativum* cultivé en 1888; j'ai obtenu pour la même plante des résultats plus nets encore dans la culture de 1889, entreprise en semant les graines récoltées avec soin des pots de l'année précédente et traitées exactement de la même façon[76]."

Here, it will be observed, there was no selection; and therefore the increased hereditary effect in the second generation must apparently be ascribed to a continuance of influence exercised by somatic tissues on germinal elements; for at the time when the changes were produced no seed had been formed. In other words, the accumulated change, like the initial change, would seem to have been exclusively of somatogenetic origin; and yet it so influenced the qualities of the seed (as this was afterwards formed), that the augmented changes were transmitted to the next generation, part for part, as the lesser changes had occurred in the preceding generation. "This experiment, therefore, like Professor Buckman's, shows that the alteration of the tissues was carried on in the second generation from the point gained in the first. In both cases no germ-plasm (in the germ-cells) existed at the time during which the alterations arose, as they were confined to the vegetative system; and in the case of the parsnips and carrots, being biennials no germ-cells are produced till the second year has arrived[77]."

Once more, Professor Bailey remarks:—

> "Squashes often show remarkable differences when grown upon different soils; and these differences can sometimes be perpetuated for a time by seeds. The writer has produced, from the same parent, squashes so dissimilar, through the simple agency of a change of soil in one season, that they might readily be taken for distinct varieties. Peas are known to vary in the same manner. The seeds of a row of peas of the same kind, last year gave the writer marked variations due to differences of soil.... Pea-growers characterize soils as 'good' and 'viney.' Upon the latter sort the plants run to vine at the expense of the fruit, and their offspring for two or three generations have the same tendency[78]."

I think these several cases are enough to show that, while the Weismannian assumption as to the seeming transmission of somatogenetic characters being restricted to the lowest kinds of plants is purely gratuitous, there is no small amount of evidence to the contrary—or evidence which seems to prove that a similar transmission occurs likewise in the higher plants. And no doubt many additional cases might be advanced by any one who is well read in the literature of economic botany.

It appears to me that the only answer to such cases would be furnished by supposing that the hereditary changes are due to an alteration of the residual "germ-plasm" in the wild seed, when this is first exposed to the changed conditions of life, due to its growth in a strange kind of soil—e.g. while germinating in an unusual kind of earth for producing the first generation. But this would be going a long way to save an hypothesis. In case, however, it should now be suggested, I may remark that it would be negatived by the following facts.[79]

In the first place, an endless number of cases might be quoted where somatogenetic changes thus produced by changed conditions of life are not hereditary. Therefore, in all these cases it is certainly not the "germ-plasm" that is affected. In other words, there can be no question that somatogenetic changes of the kinds above mentioned do very readily admit of being produced in the first generation by changes of soil, altitude, &c. And that somatogenetic changes thus produced should not always—or even generally—prove themselves to be hereditary from the first moment of their occurrence, is no more than any theory of heredity would expect. Indeed, looking to the known potency of reversion, the wonder is that in any case such changes should become hereditary in a single generation. On the other hand, there is no reason to imagine that the hypothetical germ-plasm—howsoever *unstable* we may suppose it to be—can admit of being directly affected by a change of soil in a single generation. For, on this view, it must presumably be chiefly affected during the short time that the seed is germinating; and during that time the changed conditions can scarcely be conceived as having any points of attack, so to speak, upon the residual germ-plasm. There are no roots on which the change of *soil* can make itself perceptible, nor any stem and leaves on which the change of *atmosphere* can operate. Yet the changed condition's may produce hereditary modifications in any parts of the plant, which are not only precisely analogous to non-hereditary changes similarly produced in the somatic tissues of innumerable other plants, but are always of precisely the same kind in the same lot of plants that are affected. When all the radishes grown from wild seed in Paris, for instance, varied in the direction of rotundity and dark colour, while those grown in the country presented the opposite characters, we can well understand the facts as due to an entire season's action upon the whole of the growing plant, with the result that all the changes produced in each set of plants were similar—just as in the cases where similarly "climatic" modifications are not hereditary, and therefore unquestionably due to changed conditions acting on roots, stems, leaves, or flowers, as the case may be. On the other hand, it is not thus intelligible that during the short time of germination the changed conditions should effect a re-shuffling (or any other modification) of the "germ-plasm" in the seeds—and this in such a manner that the effect on the residual germ-plasm reserved for future generations is precisely similar to that produced on the somatic tissues of the developing embryo.

In the second place, as we have seen, in some of the foregoing cases the changes were produced months—and even years—before the seeds of the first germination were formed. Therefore the hereditary effect, if subsequent to the period of embryonic germination, must have been produced on germ-plasm as this occurs diffused through the somatic tissues. But, if so, we shall have to suppose that such germ-plasm is afterwards gathered in the seeds when these are subsequently formed. This supposition, however, would be radically opposed to Weismann's theory of heredity: nor do I know of any other theory with which it would be reconcilable, save such as entertain the possibility of the Lamarckian factors.

Lastly, in the third place, I deem the following considerations of the highest importance:—

> "As other instances in which peculiar structures are now hereditary may be mentioned aquatic plants and those producing subterraneous stems. Whether they be dicotyledons or monocotyledons, there is a fundamental agreement in the anatomy of the roots and stem of aquatic plants, and, in many cases, of the leaves as well. Such has hitherto been attributed to the aquatic habit. The inference or deduction was, of course, based upon innumerable coincidences; the water being supposed to be the direct cause of the degenerate structures, which are hereditary and characteristic of such plants in the wild state. M. Costantin has, however, verified this deduction, by making terrestrial and aerial stems to grow underground and in water: the structures *at once* began to assume the subterranean or aquatic type, as the case might be; and, conversely, aquatic plants made to grow upon land *at once* began to assume the terrestrial type of structure, while analogous results followed changes from a subterranean to an aerial position, and *vice versa*."

This is also quoted from the Rev. Prof. Henslow's letters to me, and the important point in it is, that the great changes in question are proved to be of a purely "somatogenetic" kind; for they occurred "at once" *in the ready-grown plant*, when the organs concerned were exposed to the change from aquatic to terrestrial life, or *vice versa*—and also from a subterranean to an aerial position, or *vice versa*. Consequently, even the abstract possibility of the changed conditions of life having operated on the *seed* is here excluded. Yet the changes are of precisely the same kind as are now *hereditary* in the wild species. It thus appears undeniable that all these remarkable and uniform changes must originally have been somatogenetic changes; yet they have now become blastogenetic. This much, I say, seems undeniable; and therefore it goes a long way to prove that the non-blastogenetic character of the changes has been due to their originally somatogenetic character. For, if not, how did natural selection ever get an opportunity of making any of them blastogenetic, when every individual plant has always presented them as already given somatogenetically? This last consideration appears in no small measure to justify the opinion of Mr. Henslow, who concludes— "These experiments prove, not only that the influence of the environment is *at once* felt by the organ; but that it is indubitably the *cause* of the now specific and hereditary traits peculiar to normally aquatic, subterranean, and aerial stems, or roots[80]."

He continues to furnish other instances in the same line of proof—such as the distinctive "habits" of insectivorous, parasitic, and climbing plants; the difference in structure between the upper and under sides of horizontal leaves, &c. "For here, as in all organs, we discover by experiment how easily the anatomy of plants can be affected by their environment; and that, as long as the latter is constant, so are the characters of the plants constant and hereditary."

> [The following letter, contributed by Dr. Hill to *Nature*, vol. I. p. 617, may here be quoted. C. Ll. M.
>
> "It may be of interest to your readers to know that two guinea-pigs were born at Oxford a day or two before the death Dr. Romanes, both of which exhibited a well-marked droop of the left upper eyelid. These guinea-pigs were the offspring of a male and a female guinea-pig in both of which I had produced for Dr. Romanes, some months earlier, a droop of the left upper eyelid by division of the left cervical sympathetic nerve. This result is a corroboration of the series of Brown-Séquard's experiments on the inheritance of acquired characteristics. A very large series of such experiments are of course needed to eliminate all sources of error, but this I unfortunately cannot carry out at present, owing to the need of a special farm in the country, for the proper care and breeding of the animals.— LEONARD HILL.
>
> "Physiological Laboratory, Univ. Coll. London, Oct. 18, 1894."]

CHAPTER V
Characters as Hereditary and Acquired
(*continued*).

(A. and B.)
Direct and Indirect Evidence in favour of the Non-inheritance of Acquired Characters[81].

The strongest argument in favour of "continuity" is that based upon the immense difference between congenital and acquired characters in respect of heritability. For that there is a great difference in this respect is a matter of undeniable fact. And it is obvious that this difference, the importance of which must be allowed its full weight, is just what we should expect on the theory of the continuity of the germ-plasm, as opposed to that of pangenesis. Indeed it may be said that the difference in question, while it constitutes important *evidence* in favour of the former theory, is a *difficulty* in the way of the latter. But here two or three considerations must be borne in mind.

In the first place, this fact has long been one which has met with wide recognition and now constitutes the main ground on which the theory of continuity stands. That is to say, it was the previous knowledge of this contrast between congenital and acquired characters which led to the formulation of a theory of continuity by Mr. Galton, and to its subsequent development by Prof Weismann.

But, in the second place, there is a wide difference between the certainty of this fact and that of the theory based upon it. The certain fact is, that a great distinction in respect of heritability is observable between congenital and acquired characters. The theory, as formulated by Weismann, is that the distinction is not only great but absolute, or, in other words, that in no case and in no degree can any acquired character be ever inherited. This hypothesis, it will be observed, goes far beyond the observed fact, for it is obviously possible that, notwithstanding this great difference in regard to heritability between congenital and acquired characters, the latter may nevertheless, sometimes and in some degree, be inherited, however much difficulty we may experience in observing these lesser phenomena in presence of the greater. The Weismannian hypothesis of *absolute* continuity is one thing, while the observed fact of at least a *high relative degree* of continuity is quite another thing. And it is necessary to be emphatic on this point, since some of the reviewers of my *Examination of Weismannism* confound these two things. Being apparently under the impression that it was reserved for Weismann to perceive the fact of there being a great difference between the heritability of congenital and acquired characters, they deem it inconsistent in me to acknowledge this fact while at the same time questioning the hypothetical basis of his fundamental postulate touching the absolute continuity of germ-plasm. It is one merit of Galton's theory, as against Weismann's, that it does not dogmatically exclude the possible interruption of continuity on some occasions and in some degree. Herein, indeed, would seem to lie the central core of the whole question in dispute. For it is certain and has long been known that individually acquired characters are at all events much less heritable than are long-inherited or congenital ones. But Lamarckian theory supposes that congenital characters were in some cases originally acquired, and that what are now blastogenetic characters were in some cases at first somatogenetic and have become blastogenetic only in virtue of sufficiently long inheritance. Since Darwin's time, however, evolutionists (even of the so-called Lamarckian type) have supposed that natural selection greatly assists this process of determining which somatogenetic characters shall become congenital or blastogenetic. Hence all schools of evolutionists are, and have long been, agreed in regarding the continuity principle as true in the main. No evolutionist would at any time have propounded the view that one generation depends for *all* its characters on those acquired by its *immediate* ancestors, for this would merely be to unsay the theory of Evolution itself, as well as to deny the patent facts of heredity as shown, for example, in atavism. At most only some fraction of a *per cent.* could be supposed to do so. But Weismann's contention is that this principle is not only true in the main, but *absolutely* true; so that natural selection becomes all in all or not at all. Unless Weismannism be regarded as this doctrine of absolutism it permits no basis for his attempted theory of evolution.

And, whatever may be said to the contrary by the more enthusiastic followers of Prof. Weismann, I must insist that there is the widest possible difference between the truly scientific question of fact which is assumed by Weismann as answered (the base-line of the diagram on p. 43), and the elaborate structure of deductive reasoning which he has reared on this assumption (the Y-like structure). Even if the assumption should ever admit of inductive proof, the almost bewildering edifice of deductive reasoning which he has built upon it would still appear to me to present extremely little value of a scientific kind. Interesting though it may be as a monument of ingenious speculation hitherto unique in the history of science, the mere flimsiness of its material must always prevent its far-reaching conclusions from being worthy of serious attention from a biological point of view. But having already attempted to show fully in my

Examination this great distinction between the scientific importance of the question which lies at the base of "Weismannism," and that of the system which he has constructed on his assumed answer thereto, I need not now say anything further with regard to it.

Again, on the present occasion and in this connexion I should like to dissipate a misunderstanding into which some of the reviewers of the work just mentioned have fallen. They appear to have concluded that because I have criticized unfavourably a considerable number of Weismann's theories, I have shown myself hostile to his entire system. Such, however, is by no means the case; and the misunderstanding can only be accounted for by supposing that the strongly partisan spirit which these critics display on the side of neo-Darwinism has rendered them incapable of appreciating any attempt at impartial—or even so much as independent—criticism. At all events, it is a matter of fact that throughout the work in question I have been particularly careful to avoid this misunderstanding as to my own position. Over and over again it is there stated that, far from having any objection to the principle of "Continuity" as represented in the base-line of the above diagram, I have been convinced of its truth ever since reading Mr. Galton's *Theory of Heredity* in 1875. All the "hard words" which I have written against Weismann's system of theories have reference to those parts of it which go to constitute the Y-like structure of the diagram.

It is, however, desirable to recur to another point, and one which I hope will be borne in mind throughout the following discussion. It has already been stated, a few pages back, that the doctrine of continuity admits of being held in two very different significations. It may be held as absolute, or as relative. In the former case we have the Weismannian doctrine of germ-plasm: the substance of heredity is taken to be a substance *per se*, which has always occupied a separate "sphere" of its own, without any contact with that of somatoplasm further than is required for its lodgement and nutrition; hence it can never have been in any degree modified as to its hereditary qualities by use-inheritance or any other kind of somatogenetic change; it has been *absolutely* continuous "since the first origin of life." On the other hand, the doctrine of continuity may be held in the widely different sense in which it has been presented by Galton's theory of Stirp. Here the doctrine is, that while for the most part the phenomena of heredity are due to the continuity of the substance of heredity through numberless generations, this substance ("Stirp") is nevertheless not absolutely continuous, but may admit, in small though cumulative degrees, of modification by use-inheritance and other factors of the Lamarckian kind. Now this all-important distinction between these two theories of continuity has been fully explained and thoroughly discussed in my

Examination; therefore I will not here repeat myself further than to make the following remarks.

The Weismannian doctrine of continuity as absolute (base-line of the diagram) is necessary for the vast edifice of theories which he has raised upon it (the Y), first as to the minute nature and exact composition of the substance of heredity itself ("Germ-plasm"), next as to the precise mechanism of its action in producing the visible phenomena of heredity, variation, and all allied phenomena, and, lastly, the elaborate and ever-changing theory of organic evolution which is either founded on or interwoven with this vast system of hypothetic speculation. Galton's doctrine of continuity, on the other hand, is a "Theory of Heredity," and a theory of heredity alone. It does not meddle with any other matters whatsoever, and rigidly avoids all speculation further than is necessary for the bare statement and inductive support of the doctrine in question. Hence, it would appear that this, the only important respect wherein the doctrine of continuity as held by Galton differs from the doctrine as held by Weismann, arisen from the necessity under which the latter finds himself of postulating *absolute* continuity as a logical basis for his deductive theory of the precise mechanism of heredity on the one hand, and of his similarly deductive theory of evolution on the other. So far as the doctrine of continuity is itself concerned (i.e. the question of the inheritance of acquired characters), there is certainly no more inductive reason for supposing the continuity absolute "since the first origin of life," than there is for supposing it to be more or less susceptible of interruption by the Lamarckian factors. In other words, but for the sake of constructing a speculative foundation for the support of his further theories as to "the architecture of germ-plasm" and the factors of organic evolution, there is no reason why Weismann should maintain the absolute separation of the "sphere" of germ-plasm from that of somatoplasm. On the contrary, he has no reason for concluding against even a considerable and a frequent amount of cutting, or overlapping, on the part of these two spheres.

But although this seems to me sufficiently obvious, as I have shown at greater length in the *Examination of Weismannism*, it must not be understood that I hold that there is room for any large amount of such overlapping. On the contrary, it appears to me as certain as anything can well be that the amount of such overlapping from one generation to another, if it ever occur at all, must be exceedingly small, so that, if we have regard to only a few sequent generations, the effects of use-inheritance, and Lamarckian factors are, at all events as a rule, demonstrably imperceptible. But this fact does not constitute any evidence—as Weismann and his followers seem to suppose—against a possibly important influence being exercised by the Lamarckian factors, in the way of gradual increments through a long series of generations. It has long been well known that acquired characters are at best far less fully and far less certainly inherited than are congenital ones. And this fact is of itself sufficient to prove the doctrine of continuity to the extent that even the Lamarckian is rationally bound to concede. But the fact yields no proof—scarcely indeed so much as a presumption—in favour of the doctrine of continuity as absolute. For it is sufficiently obvious that the adaptive work of heredity could not be carried on at all if there had to be a discontinuity in the substance of heredity at every generation, or even after any very large number of generations.

Little more need be said concerning the arguments which fall under the headings A and B. The Indirect evidence is considered in Appendix I of the *Examination of Weismannism*; while the Direct evidence is considered in the text of that work in treating of Professor Weismann's researches on the *Hydromedusae* (pp. 71-76).

The facts of karyokinesis are generally claimed by the school of Weismann as making exclusively in favour of continuity as absolute. But this is a partisan view to take. In any impartial survey it should be seen that while the facts are fairly interpretable on Weismann's theory, they are by no means proof thereof. For any other theory of Heredity must suppose the material of heredity to be of a kind more or less specialized, and the mechanism of heredity extremely precise and well ordered. And this is all that the facts of karyokinesis prove. Granting that they prove continuity, they cannot be held to prove that continuity to be absolute. In other words, the facts are by no means incompatible with even a large amount of commerce between germ-plasm and somato-plasm, or a frequent transmission of acquired characters.

Again, Weismann's theory, that the somatic and the germ-plasm determinants may be similarly and simultaneously modified by external conditions may be extended much further than he has used it himself, so as to exclude, or at any rate invalidate, *all* evidence in favour of Lamarckianism, other than the inheritance of the effects of use and disuse. All evidence from apparently inherited effects produced by change of external conditions is thus virtually put out of court, leaving only evidence from the apparently inherited effects of functionally produced modifications. And this line of evidence is invalidated by Panmixia. Hence there remain only the arguments from selective value and co-adaptation. Weismann meets these by adducing the case of neuter insects, which have been already considered at sufficient length.

(C.)
Experimental Evidence as to the Non-inheritance of Acquired Characters.

Let us now proceed to the experimental evidence which has been adduced on the side of Weismannism.

Taking this evidence in order of date, we have first to mention that on which the school of Weismann has hitherto been satisfied almost exclusively to rely. This is the line of negative evidence, or the seeming absence of any experimental demonstration of the inheritance of acquired characters. This kind of evidence, however, presents much less cogency than is usually supposed. And it has been shown in the last chapter that the amount of experimental evidence in favour of the transmission of acquired characters is more considerable than the school of Weismann seems to be aware—especially in the vegetable kingdom. I do not think that this negative line of evidence presents much weight; and, to show that I am not biassed in forming this judgement, I may here state that few have more reason than myself for appreciating the weight of such evidence. For, as already stated, when first led to doubt the Lamarckian factors, now more than twenty years ago, I undertook a research upon the whole question—only a part of which was devoted to testing the particular case of Brown-Séquard's statements, with the result recorded in the preceding chapter. As this research yielded negative results in all its divisions—and, not only in the matter of Brown-Séquard's statements—I have not hitherto published a word upon the subject. But it now seems worth while to do so, and for the following reasons.

First, as just observed, a brief account of my old experiences in this field will serve to show what good reason I have for feeling the weight of such negative evidence in favour of Continuity as arises from failure to produce any good experimental evidence to the contrary. In the second place, now that the question has become one of world-wide interest, it would seem that even negative results deserve to be published for whatever they may be worth on the side of Neo-Darwinism. Lastly, in the third place, although the research yielded negative results in my hands, it is perhaps not undesirable to state the nature of it, if only to furnish suggestions to other physiologists, in whose hands the experiments—especially in these days of antiseptics—may lead to a different termination. Altogether I made thousands of experiments in graft-hydridization (comprising bines, bulbs of various kinds, buds, and tubers); but with uniformly negative results. With animals I tried a number of experiments in grafting characteristic congenital tissues from one variety on another—such as the combs of Spanish cocks upon the heads of Hamburgs; also, in mice and rats, the grafting together of different varieties; and, in rabbits and bitches, the transplantation of ovaries of newly-born individuals belonging to different well-marked breeds. This latter experiment seems to be one which, if successfully performed (so that the transplanted ovaries would form their attachment in a young bitch puppy and subsequently yield progeny to a dog of the same breed as herself) would furnish a crucial test as to the inheritance or non-inheritance of acquired characters. Therefore I devoted to it a large share of my attention, and tried the experiment in several different ways. But I was never able to get the foreign ovary—or even any portion thereof—to graft. Eventually the passing of the Vivisection Act caused me to abandon the whole research as far as animals were concerned—a research, indeed, of which I had become heartily tired, since in no one instance did I obtain any adhesion. During the last few years, however, I have returned to these experiments under a licence, and with antiseptic precautions, but with a similar want of success. Perhaps this prolonged and uniformly fruitless experience may now have the effect of saving the time of other physiologists, by warning them off the roads where there seems to be no thoroughfare. On the other hand, it may possibly lead some one else to try some variation in the method, or in the material, which has not occurred to me. In particular, I am not without hope that the transplantation of ovaries in very young animals may eventually prove to be physiologically possible; and, if so, that the whole issue as between the rival theories of heredity will be settled by the result of a single experiment. Possibly some of the invertebrata will be found to furnish the suitable material, although I have been unable to think of any of these which present sufficiently well-marked varieties for the purpose. But, pending the successful accomplishment of this particular experiment in the grafting of any animal tissue, I think it would be clearly unjustifiable to conclude against the Lamarckian factors on the ground of any other experiments yielding negative results in but one generation or even in a large number of sequent generations.

For instance, the latter consideration applies to the negative results of Mr. Francis Galton's celebrated *Experiments in Pangenesis.*[82]. These consisted in transfusing the blood of one variety of rabbit into the veins of both sexes of another, and then allowing the latter to breed together: in no case was there any appearance in the progeny of characters distinctive of the variety from which the transfused blood was derived. But, as Mr. Galton himself subsequently allowed, this negative result constitutes no disproof of pangenesis, seeing that only a portion of the parents' blood was replaced; that this portion, even if charged with "gemmules," would contain but a very small number of these hypothetical bodies, compared with those contained in all the tissues of the parents; and that even this small proportional number would presumably be soon overwhelmed by those contained in blood newly-made by the parents. Nevertheless the experiment was unquestionably worth trying, on the chance of its yielding a positive result; for, in this event, the question at issue would have been closed. Accordingly I repeated these experiments (with the kind help of Professor Schäfer), but with slight differences in the method, designed to give pangenesis a better chance, so to speak.

Thus I chose wild rabbits to supply the blood, and Himalayan to receive it—the former being the ancestral type (and therefore giving reversion an opportunity of coming into play), while the latter, although a product of domestication, is a remarkably constant variety, and one which differs very much in size and colour from the parent species. Again, instead of a single transfusion, there were several transfusions performed at different times. Moreover, we did not merely allow the blood of one rabbit to flow into the veins of the other (whereby little more than half the blood could be substituted); but sacrificed three wild rabbits for refilling the vascular system of each tame one on each occasion. Even as thus improved, however, the experiment yielded only negative results, which, therefore, we never published.

Subsequently I found that all this labour, both on Mr. Galton's part and our own, was simply thrown away—not because it yielded only negative results, but because it did not serve as a crucial experiment at all. The material chosen was unserviceable for the purpose, inasmuch as rabbits, even when crossed in the ordinary way, never throw intermediate characters. Needless to say, had I been aware of this fact before, I should never have repeated Mr. Galton's experiments—nor, indeed, would he have originally performed them had he been aware of it. So all this work goes for nothing. The research must begin all over again with some other animals, the varieties of which when crossed do throw intermediate characters.

Therefore I have this year made arrangements for again repeating the experiments in question—only, instead of rabbits, using well-marked varieties of dogs. A renewed attack of illness, however, has necessitated the surrender of this research to other hands, with a consequent delay in its commencement.

My ignorance of the unfortunate peculiarity displayed by rabbits in not throwing intermediate characters has led to a further waste of time in another line of experiment. On finding that mammalian ovaries did not admit of being grafted, it seemed to me that the next best thing to try would be the transplantation of fertilized ova from one variety to another, for the purpose of ascertaining whether, if a parturition should take place under such circumstances, gestation by the uterine mother would affect the characters of the ovum derived from the ovarian mother—she, of course, having been fertilized by a male of her own variety. Of course it was necessary that both the mothers should be in season at about the same time, and therefore I again chose rabbits, seeing that in the breeding season they are virtually in a chronic state of "heat." I selected Himalayans and Belgian hares, because they are well-marked varieties, breed true, and in respect of colour are very different from one another. It so happened that while I was at work upon this experiment, it was also being tried, unknown to me, by Messrs. Heape and Buckley who, curiously enough, employed exactly the same material. They were the first to obtain a successful result. Two fertilized ova of the Angora breed having been introduced into the fallopian tube of a Belgian hare, developed there in due course, and gave rise to two Angora rabbits in no way modified by their Belgian hare gestation[83].

But, interesting and suggestive as this experiment is in other connexions, it is clearly without significance in the present one, for the reason already stated. It will have to be tried on well-marked varieties of other species of animals, which are known to throw intermediate characters. Even, however, if it should then yield a similarly negative result, the fact would not tell against the inheritance of acquired characters; seeing that an ovum by the time it is ripe is a finished product, and therefore not to be expected, on any theory of heredity, to be influenced as to its hereditary potentialities by the mere process of gestation. On the other hand, if it should prove that it does admit of being thus affected, so that against all reasonable expectation the young animal presents any of the hereditary characters of its uterine mother, the fact would terminate the question of the transmission of acquired characters—and this quite as effectually as would a similarly positive result in the case of progeny from an ingrafted ovary of a different variety. In point of fact, the only difference between the two cases would be, that in the former it *might* prove possible to close the question on the side of Lamarckianism, in the latter it would *certainly* close the question, either on this side or on the opposite as the event would determine.

The only additional fact that has hitherto been published by the school of Weismann is the result of Weismann's own experiment in cutting off the tails of mice through successive generations. But this experiment does not bear upon any question that is in debate; for no one who is acquainted with the literature of the subject would have expected any positive result to follow from such a line of inquiry. As shown further back in the text, Darwin had carefully considered the case of mutilations, and explained that their non-transmissibility constitutes no valid objection to his theory of pangenesis. Furthermore, it may now be added, he expressly alluded in this connexion to the cutting off of tails, as practised by horse-breeders and dog-fanciers, "through a number of generations, without any inherited effect." He also alluded to the still better evidence which is furnished by the practice of circumcision. Therefore it is difficult to understand the object of Weismann's experiment. Yet, other than the result of this experiment, no new fact bearing on the question at issue has been even so much as alleged.

CHAPTER VI
Characters as Hereditary and Acquired
(*conclusion*[84]).

In the foregoing chapters I have endeavoured to be, before all things, impartial; and if it seems that I have been arguing chiefly in favour of the Lamarckian principles, this has been because the only way of examining the question is to consider what has to be said on the affirmative side, and then to see what the negative side can say in reply. Before we are entitled to discard the Lamarckian factors *in toto*, we must be able to destroy all evidence of their action. This, indeed, is what the ultra-Darwinians profess to have done. But is not their profession premature? Is it not evident that they have not sufficiently considered certain general facts of nature, or certain particular results of experiment, which at all events appear inexplicable by the theory of natural selection alone? In any case the present discussion has been devoted mainly to indicating such general facts and particular results. If I have fallen into errors, either of statement or of reasoning, it is for the ultra-Darwinians to correct them; but it may be well to remark beforehand, that any criticism of a merely general kind touching the comparative paucity of the facts thus adduced in favour of Lamarckian doctrine, will not stand as a valid criticism. For, as we have seen in the opening part of the discussion, even if use-inheritance and direct action of the environment have been of high importance as factors of organic evolution, it must be in almost all cases impossible to dissociate their influence from that of natural selection—at any rate where plants and animals in a state of nature are concerned. On the other hand, experiments expressly devised to test the question have not hitherto been carried out. Besides, the facts and arguments here adduced are but *comparatively* few. For, unless it can be shown that what has been said of reflex action, instinct, so-called "self-adaptation" in plants, &c., is wrong in principle, the facts which tell in favour of Lamarckian theory are *absolutely* very numerous. Only when considered in relation to cases where we are unable to exclude the conceivable possibility of natural selection having been at work, can it be said that the facts in question are not numerous.

Comparatively few, then, though the facts may be of which I have given some examples, in my opinion they are amply sufficient for the purpose in hand. This purpose is to show that the question which we are now considering is very far from being a closed question; and, therefore, that the school of Weismann is much too precipitate in alleging that there is neither any necessity for, nor evidence of, the so-called Lamarckian factors[85]. And this opinion, whatever it may be worth, is at all events both deliberate and impartial. As one of the first to doubt the transmission of acquired characters, and as one who has spent many years in experimental inquiries upon the subject, any bias that I may have is assuredly against the Lamarckian principles—seeing that nearly all my experiments have yielded negative results. It was Darwin himself who checked this bias. But if the ultra-Darwinians of the last ten years had succeeded in showing that Darwin was mistaken, I should be extremely glad to fall into line with them. As already shown, however, they have in no way affected this question as it was left by Galton in 1875. And if it be supposed a matter of but little importance whether we agree with Galton in largely diminishing the comparative potency of the Lamarckian principles, or whether we agree with Weismann in abolishing them together, it cannot be too often repeated that such is an entirely erroneous view. No matter how faintly or how fitfully acquired characters may be transmitted, in so far as they are likewise adaptive characters, their transmission (and therefore their development) must be cumulative. Hence, the only effect of attenuating our estimate of their *intensity*, is that of increasing our estimate of their *duration*—i.e. of the time over which they have to operate in order to produce important results. And, even so, it is to be remembered that the importance of such results is not to be estimated by the magnitude of modification. Far more is it to be estimated by the character of modification as adaptive. For if functionally produced changes, and changes produced in adaptive response to the environment, are ever transmitted in a cumulative manner, a time must sooner or later arrive when they will reach a selective value in the struggle for existence—when, of course, they will be rapidly augmented by natural selection. Thus, if in any degree operative at all, the great function of these principles must be that of supplying to natural selection those incipient stages of adaptive modifications in all cases where, but for their agency, there would have been nothing of the kind to select. Themselves in no way dependent on adaptive modifications having already attained a selective value, these Lamarckian principles are (under the Darwinian theory) direct causes of determinate variation in adaptive lines; and variation in those lines being cumulative, the result is that natural selection is in large part presented with the raw material of its manufacture—special material of the particular kinds required, as distinguished from promiscuous material of all kinds. And the more complex the manufacture the more important will be the work of this subordinate factory. We can well imagine how the shell of a nut, for instance, or even the protective colouring of an insect, may have been gradually built up by natural selection alone. But just in proportion as structures or organs are not merely thus of passive *use* (where, of course, the Lamarckian principles cannot obtain), but require to be actively *used*, in that proportion does it become difficult to understand the *incipient* construction of them by natural selection alone. Therefore, in many such cases, if the incipient construction is not to be explained by the Lamarckian principles, it is difficult to see how it is to be explained at all.

Furthermore, since the question as to the transmission of acquired characters stands now exactly as it did after the publication of Mr. Galton's *Theory of Heredity* twenty years ago, it would seem that our judgement with regard to it should remain exactly what it was then. Although we must "out-Darwin Darwin" to the extent of holding that he assigned too large a measure of intensity to the Lamarckian factors, no sufficient reason has been shown for denying the existence of these factors *in toto*; while, on the other hand, there are certain general considerations, and certain particular facts, which appear to render it probable that they have played a highly important part in the process of organic evolution as a whole. At the same time, and in the present state of our information, this judgement must be deemed provisional, or liable eventually to be overturned by experimental proof of the non-inheritance of acquired characters. But, even if this should ever be finally accomplished, the question would still remain whether the principle of natural selection alone is capable of explaining all the facts of adaptation; and, for my own part, I should then be disposed to believe that there must be some other, though hitherto undiscovered, principle at work, which co-operates with natural selection, by playing the subordinate role which was assigned by Darwin to the principles of Lamarck.

Finally, let it be noted that no part of the foregoing argument is to be regarded as directed against the *principle* of what Professor Weismann calls "continuity." On the contrary, it appears to be self-evident that this principle must be accepted in some degree or another by every one, whether Darwinians, Neo-Darwinians, Lamarckians, Neo-Lamarckians, or even the advocates of special creation. Yet, to hear or to read some of the followers of Weismann, one can only conclude that, prior to his publications on the subject, they had never thought about it at all. These naturalists appear to suppose that until then the belief of Darwinians was, that there could be no hereditary "continuity" between any one organic type and another (such, for instance, as between Ape and Man), but that the whole structure of any given generation must be due to "gemmules" or "somato-plasm," derived exclusively from the preceding generation. Nothing can show more ignorance, or more thoughtlessness, with regard to the whole subject. The very basis of the general theory of evolution is that there must always have been a continuity in the material substance of heredity since the time when the process of evolution began; and it was not reserved for our generation, or even for our century, to perceive the special nature of this material substance in the case of sexual organisms. No, the real and the sole question, where Weismann's theory of heredity is concerned, is simply this—Are we to hold that this material substance has been *absolutely* continuous "since the first origin of sexual propagation," always occupying a separate "sphere" of its own, at all events to the extent of never having been modified by the body substance in which it resides (Lamarckian factors); *or*, are we to hold that this "germ-plasm," "stirp," or "formative-material," has been but *relatively* continuous, so as to admit of some amount of commerce with body-substance, and therefore to admit of acquired characters, when sufficiently long continued as such, eventually becoming congenital? If this question be answered in the latter sense, of course the further question arises as to the *degree* of such commerce, or the *time* during which acquired characters must continue to be acquired in successive generations before they can sufficiently impress themselves on the substance of heredity to become congenital. But this is a subordinate question, and one which, in the present state of our information, it seems to me almost useless to speculate upon. My own opinion has always been the same as that of Mr. Galton; and my belief is that eventually both Weismann and his followers will gravitate into it. It was in order to precipitate this result as far as possible that I wrote the *Examination*. If it ever should be accomplished, Professor Weismann's elaborate theory of evolution will have had its bases removed.

SECTION II
UTILITY

CHAPTER VII
Characters as Adaptive and Specific.

One of the great changes which has been wrought in biological science by the Darwinian theory of natural selection, consists in its having furnished an intelligible explanation of the phenomena of *adaptation*. Indeed, in my opinion, this is the most important function which this theory has had to perform; and although we still find systematic zoologists and systematic botanists who hold that the chief merit of Darwin's work consists in its having furnished an explanation of the origin of *species*, a very little consideration is enough to show that such an idea is but a survival, or a vestige, of an archaic system of thought. So long as species were regarded as due to separate acts of creation, any theory which could explain their production by a process of natural evolution became of such commanding importance in this respect, that we cannot wonder if in those days the principal function of Darwin's work was held to be what the title of that work—*The Origin of Species by means of Natural Selection*—itself serves to convey. And, indeed, in those days this actually was the principal function of Darwin's work, seeing that in those days the *fact* of evolution itself, as distinguished from its *method*, had to be proved; and that the whole proof had to stand or fall with the evidence which could be adduced touching the mutability of species. Therefore, without question, Darwin was right in placing this issue as to the stability or instability of species in the forefront of his generalizations, and hence in constituting it the title of his epoch-making book. But nowadays, when the fact of evolution has been sufficiently established, one would suppose it self-evident that the theory of natural selection should be recognized as covering a very much larger field than that of explaining the origin of *species*—that it should be recognized as embracing the whole area of organic nature in respect of *adaptations*, whether these happen to be distinctive of species only, or of genera, families, orders, classes, and sub-kingdoms. For it follows from the general fact of evolution that species are merely arbitrary divisions, which present no deeper significance from a philosophical point of view than is presented by well-marked varieties, out of which they are in all cases believed to have arisen, and from which it is often a matter of mere individual taste whether they shall be separated by receiving the baptism of a specific name. Yet, although naturalists are now unanimously agreed that what they classify as species are nothing more than pronounced—and in some greater or less degree permanent—varieties, so forcible is the influence of traditional modes of thought, that many zoologists and botanists still continue to regard the origin of species as a matter of more importance than the origin of adaptations. Consequently, they continue to represent the theory of natural selection as concerned, primarily, with explaining the origin of species, and denounce as a "heretic" any one who regards the theory as primarily a theory of the origin and cumulative development of adaptations—whether structural or instinctive, and whether the adaptations are severally characteristic of species only or of any of the higher taxonomic divisions. Indeed, these naturalists appear to deem it in some way a disparagement of the theory to state that it is, primarily, a theory of adaptations, and only becomes secondarily a theory of species in those comparatively insignificant cases where the adaptations happen to be distinctive of the lowest order of taxonomic division—a view of the matter which may fitly be compared to that of an astronomer who should define the nebular hypothesis as a theory of the origin of Saturn's rings. It is indeed a theory of the origin of Saturn's rings; but only because it is a theory of the origin of the entire solar system, of which Saturn's rings form a part. Similarly, the theory of natural selection is a theory of the entire system of organic nature in respect of adaptations, whether these happen to be distinctive of particular species only, or are common to any number of species.

Now the outcry which has been raised over this definition of the theory of natural selection is a curious proof of the opposition which may be furnished by habitual modes of thought to an exceedingly plain matter of definition. For, I submit, that no one can deny any of the following propositions; nor can it be denied that from these propositions the foregoing definition of the theory in question follows by way of necessity. The propositions are, first, that natural selection is taken to be the agency which is mainly, if not exclusively, concerned in the evolution of adaptive characters: secondly, that these characters, when evolved, are in some cases peculiar to single species only, while in other cases, and in process of time, they become the common property of many species: thirdly, that in cases where they are peculiar to single species only, they constitute at all events one of the reasons (or even, as the ultra-Darwinians believe, the only reason) why the particular species presenting them have come to be species at all. Now, these being the propositions on which we are all agreed, it obviously follows, of logical necessity, that the theory in question is primarily one which explains the existence of adaptive characters wherever these occur; and, therefore, whether they happen to be restricted to single species, or are common to a whole group of species. Of course in cases where they are restricted to single species, the theory which explains the origin of these particular adaptations becomes also a theory which explains the origin of these particular species; seeing that, as we are all agreed, it is in virtue of such particular adaptations that such particular species exist. Yet even in these cases the theory is, primarily, a theory of the adaptations in virtue of which the particular species exists; for, *ex hypothesi*, it is the adaptations which condition the species, not the species the adaptations. But, as just observed, adaptations may be the common property of whole groups of species; and thus the theory of natural selection becomes a theory of the origin of genera, of families, of orders, and of classes, quite as much as it is a theory of the origin of species. In other words, it is everywhere a theory of adaptations; and it is only where the adaptations happen to be restricted to single species that the theory therefore and incidentally becomes also a theory of the particular species which presents them. Hence it is by no means the same proposition to affirm that the theory of natural selection is a theory of the origin of species, and that it is a theory of the origin of adaptations, as some of my critics have represented it to be; for these two things are by no means conterminous. And in as far as the two propositions differ, it is perfectly obvious that the latter is the true one.

Possibly, however, it may be said—Assuredly natural selection is a theory of the origin (i.e. cumulative development) of adaptations; and, no less assuredly, although species owe their origin to such adaptations, there is now no common measure between these two things, seeing that in numberless cases the same adaptations are the common property of numberless species. But, allowing all this, we must still remember that in their *first beginnings* all these adaptations must have been distinctive of, or peculiar to, some one particular species, which afterwards gave rise to a whole genus, family, order, or class of species, all of which inherited the particular adaptations derived from this common ancestor, while progressively gaining additional adaptive characters severally distinctive of their subsequently diverging lines of descent. So that really all adaptive characters must originally have been specific characters; and therefore there is no real distinction to draw between natural selection as a theory of species and as a theory of adaptations.

Well, if this objection were to be advanced, the answer would be obvious. Although it is true that every adaptive character which is now common to a group of species must originally have been distinctive of a single parent species, it by no means follows that in its first beginning as a specific character it appeared in the fully developed form which it now presents as a generic, family, ordinal, or yet higher character. On the contrary, it is perfectly certain that in the great majority of instances such cannot possibly have been the case; and the larger the group of species over which any particular adaptive character now extends, the more evidently do we perceive that this character must itself have been the product of a gradual evolution by natural selection through an innumerable succession of species in branching lines. The wing of a bird, for example, is an adaptive structure which cannot possibly have ever appeared suddenly as a merely specific character: it must have been slowly elaborated through an incalculable number of successive species, as these branched into genera, families, and orders of the existing class. So it is with other class distinctions of an adaptive kind; and so, in progressively lessening degrees, is it with adaptive characters of an ordinal, a family, or a generic value. That is to say, in *all* cases where an adaptive structure is common to any considerable group of species, we meet with clear evidence that the structure has been the product of evolution through the ancestry of those species; and this evidence becomes increasingly cogent the higher the taxonomic value of the structure. Indeed, it may be laid down as a general rule, that the greater the *degree* of adaptation the greater is its *diffusion*—both as regards the number of species which present it now, and the number of extinct species through which it has been handed down, in an ever ramifying extension and in an ever improving form. Species, therefore, may be likened to leaves: successive and transient crops are necessary for the gradual building up of adaptations, which, like the woody and permanent branches, grow continuously in importance and efficiency through all the tree of life. Now, in my view, it is the great office of natural selection to see to the growth of these permanent branches; and although natural selection has likewise had an enormously large share in the origination of each successive crop of leaves—nay, let it be granted to the ultra-Darwinians for the sake of argument, an exclusive prerogative in this respect—still, in my view, this is really the least important part of its work. Not as an explanation of those merely permanent varieties which we call species, but as an explanation of the adaptive machinery of organic nature, which has led to the construction both of the animal and vegetable kingdoms in all their divisions do I regard the Darwinian theory as one of the greatest generalizations in the history of science.

I have dwelt thus at some length upon a mere matter of definition because, as we shall now find, although it is but a matter of definition, it is fraught with consequences of no small importance to the general theory of descent. Starting from an erroneous definition of the theory of natural selection as primarily a theory of the origin of species, both friends and foes of the theory have concluded that the principle of utility must by hypothesis be of universal occurrence so far as species are concerned; whereas, if once these naturalists were to perceive that their definition of the theory is erroneous, they would likewise perceive that their conclusion cannot follow deductively from the theory itself. If such a conclusion is to be established at all, it can only be by other and independent evidence of the inductive kind—to wit, by actual observation.

Hence we see the importance of starting with an accurate definition of the theory before proceeding to examine the doctrine of utility as of universal application to species—a doctrine which, as just stated, has been habitually and expressly deduced from the theory. This doctrine occurs in two forms; or, more correctly, there are with reference to this subject two distinct doctrines, which partly coincide and partly exclude one another. First, it is held by some naturalists that all species must necessarily owe their origin to natural selection. And secondly, it is held by other naturalists, that not only all species, but likewise all specific characters must necessarily do the same. Let us consider these two doctrines separately.

The first, and less extensive doctrine, rests on the deduction that every species must owe its differentiation as a species to the evolution of at least one adaptive character, which is peculiar to that species. Although, when thus originated, a species may come to present any number of other peculiar characters of a non-adaptive kind, these merely indifferent peculiarities are supposed to hang, as it were, on the peg supplied by the one adaptive peculiarity; it is the latter which conditions the species, and so furnishes an opportunity for any number of the former to supervene. But without the evolution of at least one adaptive character there could have been no distinct species, and therefore no merely adventitious characters as belonging to that species. I will call this the Huxleyan doctrine, because Professor Huxley is its most express and most authoritative supporter.

The second and more extensive doctrine I will call, for the same reason, the Wallacean doctrine. This is, as already stated, that it follows deductively from the theory of natural selection, that not only all species, but even all the distinctive characters of every species, must necessarily be due to natural selection; and, therefore, can never be other than themselves useful, or, at the least, correlated with some other distinctive characters which are so.

Here, however, I should like to remark parenthetically, that in choosing Professor Huxley and Mr. Wallace as severally representative of the doctrines in question, I earnestly desire to avoid any appearance of discourtesy towards such high authorities.

I am persuaded—as I shall hereafter seek to show Darwin was persuaded—that the doctrine of utility as universal where species are concerned, is, in both the above forms, unsound. But it is less detrimental in its Huxleyan than in its Wallacean form, because it does not carry the erroneous deduction to so extreme a point. Therefore let us first consider the doctrine in its more restricted form, and then proceed, at considerably greater length, to deal with it in its more extended form.

The doctrine that all *species* must necessarily be due to natural selection, and therefore must severally present at least one adaptive character, appears to me doubly erroneous.

In the first place, it is drawn from what I have just shown to be a false premiss; and, in the second place, the conclusion does not follow even from this premiss. That the premiss—or definition of the theory as primarily a theory of the origin of species—is false, I need not wait again to argue. That the conclusion does not follow even from this erroneous premiss, a very few words will suffice to prove. For, even if it were true that natural selection is primarily a theory of the origin of species, it would not follow that it must therefore be a theory of the origin of *all* species. This would only follow if it were first shown that the theory is not merely *a* theory of the origin of species, but *the* theory of the origin of species—i.e. that there can be no further theory upon this subject, or any cause other than natural selection which is capable of transforming any single specific type.

Needless to say, this cannot be shown by way of deduction from the theory of natural selection itself—which, nevertheless, is the only way whereby it is alleged that the doctrine is arrived at[86].

From the doctrine of utility as advocated by Professor Huxley, we may now pass on to consider it in the much more comprehensive form advocated by Mr. Wallace. Of course it is obvious that if the doctrine is erroneous in its Huxleyan form, much more must it be so in its Wallacean; and, therefore, that having shown its erroneousness in its less extended application, there is little need to consider it further in its more extended form. Looking, however, to its importance in this more extended application, I think we ought to examine it independently as thus presented by Mr. Wallace and his school. Let us therefore consider, on its own merits, the following statement:—It follows directly from the theory of natural selection that not only all species, but likewise all specific characters, must be due to natural selection, and, therefore, must all be of use to the species which present them, or else correlated with other characters which are so.

It seems worth while to observe, *in limine*, that this doctrine is contradicted by that of Professor Huxley. For supposing natural selection to be the only principle concerned in the origin of all species, it by no means follows that it is the sole agency concerned in the origin of all specific characters. It is enough for the former proposition if only some of the characters distinctive of any given species—nay, as he very properly expresses it, if only one such character—has been due to natural selection; for it is clear that, as he adds, "any number of indifferent [specific] characters" may thus have been furnished with an opportunity, so to speak, of being produced by causes other than natural selection. Hence, as previously remarked, the Huxleyan doctrine, although coinciding with the Wallacean up to the point of maintaining utility as the only principle which can be concerned in the origin of species, designedly excludes the Wallacean doctrine where this proceeds to extend any similar deduction to the case of specific characters[87].

In the next place, and with special reference to the Wallacean doctrine, it is of importance to observe that, up to a certain point there is complete agreement between Darwinists of all schools. We all accept natural selection as a true cause of the origin of species (though we may not all subscribe to the Huxleyan deduction that it is necessarily a cause of the origin of *all* species). Moreover, we agree that specific characters are often what is called rudimentary or vestigial; and, once more, that our inability to detect the use of any given structure or instinct is no proof that such a structure or instinct is actually useless, seeing that it may very probably possess some function hitherto undetected, or possibly undetectable. Lastly, we all agree that a structure which is of use may incidentally entail the existence of some other structure which is not of use; for, in virtue of the so-called principle of correlation, the useless structure may be an indirect consequence of natural selection, since its development may be due to that of the useful structure, with the growth of which the useless one is correlated.

Nevertheless, while fully conceding all these facts and principles to the Wallacean party, those who think with Professor Huxley—and still more, of course, those few naturalists who think as I do——are unable to perceive that they constitute any grounds for holding the doctrine that all specific *characters* are, or formerly have been, directly or indirectly due to natural selection. My own reasons for dissenting from this Wallacean doctrine are as follows.

From what has just been said, it will be apparent that the question in debate is not merely a question of fact which can be settled by a direct appeal to observation. If this were the case, systematic naturalists could soon settle the question by their detailed knowledge of the structures which are severally distinctive of any given group of species. But so far is this from being the case, that systematic naturalists are really no better qualified to adjudicate upon the matter than are naturalists who have not devoted so much of their time to purely diagnostic work. The question is one of general principles, and as such cannot be settled by appeals to special cases. For example, suppose that the rest of this chapter were devoted to a mere enumeration of cases where it appears impossible to suggest the utility of certain specific characters, although such cases could be adduced by the thousand, how should I be met at the end of it all? Not by any one attempting to suggest the utility, past or present, of the characters named; but by being told that they must all present some *hidden* use, must be *vestigial*, or else must be due to *correlation*. By appealing to one or other of these assumptions, our opponents are always able to escape the necessity of justifying their doctrine in the presence of otherwise inexplicable facts. No matter how many seemingly "indifferent characters" we may thus accumulate, Mr. Wallace and his followers will always throw upon us the impossible burden of proving the negative, that these apparently useless characters do *not* present some hidden or former use, are *not* due to correlation, and therefore have *not* been produced by natural selection. It is in vain to retort that the burden of proof really lies the other way, or on the side of those who affirm that there is utility where no man can see it, or that there is correlation where no one can detect it. Thus, so far as any appeal to particular facts is concerned, it does not appear that there is any *modus vivendi*. Our opinions upon the question are really determined by the views which we severally take on matters of general principle. The issue, though it has a biological bearing, is a logical issue, not a biological one: it turns exclusively on those questions of definition and deduction with which we have just been dealing.

But although it thus follows that we cannot determine in fact what proportion of apparently useless characters are or are not really useful, we may very easily determine in fact what proportion of specific characters *fail to present any observable evidences of utility*. Yet, even upon this question of observable fact, it is surprising to note the divergent statements which have of late years been made by competent writers; statements in fact so divergent that they can only be explained by some want of sufficient thought on the part of those naturalists who are antecedently persuaded that all specific characters must be either directly or indirectly due to natural selection. Hence they fail to give to apparently useless specific characters the attention which, apart from any such antecedent persuasion, they deserve. For example, a few years ago I incidentally stated in a paper before the Linnaean Society, that "a large proportional number of specific characters" are of a trivial and apparently unmeaning kind, to which no function admits of being assigned, and also stated that Darwin himself had expressly given utterance to the same opinion. When these statements were made, I did not anticipate that they would be challenged by anybody, except perhaps, by Mr. Wallace. And, in order now to show that my innocence at that time was not due to ignorance of contemporary thought on such matters, a sentence may here be quoted from a paper which was read at the meeting of the British Association of the same year, by a highly competent systematic naturalist, Mr. Henry Seebohm, and soon afterwards extensively republished. Criticizing adversely my then recently published paper, he said:—

> "I fully admit the truth of this statement; and I presume
> that few naturalists would be prepared to deny that
> 'distinctions of specific value frequently have reference to
> structures which are without any utilitarian
> significance[88].'"

But since that time the course of Darwinian speculation has been greatly influenced by the writings of Weismann, who, among other respects in which he out-darwins Darwin, maintains the doctrine of utility as universal. In consequence of the influence which these writings have exercised, I have been more recently and extensively accused of "heresy" to Darwinian principles, for having stated that "a large proportional number of specific characters" do not admit of being proved useful, or correlated with other characters that are useful. Now, observe, we have here a simple question of fact. We are not at present concerned with the question how far the argument from ignorance may be held to apply in mitigation of such cases; but we are concerned only with the question of fact, as to what proportional number of cases actually occur where we are *unable to suggest* the use of specific characters, or the useful characters with which these apparently useless ones are correlated. I maintain, as a matter of fact, that the cases in question embrace "a large proportional number of specific characters." On the other hand, I am accused of betraying ignorance of species, and of the work of "species-makers," in advancing this statement; and have been told by Mr. Wallace, and others of his school, that there is absolutely no evidence to be derived from nature in support of my views. Well, in the first place, if this be the case, it is somewhat remarkable that a large body of competent naturalists, such as Bronn, Broca, Nägeli, Kerner, Sachs, De Vries, Focke, Henslow, Haeckel, Kölliker, Eimer, Giard, Pascoe, Mivart, Seebohm, Lloyd Morgan, Dixon, Beddard, Geddes Gulick, and also, as we shall presently see, Darwin himself, should have fallen into the same error. And it is further remarkable that the more a man devotes himself to systematic work in any particular department—whether as an ornithologist, a conchologist, an entomologist, and so forth—the less is he disposed to accept the dogma of specific characters as universally adaptive characters. But, in the second place, and quitting considerations of mere authority, I appeal to the facts of nature themselves; and will now proceed, as briefly as possible, to indicate the result of such an appeal.

For the following reasons, that birds and mammals seem to furnish the best field for testing the question by direct observation. First, these classes present many genera which have been more carefully worked out than is usually the case with genera of invertebrates, or even of cold-blooded vertebrates. Secondly, they comprise many genera each including a large number of species, whose habits and conditions of life are better known than is the case with species belonging to large genera of other classes. Thirdly, as birds and mammals represent the highest products of evolution in respect of organization, a more severe test is imposed than could be imposed elsewhere, when the question is as to the utility of specific characters; for if these highest products of organization fail to reveal, in a large proportional number of cases, the utility of their specific characters, much more is this likely to be the case among organic beings which stand lower in the scale of organization, and therefore, *ex hypothesi*, are less elaborate products of natural selection. Fourthly, and lastly, birds and mammals are the classes which Mr. Wallace has expressly chosen to constitute his ground of argument with regard to the issue on which we are now engaged.

It would take far too long to show, even in epitome, the results of this inquiry. Therefore I will only state the general upshot. Choosing genera of birds and mammals which contain a large number of species whose diagnostic characters have been worked out with most completeness, I restricted the inquiry to specific distinctions of colour, not only for the sake of having a uniform basis for comparisons, but still more because it seemed that the argument from our ignorance of possibly unknown uses could be more successfully met in the case of slight differences of colour or of shading, than in that of any differences of structure or of form. Finally, after tabulating all the differences of colour which are given as diagnostic of each species in a genus, and placing in one column those which may conceivably be useful, while placing in another column those of which it appeared inconceivable that any use could be suggested, I added up the figures in the two columns, and thus obtained a grand total of all the specific characters of the genus in respect of colours, separated into the two classes of conceivably useful and apparently useless. Now, in all cases the apparently useless characters largely preponderated over the conceivably useful ones; and therefore I abundantly satisfied myself regarding the accuracy of my previous statement, that a large proportional number—if not an actual majority—of specific characters belong to the latter category.

The following is a brief abstract of these results.

With respect to Birds, a large number of cases were collected wherein the characters of allied species differ from one another in such minute respects of colour or shading, that it seemed unreasonable to suppose them due to any selective value to the birds in question. It is needless—even if it were practicable on the present occasion—to adduce this evidence in detail, since an exceedingly good sample of it may be found in a small book which is specially devoted to considering the question in its relation to birds. I allude to an essay by Mr. Charles Dixon, entitled *Evolution without Natural Selection* (1885). In this work Mr. Dixon embodies the results of five years' "careful working at the geographical distribution and variations of plumage of Palaearctic birds and their allies in various other parts of the world"; and shows, by a large accumulation of facts, not only that there is no utility to be suggested in reference to the minute or trivial differences of colouration which he describes; but also that these differences are usually correlated with isolation on the one hand, or with slight differences of climate on the other. Now it will be shown later on that both these agents can be proved, by independent evidence, capable of inducing changes of specific type without reference to utility: therefore the correlation which Mr. Dixon unquestionably establishes between apparently useless (because utterly trivial) specific distinctions on the one hand, and isolation or climatic change on the other, constitutes additional evidence to show that the uselessness is not only apparent, but real. Moreover I have collected a number of cases where such minute differences of colour between allied species of birds happen to affect parts of the plumage which are *concealed*— as for instance, the breast and abdomen of creepers. In such cases it seems impossible to suggest how natural selection can have operated, seeing that the parts affected are not exposed to the view either of enemies or of prey.

Analogous illustrations to any amount may be drawn from Mammals. For instance, I have worked through the Marsupials with the aid of Mr. Oldfield Thomas' diagnostic description of their numerous species. Now, let us take any one of the genera, such as the kangaroos. This comprises 23 species living on an island continent of high antiquity, and not exposed to the depredations of any existing carnivorous enemies; so that there is here no present need to vary colour for purposes of protection. Moreover, in all cases the diagnostic distinctions of colour are so exceedingly trivial, that even if large carnivora were recently abundant in Australia, no one could reasonably suggest that the differences in question would then have been protective. On an average, each of the 23 species presents rather more than 20 peculiarities of shading, which are quoted as specifically diagnostic. Altogether there are 474 of these peculiarities distributed pretty evenly among the 23 species; and in no case can I conceive that utility can be suggested.

Hitherto we have been considering the question of fact, as to whether "a large proportional number of specific characters" do or do not admit of having their utility demonstrated, or even so much as plausibly suggested. In the result, I can only conclude that this question of fact is really not an open one, seeing that it admits of an abundantly conclusive answer by any naturalist who will take the trouble to work through the species of any considerable number of genera in the way above indicated. But although the question of fact is thus really closed, there remains a more ultimate question as to its theoretical interpretation. For, as already pointed out, no matter how great an accumulation of such facts may be collected, our opponents are always able to brush them aside by their *a priori* appeal to the argument from ignorance. In effect they say—We do not care for any number of thousands of such facts; it makes no difference to us what "proportional number" of specific characters fail to show evidence of utility; you are merely beating the air by adducing them, for we are already persuaded, on antecedent grounds, that *all* specific characters *must* be either themselves useful, or correlated with others that are, whether or not we can perceive the utility, or suggest the correlation.

To this question of theoretical interpretation, therefore, we must next address ourselves. And here, first of all, I should like to point out how sturdy must be the antecedent conviction of our opponents, if they are to maintain it in the face of such facts as have just been adduced. It must be remembered that this antecedent conviction is of a most uncompromising kind. By its own premisses it is committed to the doctrine that *all* specific characters, without a single exception, *must* be either useful, vestigial, or correlated. Well, if such be the case, is it not somewhat astonishing that out of 474 differences of colour which are distinctive of the 23 species of the genus Macropus, no single one appears capable of having any utility demonstrated, or indeed so much as suggested? For even the recent theory that slight differences of colour, which cannot be conceived as serving any other purpose, may enable the sexes of the same species quickly to recognize each other, is not here available. The species of the genus Macropus are more conspicuously distinguished by differences of size and form than by these minute differences of colour; and therefore no such use can be attributed to the latter. And, as previously stated, even within the order Marsupialia the genus Macropus is not at all exceptional in this respect; so that by including other genera of the order it would be easy to gather such apparently indifferent specific characters by the hundred, without any one of them presenting evidence—or even suggestion—of utility. How robust therefore is the faith of an *a priori* conviction which can stand against such facts as these! What, then, are the *a priori* grounds on which it stands? Mr. Wallace, the great leader of this school of thought, says:—

> "It is a necessary deduction from the theory of natural selection, that none of the definite facts of organic nature, no special organ, no characteristic form or marking, no peculiarities of instinct or of habit, no relations between species or between groups of species, can exist, but which must now be, or once have been, *useful* to the individuals or the races which possess them[89]."

Here, then, we have in brief compass the whole essence of our opponents' argument. It is confessedly an argument *a priori*, a deduction from the theory of natural selection, a supposed consequence of that theory which is alleged to be so necessary that to dispute the consequence is tantamount to denying the theory from which it is derived. In short, as before stated, it is a question of theory, not a question of fact: our difference of opinion is logical, not biological: it depends on our interpretation of principles, not on our observation of species. It will therefore be my endeavour to show that the reasoning in question is fallacious: that it is *not* a necessary deduction from the theory of natural selection that no characteristic form or marking, no peculiarities of instinct or of habit, can exist, but which must now be, or once have been, useful, or correlated with some other peculiarity that is useful.

"The tuft of hair on the breast of a wild turkey-cock *cannot be of any use*, and it is doubtful whether it can be ornamental in the eyes of the female bird;—indeed, had the tuft appeared under domestication, it would have been called a monstrosity[90]."

As a matter of common sense, unprejudiced by dogma, this appears to be a perfectly sound judgement; but if Wallace had asked Darwin to prove such a negative, Darwin could only have replied that it was for Wallace to prove the affirmative—and thus the issue would have been thrown back upon a discussion of general principles. Then Wallace would have said— "The assertion of inutility in the case of any organ or peculiarity which is not a rudiment or a correlation *is not, and can never be*, the statement of a fact, but *merely an expression of our ignorance of its purpose or origin[91]*." Darwin, however, would have replied:—"Our ignorance of the laws of variation is profound"; and while, on this account, we ought "to be extremely cautious in *pretending to decide what structures are now, or have formerly been, of use to each species*," in point of fact "there can be little doubt that the tendency to vary in the same manner has *often* been so strong, that *all* individuals of the same species have been similarly modified *without the aid of any form of selection[92]*."

It will be my endeavour in the following discussion to show that Darwin would have had an immeasurable advantage in this imaginary debate.

To begin with, Wallace's deductive argument is a clear case of circular reasoning. We set out by inferring that natural selection is a cause from numberless cases of observed utility as an effect: yet, when "in a large proportional number" of cases we fail to perceive any imaginable utility, it is argued that nevertheless utility must be there, since otherwise natural selection could not have been the cause.

Be it observed, in any given case we may properly anticipate utility as *probable*, even where it is not perceived; because there are already so enormous a number of cases where it is perceived, that, if the principle of natural selection be accepted at all, we must conclude with Darwin that it is "the *main* means of modification." Therefore, in particular cases of unperceived utility we may take this antecedent probability as a guide in our biological researches—as has been done with such brilliant success both by Darwin and Wallace, as well as by many of their followers. But this is a very different thing from laying down the universal maxim, that in *all* cases utility *must* be present, whether or not we shall ever be able to detect it[93]. For this universal maxim amounts to an assumption that natural selection has been the "*exclusive* means of modification." That it has been "the main means of modification" is proved by the generality of the observed facts of adaptation. That it has been "the exclusive means of modification," with the result that these facts are universal, cannot be thus proved by observation. Why, then, is it alleged? Confessedly it is alleged by way of deduction from the theory of natural selection itself. Or, as above stated, after having deduced the theory from the facts, it is sought to deduce the facts from the theory.

Thus far I have been endeavouring to show that the universality of adaptation cannot be inferred from its generality, or from the theory of natural selection itself. But, of course, the case would be quite different if there were any independent evidence—or rather, let us say, any logical argument—to show that natural selection is "the exclusive means of modification." For in this event it would no longer involve circular reasoning to maintain that all specific characters are likewise adaptive characters. It might indeed appear antecedently improbable that no other principle than natural selection can possibly have been concerned in the differentiation of those relatively permanent varieties which we call species—that in all the realm of organic nature, and in all the complexities of living processes, there is no room for any other influence in the production of change, even of the most trivial and apparently unmeaning kind. But if there were any good evidence or logical argument to the contrary, this antecedent presumption would have to give way; and the certainty that all specific characters are likewise adaptive characters would be determined by the cogency of such evidence or argument as could be adduced. In short, we are not entitled to conclude—and still less does it follow "as a necessary deduction from the theory of natural selection"— that all the details of specific differentiation must in every case be either useful, vestigial, or correlated, *unless it has been previously shown, by independent evidence, or accurate reasoning, that there is no room for any other principle of specific change.*

This, apparently, is the central core of the question. Therefore I will now proceed to consider such arguments as have been adduced to prove that, other than natural selection, there *can* have been no "means of modification." And, after having exhibited the worthlessness of these arguments, I will devote the next chapter to showing that, as a matter of observable fact, there *are* a considerable number of other principles, which can be proved to be capable of producing such minute differences of form and colour as "in a large proportional number" of cases constitute diagnostic distinctions between species and species.

First, then, for the reasons *a priori*—and they are confessedly *a priori*—which have been adduced to prove that natural selection has been what in Darwin's opinion it has not been,—"the *exclusive* means of modification." Disregarding the Lamarckian factors—which, even if valid, have but little relation to the present question, seeing that they are concerned, almost exclusively, with the evolution of *adaptive* characters—it is alleged that natural selection must occupy the whole field, because no other principle of change can be allowed to operate in the presence of natural selection. Now, I fully agree that this statement may hold as regards any principle of change which is deleterious; but clearly it does not hold as regards any principle which is merely neutral. If any one were to allege that specific characters are frequently detrimental to the species presenting them, he would no doubt lay himself open to the retort that natural selection could not allow such characters to persist; or, which amounts to the same thing, that it *does* "necessarily follow from the theory of natural selection" that specific characters can never be in any large number, or in any large measure, *harmful* to the species presenting them. But where the statement is that specific characters are frequently *indifferent*—again to use Professor Huxley's term—the retort loses all its relevancy. No reason has ever been shown why natural selection should interfere with merely indifferent characters, supposing such to have been produced by any of the agencies which we shall presently have to consider. Therefore this argument—or rather assertion—goes for nothing.

The only other argument I have met with on this side of the question is one that has recently been adduced by Mr. Wallace. He says:—

> "One very weighty objection to the theory that *specific* characters can ever be wholly useless appears to have been overlooked by those who have maintained the frequency of such characters, and that is, their almost necessary instability[94]."

This argument he proceeds to elaborate at considerable length, but fails to perceive what appears to me the obvious answer. Provided that the cause of the useless character is constant, there is no difficulty in understanding why the character is stable. Utility is not the only principle that can lead to stability: any other principle must do the same, provided that it acts for a sufficient length of time, and with a sufficient degree of uniformity, on all the individuals of a species. This is a consideration the cogency of which was clearly recognized by Darwin, as the following quotations will show. Speaking of unadaptive characters, he says they may arise as merely

> "fluctuating variations, which sooner or later become *constant* through the nature of the organism and of surrounding conditions, *but not through natural selection*[95]."

Elsewhere we read:—

> "Each of the endless variations which we see in the plumage of our fowls must have had some efficient cause; and if the *same* cause were to act *uniformly* during a long series of generations on *many* individuals, *all* probably would be modified in the same manner."

As special illustrations of this fact I may quote the following cases from Darwin's works.

> "Dr. Bachman states that he has seen turkeys raised from the eggs of wild species, lose their metallic tints, and become spotted in the third generation. Mr. Yarrell many years ago informed me that the wild ducks bred in St James' Park lost their true plumage after a few generations. An excellent observer (Mr. Hewitt) ... found that he could not breed wild ducks true for more than five or six generations, as they proved so much less beautiful. The white collar round the neck of the mallard became broader and more irregular, and white feathers appeared in the duckling's wings &c.[96]"

Now, such cases—to which numberless others might be added—prove that even the subtle and inconspicuous causes incidental to domestication are capable of inducing changes of specific character quite as great, and quite as "stable," as any that in a state of nature are taken to constitute specific distinctions. Yet there can here be no suggestion of utility, inasmuch as the change takes place in the course of a few generations, and therefore without leaving time for natural selection to come into play— even if it ever could come into play among the sundry domesticated birds in question.

But the facts of domestication also make for the same conclusion in another way—namely, by proving that when time enough *has* been allowed for the production of useless changes of greater magnitude, such changes are not infrequently produced. And the value of this line of evidence is that, great as are the changes, it is impossible that either natural or artificial selection can have been concerned in their production. It will be sufficient to give two examples—both with regard to structure.

The first I will render in the words whereby it has already been stated in my own paper on *Physiological Selection*, because I should like to take this opportunity of answering Mr. Wallace's objection to it.

"Elsewhere (*Origin of Species*, p. 158) Mr. Darwin points out that modifications which appear to present obvious utility are often found on further examination to be really useless. This latter consideration, therefore, may be said to act as a foil to the one against which I am arguing, namely, that modifications which appear to be useless may nevertheless be useful. But here is a still more suggestive consideration, also derived from Mr. Darwin's writings. Among our domesticated productions changes of structure—or even structures wholly new—not unfrequently arise, which are in every way analogous to the apparently useless distinctions between wild species. Take, for example, the following most instructive case:—

FIG. 2.—Old Irish Pig, showing jaw-appendages (after Richardson).

"'Another curious anomaly is offered by the appendages described by M. Eudes-Deslongchamps as often characterizing the Normandy pigs. These appendages are always attached to the same spot, to the corners of the jaws; they are cylindrical, about three inches in length, covered with bristles, and with a pencil of bristles rising out of a sinus on one side; they have a cartilaginous centre with two small longitudinal muscles; they occur either symmetrically on both sides of the face, or on one side alone. Richardson figures them on the gaunt old Irish Greyhound pig; and Nathusius states that they occasionally appear in all the long-eared races, but are not strictly inherited, for they occur or fail in the animals of the same litter. As no wild pigs are known to have analogous appendages, we have at present no reason to suppose that their appearance is due to reversion; and if this be so, we are forced to admit that a somewhat complex, though apparently useless, structure may be suddenly developed without the aid of selection[97].'"

To this case Mr. Wallace objects:—

"But it is expressly stated that they are not constant; they appear 'frequently' or 'occasionally,' they are 'not strictly inherited, for they occur or fail in animals of the same litter'; and they are not always symmetrical, sometimes appearing on one side of the face alone. Now, whatever may be the cause or explanation of these anomalous appendages, they cannot be classed with 'specific characters,' the most essential features of which are, that they *are* symmetrical, that they *are* inherited, and that they *are* constant[98]."

But, to begin with, I have not classed these appendages with "specific characters," nor maintained that Normandy pigs ought to be regarded as specifically distinct on account of them. What I said was:—

"Now, if any such structure as this occurred in a wild species, and if any one were to ask what is the use of it, those who rely on the argument from ignorance would have a much stronger case than they usually have; for they might point to the cartilage supplied with muscles, and supporting a curious arrangement of bristles, as much too specialized a structure to be wholly meaningless. Yet we happen to know that this particular structure is wholly meaningless[99]."

In the next place, is it either fair or reasonable to expect that a varietal character of presumably very recent origin should be as strongly inherited—and therefore as constant both in occurrence and symmetry—as a true specific character, say, of a thousand times its age? Even characters of so-called "constant varieties" in a state of nature are usually less constant than specific characters; while, again, as Darwin says, "it is notorious that specific characters are more variable than generic,"—the reason in both cases being, as he proceeds to show, that the less constant characters are characters of more recent origin, and therefore less firmly fixed by heredity[100]. Hence I do not understand how Mr. Wallace can conclude, as he does, "that, admitting that this peculiar appendage is wholly useless and meaningless, the fact would be rather an argument against specific characters being also meaningless, because the latter never have the characteristics [i.e. inconstancy of occurrence, form, and transmission] which this particular variation possesses[101]." Mr. Wallace can scarcely suppose that when specific characters first arise, they present the three-fold kind of constancy to which he here alludes. But, if not, can it be denied that these peculiar appendages appear to be passing through a phase of development which all "specific characters" must have passed through, before they have had time enough to be firmly fixed by heredity[102]?

If, however, even this should be denied, what will be said of the second case, that of the niata cattle?

> "I saw two herds on the northern bank of the Plata.... The forehead is very short and broad, with the nasal end of the skull, together with the whole plane of the upper molar-teeth, curved upwards. The lower jaw projects beyond the upper, and has a corresponding upward curvature.... The skull which I presented to the College of Surgeons has been thus described by Professor Owen. 'It is remarkable from the stunted development of the nasals, premaxillaries, and fore part of the lower jaw, which is unusually curved upwards to come into contact with the premaxillaries. The nasal bones are about one-third the ordinary length, but retain almost their normal breadth. The triangular vacuity is left between them and the frontal and lachrymal, which latter bone articulates with the premaxillary, and thus excludes the maxillary from any junction
> with the nasal.' So that even the connexion of some of the bones is changed. Other differences might be added: thus the plane of the condyles is somewhat modified, and the terminal edge of the premaxillaries forms an arch. In fact, on comparison with the skull of a common ox, scarcely a single bone presents the same exact shape, and the whole skull has a wonderfully different appearance[103]."

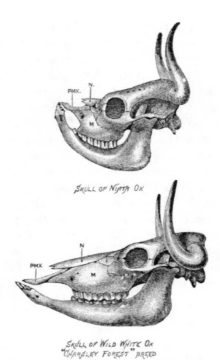

SKULL OF NIATA OX

SKULL OF WILD WHITE OX
"CHARSLEY FOREST" BREED

FIG. 3.—Drawn from nature. R. Coll. Surg. Mus.

As I cannot find that this remarkable skull has been figured before, I have had the accompanying woodcut made in order to compare it with the skull of a Charsley Forest ox; and a glance is sufficient to show what "a wonderfully different appearance" it presents.

Now the important points in the present connexion with regard to this peculiar race of cattle are the following.

Their origin is not known; but it must have been subsequent to the year 1552, when cattle were first introduced to America from Europe, and it is known that such cattle have been in existence for at least a century. The breed is very true, and a niata bull and cow invariably produce niata calves. A niata bull crossed with a common cow, and the reverse cross, yield offspring having an intermediate character, but with the niata peculiarities highly conspicuous[104].

Here, then, we have unquestionable evidence of a whole congeries of very distinctive characters, so unlike anything that occurs in any other cattle, that, had they been found in a state of nature, they would have been regarded as a distinct species. And the highly peculiar characters which they present conform to all "the most essential features of specific characters," as these are stated by Mr. Wallace in his objection to the case of the pig's appendages. That is to say, "they *are* symmetrical, they *are* inherited, and they *are* constant." In point of fact, they are *always* "constant," both as to occurrence and symmetry, while they are so completely "inherited" that not only does "a niata bull and cow *invariably* produce niata calves"; but even when crossed with other cattle the result is a *hybrid*, "with the niata character *strongly* displayed."

Hence, if we were to follow Mr. Wallace's criteria of specific characters, which show that the pig's appendages "cannot be classed with specific characters" (or with anything of the nature of specific characters), it would follow that the niata peculiarities *can* be so classed. This, therefore, is a case where he will find all the reasons which in other cases he takes to justify him in falling back upon the argument from ignorance. The cattle are half wild, he may urge; and so the three-fold constancy of their peculiar characters may very well be due, either directly or indirectly, to natural selection—i.e. they may either be of some hidden use themselves, or correlated with some other modifications that are of use: it is, he may say, as in such cases he often does say, for us to disprove both these possibilities.

Well, here we have one of those rare cases where historical information, or other accidents, admit of our discharging this burden of proving a negative. Darwin's further description shows that this customary refuge in the argument from ignorance is most effectually closed. For—

> "When the pasture is tolerably long, these cattle feed as well as common cattle with their tongue and palate; but during the great droughts, when so many animals perish on the Pampas, the niata breed lies under a great disadvantage, and would, if not attended to, become extinct; for the common cattle, like horses, are able to keep alive by browsing with their lips on the twigs of trees and on reeds; this the niatas cannot so well do, as their lips do not join, and hence they are found to perish before the common cattle. This strikes me as a good illustration of how little we are able to judge from the ordinary habits of an animal, on what circumstances, occurring only at long intervals of time, its rarity or extinction may depend. It shows us, also, how natural selection would have determined the rejection of the niata modification, had it arisen in a state of nature[105]."

Hence, it is plainly *impossible* to attribute this modification to natural selection, either as acting directly on the modified parts themselves, or indirectly through correlation of growth. And as the modification is of specific magnitude on the one hand, while it presents all "the most essential features of specific characters" on the other, I do not see any means whereby Mr. Wallace can meet it on his *a priori* principles. It would be useless to answer that these characters, although conforming to all his tests of specific characters, differ in respect of being deleterious, and would therefore lead to extermination were the animals in a wholly wild state; because, considered as an argument, this would involve the assumption that, apart from natural selection, only deleterious characters can arise under nature—i. e. that merely "indifferent" characters can never do so, which would be absurd. Indeed, I have chosen this case of the niata cattle expressly because their strongly marked peculiarities *are* deleterious, and therefore exclude Mr. Wallace's appeal to the argument from ignorance of a possible utility. But if even these pronounced and deleterious peculiarities can arise and be perpetuated with such constancy and fidelity, much more is this likely to be the case with less pronounced and merely neutral peculiarities.

It may, however, be further objected that these cattle are not improbably the result of *artificial* selection. It may be suggested that the semi-monstrous breed originated in a single congenital variation, or "sport," which was isolated and multiplied as a curiosity by the early settlers. But even if such be the explanation of this particular case, the fact would not weaken our illustration. On the contrary, it would strengthen our general argument, by showing an additional means whereby indifferent specific characters can arise and become fixed in a state of nature. As it seems to me extremely probable that the niata cattle did originate in a congenital monstrosity, which was then isolated and multiplied by human agency (as is known to have been the case with the "ancon sheep"), I will explain why this tends to strengthen our general argument.

It is certain that if these animals were ever subject to artificial isolation for the purpose of establishing their breed, the process must have ceased a long time ago, seeing that there is no memory or tradition of its occurrence. Now this proves that, however the breed may have originated, it has been able to maintain its many and highly peculiar characters for a number of generations without the help of selection, either natural or artificial. This is the first point to be clear upon. Be its origin what it may, we know that this breed has proved capable of perpetuating itself with uniform "constancy" for a number of generations after the artificial selection has ceased— supposing such a process ever to have occurred. And this certain fact that artificial selection, even if it was originally needed to establish the type, has not been needed to perpetuate the type, is a full answer to the supposed objection. For, in view of this fact, it is immaterial what the origin of the niata breed may have been. In the present connexion, the importance of this breed consists in its proving the subsequent "stability" of an almost monstrous form, continued through a long series of generations by the force of heredity alone, without the aid of any form of selection.

The next point is, that not only is a seeming objection to the illustration thus removed, but that, if we do entertain the question of origin, and if we do suppose the origin of these cattle to have been in a congenital "sport," afterwards multiplied by artificial isolation, we actually strengthen our general argument by increasing the importance of this particular illustration. For the illustration then becomes available to show how indifferent specific characters may sometimes originate in merely individual sports, which, if not immediately extinguished by free intercrossing, will perpetuate themselves by the unaided force of heredity. But this is a point to which we shall recur in the ensuing chapter.

In conclusion, it is worth while to remark, with regard to Mr. Wallace's argument from constancy, that, as a matter of fact, utility does not seem to present any greater power in securing "stability of characters" than any other cause of like constancy. Thus, for instance, whatever the causes may have been which have produced and perpetuated the niata breed of cattle, they have certainly produced a wonderful "stability" of a great modification in a wonderfully short time. And the same has to be said of the ducks in St. James' Park, as well as sundry other cases. On the other hand, when, as in the case of numberless natural species, modification has been undoubtedly produced by natural selection, although the modification must have had a very much longer time in which to have been fixed by heredity, it is often far from being stable—notwithstanding that Mr. Wallace regards stability as a criterion of specific characters. Indeed—and this is more suggestive still—there even seems to be a kind of *inverse* proportion between the utility and the stability of a specific character. The explanation appears to be (*Origin of Species*, pp. 120-2), that the more a specific character has been forced on by natural selection on account of its utility, the less time will it have had to become well fixed by heredity before attaining a full development. Moreover, as Darwin adds, in cases where the modification has not only been thus "comparatively recent," but also "extraordinarily great," the probability is that the parts so modified must have been very variable in the first instance, and so are all the more difficult to render constant by heredity. Thus we see that utility is no better—even if it be so good—a cause of stability in specific characters, as are the unknown causes of stability in many varietal characters[106].

CHAPTER VIII
Characters as Adaptive and Specific
(continued).

Let us now proceed to indicate some of the causes, other than natural selection, which may be regarded as adequate to induce such changes in organic types as are taken by systematists to constitute diagnostic distinctions between species and species. We will first consider causes external to organisms, and will then go on to consider those which occur within the organisms themselves: following, in fact, the classification which Darwin has himself laid down. For he constantly speaks of such causes as arising on the one hand, from "changed conditions of life" and, on the other hand, from "the nature of the organism"—that is, from internal processes leading to "variations which seem to us in our ignorance to arise spontaneously."

In neither case will it be practicable to give more than a brief *résumé* of all that might be said on these interesting topics.

I. Climate.

There is an overwhelming mass of evidence to prove that the assemblage of external conditions of life conveniently summarized in the word Climate, exercise a potent, an uniform, and a permanent influence on specific characters.

With regard to plants, Darwin adduces a number of facts to show the effects of climate on wheat, cabbages, and other vegetables. Here, for example, is what he says with regard to maize imported from America to Germany:—

> "During the first year the plants were twelve feet high, and a few seeds were perfected; the lower seeds in the ear kept true to their proper form, but the upper seeds became slightly changed. In the second generation the plants were from nine to ten feet high, and ripened their seed better; the depression on the outer side of the seed had almost disappeared, and the original beautiful white colour had become duskier. Some of the seeds had even become yellow, and in their now rounded form they approached the common European maize. In the third generation nearly all resemblance to the original and very distinct American parent-form was lost[107]."

As these "highly remarkable" changes were effected in but three generations, it is obvious that they cannot have been dependent on selection of any kind. The same remark applies to trees. Thus,—

> "Mr. Meehan has compared twenty-nine kinds of American trees with their nearest European allies, all grown in close proximity and under as nearly as possible the same conditions. In the American species he finds, with the rarest exceptions, that the leaves fall earlier in the season, and assume before their fall a brighter tint; that they are less deeply toothed or serrated; that the buds are smaller; that the trees are more diffuse in growth and have fewer branchlets; and, lastly, that the seeds are smaller—all in comparison with the corresponding European species. Now, considering that these corresponding trees belong to several distinct orders, and that they are adapted to widely different stations, it can hardly be supposed that their differences are of any special service to them in the New and Old worlds; and, if so, such differences cannot have been gained through natural selection, and must be

attributed to the long continued action of a different climate[108]."

These cases, however, I quote mainly in order to show Darwin's opinion upon the matter, with reference to the absence of natural selection. For, where the vegetable kingdom is concerned, the fact of climatic variation is so general, and in its relation to diagnostic work so important, that it constitutes one of the chief difficulties against which species-makers have to contend. And the more carefully the subject is examined the greater does the difficulty become. But, as to this and other general facts, it will be best to allow a recognized authority to speak; and therefore I will give a few extracts from Kerner's work on *Gute und schlechte Arten*.

He begins by showing that geographical (or it may be topographical) varieties of species are often so divergent, that without a knowledge of intermediate forms there could be no question as to their being good species. As a result of his own researches on the subject, he can scarcely find language strong enough to express his estimate of the extent and the generality of this source of error. In different parts of Europe, or even in different parts of the Alps, he has found these climatic varieties in such multitudes and in such high degrees both of constancy and divergence, that, after detailing his results, he finishes his essay with the following remarkable conclusions:—

"Die Wissenchaft geht aber ihren Entwicklungsgang im grossen Ganzen gerade so, wie die Erkenntniss bei jedem einzelnen Naturforscher. Fast jeder Botaniker muss seinen Entwicklungsgang durchmachen und gelangt endlich mehr oder weniger nahe zu demselben Ziele. Die Ungleichheit besteht nur darin, dass der eine langsamer, der andere aber rascher bei dem Ziele ankommt. Anfänglich müht sich jeder ab, die Formen in hergebrachter Weise zu gliedern und die 'guten Arten' herauszulesen. Mit der Erweiterung des Gesichtskreises und mit der Vermehrung der Anschauungen aber schwindet auch immer mehr der Boden unter den Füssen, die bisher für unverrückbar gehaltenen Grenzen der gut geglaubten Arten stellen sich als eine der Natur angelegte Zwangsjacke heraus, die Uebcrzeugung, dass die Grenzen, welche wir ziehen, eben nur künstliche sind, gewinnt immer mehr und mehr die Oberhand, und wer nicht gerade zu den hartgesottenen Eigensinnigen gehört, und wer die Wahrheit höher stellt als das starre Festhalten an seinen früheren Ansichten, geht schliesslich bewusst oder unbewusst in das Lager derjenigen über, in welchem auch ich mir ein bescheidenes Plätzchen aufgesucht habe."

By these "hard-boiled" botanists he means those who entertain the traditional notion of a species as an assemblage of definite characters, always and everywhere associated together. This notion (Artsbeständigkeit) must be entirely abandoned. Summarizing Kerner's facts for their general results we find that his extensive investigations have proved that in his numberless kinds of European plants the following relations frequently obtain. Supposing that there are two or more allied species, A and B, then A' and B' may be taken to represent their respective types as found in some particular area. It does not signify whether A' and B' are geographically remote from, or close to, A and B; the point is that, whether in respect of temperature, altitude, moisture, character of soil, &c., there is some difference in the conditions of life experienced by the plants growing at the different places. Now, in numberless plants it is found that the typical or constant peculiarities of A' differ more from those of A than they do from those of B; while, conversely, the characters of A' may bear more resemblance to those of B' than they do to those of A—on account of such characters being due to the same external causes in both cases. The consequence is that A' might more correctly be classified with B', or *vice versa*. Another consequence is that whether A and B, or A' and B', be recorded as the "good species" usually depends upon which has happened to have been first described.

Such a mere abstract of Kerner's general results, however, can give no adequate idea of their cogency: for this arises from the number of species in which specific characters are thus found to change, and even to *interchange*, with different conditions of life. Thus he gives an amusing parable of an ardent young botanist, Simplicius, who starts on a tour in the Tyrol with the works of the most authoritative systematists to assist him in his study of the flora. The result is that Simplicius becomes so hopelessly bewildered in his attempts at squaring their diagnostic descriptions with the facts of nature, that he can only exclaim in despair—"Sonderbare Flora, diese tirolische, in welcher so viele characteristische Pflanzen nur schlechte Arten, oder gar noch schlechter als schlechte Arten, sind." Now, in giving illustrations of this young man's troubles, Kerner fills five or six pages with little else than rows of specific names.

Upon the whole, Kerner concludes that the more the subject is studied, the more convinced must the student become that all distinction between species as "good" and "bad" vanishes. In other words, the more that our knowledge of species and of their diagnostic characters increases, the more do we find that "bad species" multiply at the expense of "good species"; so that eventually we must relinquish the idea of "good species" altogether.

Or, conversely stated, we must agree to regard as equally "good species" any and every assemblage of individuals which present the same peculiarities: provided that these peculiarities do not rise to a generic value, they equally deserve to be regarded as "specific characters," no matter how trivial, or how local, they may be. In fact, he goes so far as to say that when, as a result of experiments in transplantation from one set of physical conditions to another, seedlings are found to present any considerable and constant change in their specific characters, these seedlings are no less entitled to be regarded as a "good species" than are the plants from which they have been derived. Probably few systematists will consent to go quite so far as this; but the fact that Kerner has been led deliberately to propound such a statement as a result of his wide observations and experiments is about as good evidence as possible on the points with which we are here concerned. For even Simplicius would hardly be quite so simple as to suppose that each one of all the characters which he observes in his "remarkable flora," so largely composed of "bad or even worse than bad species," is of utilitarian significance.

Be it noted, however, that I am not now expressing my own opinion. There are weighty reasons against thus identifying climatic variations with good species—reasons which will be dealt with in the next chapter. Kerner does not seem to appreciate the weight of these reasons, and therefore I do not call him as a witness to the subject as a whole; but only to that part of it which has to do with the great and general importance of climatic variability in relation to diagnostic work. And thus far his testimony is fully corroborated by every other botanist who has ever attended to the subject. Therefore it does not seem worth while to quote further authorities in substantiation of this point, such as Gärtner, De Candolle, Nägeli, Peter, Jordan, &c. For nowadays no one will dispute the high generality and the frequently great extent of climatic variation where the vegetable kingdom is concerned. Indeed, it may fairly be doubted whether there is any one species of plant, whose distribution exposes it to any considerable differences in its external conditions of life, which does not present more or less considerable differences as to its characters in different parts of its range. The principal causes of such climatic variation appear to be the chemical, and, still more, the mechanical nature of soil; temperature; intensity and diurnal duration of light in spring and summer; moisture; presence of certain salts in the air and soil of marine plants, or of plants growing near mineral springs; and sundry other circumstances of a more or less unknown character.

Before closing these remarks on climatic variation in the vegetable kingdom, prominent attention must be directed to a fact of broad generality and, in relation to our present subject, of considerable importance. This is that the same external causes very frequently produce the same effects in the way of specific change throughout large numbers of *unrelated* species— i.e. species belonging to different genera, families, and orders. Moreover, throughout all these unrelated species, we can frequently trace a uniform correlation between the degrees of change and the degrees to which they have been subjected to the causes in question.

As examples, all botanists who have attended to the subject are struck by the similarity of variation presented by different species growing on the same soils, altitudes, latitudes, longitudes, and so forth. Plants growing on chalky soils, when compared with those growing on richer soils, are often more thickly covered with down, which is usually of a white or grey colour. Their leaves are frequently of a bluish-green tint, more deeply cut, and less veined, while their flowers tend to be larger and of a lighter tint. There are similarly constant differences in other respects in varieties growing on sundry other kinds of soils. Sea-salt has the general effect, on many different kinds of plants, of producing moist fleshy leaves, and red tints. Experiments in transplantation have shown that these changes may be induced artificially; so there can be no doubt as to its being this that and the other set of external conditions which produces them in nature. Again, dampness causes leaves to become smoother, greener, less cut, and the flowers to become darker; while dryness tends to produce opposite effects. I need not go on to specify the particular results on all kinds of plants of altitude, latitude, longitude, and so forth. For we are concerned only with the fact that these two correlations may be regarded as general laws appertaining to the vegetable kingdom—namely, (A) that the same external causes produce similar varietal effects in numerous unallied species of plants; and, (B) that the more these species are exposed to such causes the greater is the amount of varietal effect produced—so that, for instance, on travelling from latitude to latitude, longitude to longitude, altitude to altitude, &c., we may see greater and greater degrees of such definite and more or less common varietal changes affecting the unallied species in question. Now these general laws are of importance for us, because they prove unequivocally that it is the direct action of external conditions of life which produce climatic variations of specific types. And, taken in connexion with the results of experiments in transplantation (which in a single generation may yield variations similar to those found in nature under similar circumstances), these general laws still further indicate that climatic variations are "indifferent" variations. In other words, we find that changes of specific characters are of widespread occurrence in the vegetable kingdom, that they are constantly and even proportionally related to definite external circumstances, but yet that, in as far as they are climatic, they cannot be attributed to the agency of natural selection[109].

Turning next to animals, it may first be observed that climatic conditions do not appear to exercise an influence either so general or so considerable as in the case of plants. Nevertheless, although these influences are relatively more effective in the vegetable kingdom than they are in the animal, absolutely considered they are of high generality and great importance even in the latter. But as this fact is so well recognized by all zoologists, it will be needless to give more than a very few illustrations. Indeed, throughout this discussion on climatic influences my aim is merely to give the general reader some idea of their importance in regard to systematic natural history; and, therefore, such particular cases as are mentioned are selected only as samples of whole groups of cases more or less similar.

With regard to animals, then, we may best begin by noticing that, just as in the case of plants, there is good evidence of the same external causes producing the same effects in multitudes of species belonging to different genera, families, orders, and even classes. Moreover, we are not without similarly good evidence of *degrees* of specific change taking place in correlation with *degrees* of climatic change, so that we may frequently trace a gradual progress of the former as we advance, say, from one part of a large continent to another. Instances of these correlations are not indeed so numerous in the animal kingdom as they are in the vegetable. Nevertheless they are amply sufficient for our present purposes.

For example, Mr. Allen has studied in detail changes of size and colour among birds and mammals on the American continent; and he finds a wonderfully close sliding scale of both, corresponding stage by stage with gradual changes of climate. Very reasonably he attributes this to the direct influence of climatic conditions, without reference to natural selection—as does also Mr. Gould with reference to similar facts which he has observed among the birds of Australia. Against this view Mr. Wallace urges, "that the effects are due to the greater or less need of protection." But it is difficult to believe that such can be the case where so innumerable a multitude of widely different species are concerned—presenting so many diverse habits, as well as so many distinct habitats. Moreover, the explanation seems incompatible with the *graduated* nature of the change, and also with the fact that not only colouration but size, is implicated.

We meet with analogous facts in butterflies. Thus *Lycaena agestis* not only presents seasonal variations, (A) and (B); but while (A) and (B) are respectively the winter and summer forms in Germany, (B) and (C) are the corresponding forms in Italy. Therefore, (B) is in Germany the summer form, and in Italy the winter form—the German winter form (A) being absent in Italy, while the Italian summer form (C) is absent in Germany. Probably these facts are due to differences of temperature in the two countries, for experiments have shown that when pupae of sundry species of moths and butterflies are exposed to different degrees of temperature, the most wonderful changes of colour may result in the insects which emerge. The remarkable experiments of Dorfmeister and Weismann in relation to this subject are well known. More recently Mr. Merrifield has added to their facts, and concludes that the action of cold upon the pupae—and also, apparently, upon the larvae—has a tendency to produce dark hues in the perfect insect[110].

But, passing now from such facts of climatic variations over wide areas to similar facts within small areas, in an important *Memoir on the Cave Fauna of North America*, published a few years ago by the American Academy of Sciences, it is stated:—

> "As regards change of colour, we do not recall an exception to the general rule that all cave animals are either colourless or nearly white, or, as in the case of Arachnida and Insects, much paler than their out-of-door relatives."

Now, when we remember that these cave faunas comprise representatives of nearly all classes of the animal kingdom, it becomes difficult, if not impossible, to imagine that so universal a discharge of colouring can be due to natural selection. It must be admitted that the only way in which natural selection could act in this case would be indirectly through the principle of correlation. There being no light in the caves, it can be of no advantage to the animals concerned that they should lose their colour for the sake of protection, or for any other reason of a similarly direct kind. Therefore, if the loss of colour is to be ascribed to natural selection, this can only be done by supposing that natural selection has here acted indirectly through the principle of correlation. There is evidence to show that elsewhere modification or loss of colour is in some cases brought about by natural selection, on account of the original colour being correlated with certain physiological characters (such as liability to particular diseases, &c.); so that when natural selection operates directly upon these physiological characters, it thereby also operates indirectly upon the correlated colours. But to suppose that this can be the explanation of the uniform diminution of colour in all inhabitants of dark caves would be manifestly absurd. If there were only one class of animals in these caves, such as Insects, it might be possible to surmise that their change of colour is due to natural selection acting directly upon their physiological constitutions, and so indirectly upon their colours. But it would be absurd to suppose that such can be the explanation of the facts, when these extend in so similar a manner over so many scores of species belonging to such different types of animal life.

With more plausibility it might be held that the universal discharge of colour in these cave-faunas is due, not to the presence, but to the absence of selection—i. e. to the cessation of selection, or panmixia. But against this—at all events as a full or general explanation—lie the following facts. First, in the case of Proteus—which has often been kept for the purposes of exhibition &c., in tanks—the skin becomes dark when the animal is removed from the cave and kept in the light. Secondly, deep-sea faunas, though as much exposed as the cave-faunas, to the condition of darkness, are not by any means invariably colourless. On the contrary, they frequently present brilliant colouration. Thus it is evident that if panmixia be suggested in explanation of the discharge of colouring in cave-faunas, the continuance of colour in deep-sea faunas appears to show the explanation insufficient. Thirdly, according to my view of the action of panmixia as previously explained, no *total* discharge of colouration is likely to be caused by such action alone. At most the bleaching as a result of the mere withdrawal of selection would proceed only to some comparatively small extent. Fourthly, Mr. Packard in the elaborate *Memoir on Cave Fauna*, already alluded to, states that in some of the cases the phenomena of bleaching appear to have been induced within very recent times—if not, indeed, within the limits of a single generation. Should the evidence in support of this opinion prove trustworthy, of course in itself it disposes of any suggestion either of the presence or the absence of natural selection as concerned in the process.

Nevertheless, I myself think it inevitable that to some extent the cessation of selection must have helped in discharging the colour of cave faunas; although for the reasons now given it appears to me that the main causes of change must have been of that direct order which we understand by the term climatic.

As regards dogs, the Rev. E. Everest found it impossible to breed Scotch setters in India true to their type. Even in the second generation no single young dog resembled its parents either in form or shape. "Their nostrils were more contracted, their noses more pointed, their size inferior, and their limbs more slender[111]." Similarly on the coast of New Guinea, Bosman says that imported breeds of dogs "alter strangely; their ears grow long and stiff like those of foxes, to which colour they also incline ... and in three or four broods their barking turns into a howl[112]."

Darwin gives numerous facts showing the effects of climate on horses, cattle, and sheep, in altering, more or less considerably, the characters of their ancestral stocks. He also gives the following remarkable case with regard to the rabbit. Early in the fifteenth century a common rabbit and her young ones were turned out on the island of Porto Santo, near Madeira. The feral progeny now differ in many respects from their parent stock. They are only about one-third of the weight, present many differences in the relative sizes of different parts, and have greatly changed in colour. In particular, the black on the upper surface of the tail and tips of the ears, which is so constant in all other wild rabbits of the world as to be given in most works as a specific character, has entirely disappeared. Again, "the throat and certain parts of the under surface, instead of being pure white, are generally grey or leaden colour," while the upper surface of the whole body is redder than in the common rabbit. Now, what answer have our opponents to make to such a case as this? Presumably they will answer that the case simply proves the action of natural selection during the best part of 400 years on an isolated section of a species. Although we cannot say of what use all these changes have been to the rabbits presenting them, nevertheless we *must* believe that they have been produced by natural selection, and therefore *must* present some hidden use to the isolated colony of rabbits thus peculiarly situated. Four centuries is long enough to admit of natural selection effecting all these changes in the case of so rapidly breeding an animal as the rabbit, and therefore it is needless to look further for any explanation of the facts. Such, I say, is presumably the answer that would be given by the upholders of natural selection as the only possible cause of specific change. But now, in this particular case it so happens that the answer admits of being conclusively negatived, by showing that the great assumption on which it reposes is demonstrably false. For Darwin examined two living specimens of these rabbits which had recently been sent from Porto Santo to the Zoological Gardens, and found them coloured as just described. Four years afterwards the dead body of one of them was sent to him, and then he found that the following changes had taken place. "The ears were plainly edged, and the upper surface of the tail was covered with blackish-grey fur, and the whole body was much less red; so that under the English climate this individual rabbit has recovered the proper colour of its fur in rather less than four years!"

Mr. Darwin adds:—

> "If the history of these Porto Santo rabbits had not been known, most naturalists, on observing their much reduced size, their colour, reddish above and grey beneath, their tails and ears not tipped with black, would have ranked them as a distinct species. They would have been strongly confirmed in this view by seeing them alive in the Zoological Gardens, and hearing that they refused to couple with other rabbits. Yet this rabbit, which there can

be little doubt would thus have been ranked as a distinct species, as certainly originated since the year 1420[113]."

Moreover, it certainly originated as a direct result of climatic influences, independent of natural selection; seeing that, as soon as individual members of this apparently new species were restored to their original climate, they recovered their original colouration.

As previously remarked, it is, from the nature of the case, an exceedingly difficult thing to prove in any given instance that natural selection has not been the cause of specific change, and so finally to disprove the assumption that it must have been. Here, however, on account of historical information, we have a crucial test of the validity of this assumption, just as we had in the case of the niata cattle; and, just as in their case, the result is definitely and conclusively to overturn the assumption. If these changes in the Porto Santo rabbits had been due to the gradual influence of natural selection guided by inscrutable utility, it is simply impossible that the same individual animals, in the course of their own individual life-times, should revert to the specific characters of their ancestral stock on being returned to the conditions of their ancestral climate. Therefore, unless any naturalist is prepared to contradict Darwin's statement that the changes in question amount to changes of specific magnitude, he can find no escape from the conclusion that distinctions of specific importance may be brought about by changes of habitat alone, without reference to utility, and therefore independently of natural selection.

II. Food.

Although, as yet, little is definitely known on the subject, there can be no doubt that in the case of many animals differences of food induce differences of colour within the life-time of individuals, and therefore independently of natural selection.

Thus, sundry definite varieties of the butterfly *Euprepia caja* can be reared according to the different nourishment which is supplied to the caterpillar; and other butterflies are also known on whose colouring and markings the food of the caterpillar has great influence[114].

Again, I may mention the remarkable case communicated to Darwin by Moritz Wagner, of a species of *Saturnia*, some pupae of which were transported from Texas to Switzerland in 1870. The moths which emerged in the following year were like the normal type in Texas. Their young were supplied with leaves of *Juglans regia*, instead of their natural food, *J. nigra*; and the moths into which these caterpillars changed were so different from their parents, both in form and colour, "that they were reckoned by entomologists as a distinct species[115]."

With regard to mollusks, M. Costa tells us that English oysters, when turned down in the Mediterranean, "*rapidly* became like the true Mediterranean oyster, altered their manner of growth, and formed prominent diverging rays." This is most probably due to some change of food. So likewise may be the even more remarkable case of *Helix nemoralis*, which was introduced from Europe to Virginia a few years ago. Under the new conditions it varied to such an extent that up to last year no less than 125 varieties had been discovered. Of these 67, or more than half, are new—that is, unknown in the native continent of the species[116].

In the case of Birds, the Brazilian parrot *Chrysotis festiva* changes the green in its feathers to red or yellow, if fed on the fat of certain fishes; and the Indian Lori has its splendid colouring preserved by a peculiar kind of food (Wallace). The Bullfinch is well known to turn black when fed on hemp seeds, and the Canary to become red when fed on cayenne pepper (Darwin). Starting from these facts, Dr. Sauermann has recently investigated the subject experimentally; and finds that not only finches, but likewise other birds, such as fowls, and pigeons, are subject to similar variations of colour when fed on cayenne pepper; but in all cases the effect is produced only if the pepper is given to the young birds before their first moult. Moreover, he finds that a moist atmosphere facilitates the change of colour, and that the ruddy hue is discharged under the influence either of sunlight or of cold. Lastly, he has observed that sundry other materials such as glycerine and aniline dyes, produce the same results; so there can be no doubt that organic compounds probably occur in nature which are capable of directly affecting the colours of plumage when eaten by birds. Therefore the presence of such materials in the food-stuffs of birds occupying different areas may very well in many cases determine differences of colouration, which are constant or stable so long as the conditions of their production are maintained.

III. Sexual Selection.

Passing on now to causes of specific change which are internal, or comprised within the organisms themselves, we may first consider the case of Sexual Selection.

Mr. Wallace rejects the theory of sexual selection *in toto*, and therefore nothing that can be said under this head would be held by him to be relevant. Many naturalists, however, believe that Darwin was right in the large generalization which he published under this title; and in so far as any one holds that sexual selection is a true cause of specific modification, he is obliged to believe that innumerable specific characters—especially in birds and mammals—have been produced without reference to utility (other, of course, than utility for sexual purposes), and therefore without reference to natural selection. This is so obvious that I need not pause to dilate upon it. One remark, however, may be useful. Mr. Wallace is able to make a much more effective use of his argument from "necessary instability" when he brings it against the Darwinian doctrine of sexual selection, than he does when he brings it against the equally Darwinian doctrine of specific characters in general not being all necessarily due to natural selection. In the latter case, it will be remembered, he is easily met by showing that the causes of specific change other than natural selection, such as food, climate, &c., may be quite as general, persistent, and uniform, as natural selection itself; and therefore in this connexion Mr. Wallace's argument falls to the ground. But the argument is much more formidable as he brings it to bear against the theory of sexual selection. Here he asks, What is there to guarantee the uniformity and the constancy of feminine taste with regard to small matters of embellishment through thousands of generations, and among animals living on extensive areas? And, as we have seen in Part 1, it is not easy to supply an answer. Therefore this argument from the "necessary instability of character" is of immeasurably greater force as thus applied against Darwin's doctrine of sexual selection, than it is when brought against his doctrine that all specific characters need not necessarily be due to natural selection. Therefore, also, if any one feels disposed to attach the smallest degree of value to this argument in the latter case, consistency will require him to allow that in the former case it is simply overwhelming, or in itself destructive of the whole theory of sexual selection. And, conversely, if his belief in the theory of sexual selection can survive collision with this objection from instability, he ought not to feel any tremor of contact when the objection is brought to bear against his scepticism regarding the alleged utility of all specific characters. For assuredly no specific character which is apparent to our eyes can be supposed to be so refined and complex (and therefore so presumably inconstant and unstable), as are those minute changes of cerebral structure on which a psychological preference for all the refined shadings and many pigments of a complicated pattern must be held ultimately to depend. For this reason, then, as well as for those previously adduced, if any one agrees with Darwin in holding to the theory of sexual selection notwithstanding this objection from the necessary instability of unuseful embellishments, *a fortiori* he ought to disregard the objection altogether in its relation to useless specific characters of other kinds.

But quite apart from this consideration, which Mr. Wallace and his followers may very properly say does not apply to them, let us see what they themselves have made of the facts of secondary sexual characters— which, of course, are for the most part specific characters—in relation to the doctrine of utility.

Mr. Wallace himself, in his last work, quotes approvingly a letter which he received in 1869 from the Rev. O Pickard-Cambridge, as follows:—

> "I myself doubt that particular application of the Darwinian theory which attributes male peculiarities of form, structure, colour, and ornament to female appetency or predilection. There is, it seems to me, undoubtedly something in the male organization of a special and sexual nature, which, of its own vital force, develops the remarkable male peculiarities so commonly seen, *and of no imaginable use to that sex.* In as far as these peculiarities show a great vital power, they point out to us the finest and strongest individuals of the sex, and show us which of them would most certainly appropriate to themselves the best and greatest number of females, and leave behind them the strongest and greatest number of progeny. And here would come in, as it appears to me, the proper application of Darwin's theory of Natural Selection; *for the possessors of greatest vital power being those most frequently produced and reproduced, the external signs of it would go on developing in an ever increasing exaggeration,* only to be checked where it became really detrimental in some respect or other to the individual[117]."

Here then the idea is, as more fully expressed by Mr. Wallace in the context, that all the innumerable, frequently considerable, and generally elaborate "peculiarities of form, structure, colour, and ornament," which Darwin attributed to sexual selection, are really due to "the laws of growth." Diverse, definite, and constant though these specific peculiarities be, they are all but the accidental or adventitious accompaniments of "vigour," or "vital power," due to natural selection. Now, without waiting to dispute this view, which has already been dealt with in the chapter on Sexual Selection in Part I, it necessarily follows that "a large proportional number of specific characters," which, while presenting "no imaginable use," are very much less remarkable, less considerable, less elaborate, &c., must likewise be due to this "correlation with vital power." But if the principle of correlation is to be extended in this vague and general manner, it appears to me that the difference between Mr. Wallace and myself, with respect to the principle of utility, is abolished. For of course no one will dispute that the prime condition to the occurrence of "specific characters," whether useful or useless, is the existence of some form which has been denominated a "species" to present them; and this is merely another way of saying that such characters cannot arise except in correlation with a general fitness due to natural selection. Or, to put the case in Mr. Wallace's own words—"This development [of useless specific characters] will necessarily proceed by the agency of natural selection [as a necessary condition] *and the general laws which determine the production of colour and of ornamental appendages.*" The case, therefore, is just the same as if one were to say, for example, that all the ailments of animals and plants proceed from correlation with life (as a necessary condition), "and the general laws which determine the production" of ill-health, or of specific disease. In short, the word "correlation" is here used in a totally different sense from that in which it is used by Darwin, and in which it is elsewhere used by Wallace for the purpose of sustaining his doctrine of specific characters as necessarily useful. To say that a useless character A is correlated with a useful one B, is a very different thing from saying that A is "correlated with vital power," or with the general conditions to the existence of the species to which it belongs. So far as the present discussion is concerned, no exception need be taken to the latter statement. For it simply surrenders the doctrine against which I am contending.

IV. Isolation.

It is the opinion of many naturalists who are well entitled to have an opinion upon the subject, that, in the words of Mr. Dixon, "Isolation can preserve a non-beneficial as effectually as natural selection can preserve a beneficial variation[118]." The ground on which this doctrine rests is thus clearly set forth by Mr. Gulick:—"The fundamental cause of this seems to lie in the fact that no two portions of a species possess exactly the same average characters; and, therefore, that the initial differences are for ever reacting on the environment and on each other in such a way as to ensure increasing divergence in each generation, as long as the individuals of the two groups are kept from intergenerating[119]." In other words, as soon as a portion of a species is separated from the rest of that species, so that breeding between the two portions is no longer possible, the general average of characters in the separated portion not being in all respects precisely the same as it is in the other portion, the result of in-breeding among all individuals of the separated portion will eventually be different from that which obtains in the other portion; so that, after a number of generations, the separated portion may become a distinct species from the effect of isolation alone. Even without the aid of isolation, any original difference of average characters may become, as it were, magnified in successive generations, provided that the divergence is not harmful to the individuals presenting it, and that it occurs in a sufficient proportional number of individuals not to be immediately swamped by intercrossing. For, as Mr. Murphy has pointed out, in accordance with Delbœuf's law, "if, in any species, a number of individuals, bearing a ratio not infinitely small to the entire number of births, are in every generation born with a particular variation which is neither beneficial nor injurious, and if it be not counteracted by reversion, then the proportion of the new variety to the original form will increase till it approaches indefinitely near to equality[120]." Now even Mr. Wallace himself allows that this must be the case; and thinks that in these considerations we may find an explanation of the existence of certain definite varieties, such as the melanic form of the jaguar, the brindled or ring-eyed guillemot, &c. But, on the other hand, he thinks that such varieties must always be unstable, and continually produced in varying proportions from the parent forms. We need not, however, wait to dispute this arbitrary assumption, because we can see that it fails, even as an assumption, in all cases where the superadded influence of isolation is concerned. Here there is nothing to intercept the original tendency to divergent evolution, which arises directly out of the initially different average of qualities presented by the isolated section of the species, as compared with the rest of that species[121].

As we shall have to consider the important principle of isolation more fully on a subsequent occasion, I need not deal with it in the present connexion, further than to remark that in this principle we have what appears to me a full and adequate condition to the rise and continuance of specific characters which need not necessarily be adaptive characters. And, when we come to consider the facts of isolation more closely, we shall find superabundant evidence of this having actually been the case.

V. Laws of Growth.

Under this general term Darwin included the operation of all unknown causes internal to organisms leading to modifications of form or structure—such modifications, therefore, appearing to arise, as he says "spontaneously," or without reference to utility. That he attributed no small importance to the operation of these principles is evident from the last edition of the *Origin of Species*. But as these "laws of growth" refer to causes confessedly unknown, I will not occupy space by discussing this division of our subject—further than to observe that, as we shall subsequently see, many of the facts which fall under it are so irreconcilably adverse to the Wallacean doctrine of specific characters as universally adaptive, that in the face of them Mr. Wallace himself appears at times to abandon his doctrine *in toto*.

CHAPTER IX
Characters as Adaptive and Specific
(*continued*).

It must have appeared strange that hitherto I should have failed to distinguish between "true species" and merely "climatic varieties." But it will conduce to clearness of discussion if we consider our subject point by point. Therefore, having now given a fair statement of the facts of climatic variation, I propose to deal with their theoretical implications—especially as regards the distinction which naturalists are in the habit of drawing between them and so-called true species.

First of all, then, what is this distinction? Take, for example, the case of the Porto Santo rabbits. To almost every naturalist who reads what has been said touching these animals, it will have appeared that the connexion in which they are adduced is wholly irrelevant to the question in debate. For, it will be said that the very fact of the seemingly specific differentiation of these animals having proved to be illusory when some of them were restored to their ancestral conditions, is proof that their peculiar characters are not specific characters; but only what Mr. Wallace would term "individual characters," or variations that are not *inherited*. And the same remark applies to all the other cases which have been adduced to show the generality and extent of climatic variation, both in other animals and also in plants. Why, then, it will be asked, commit the absurdity of adducing such cases in the present discussion? Is it not self-evident that however general, or however considerable, such merely individual, or non-heritable, variations may be, they cannot possibly have ever had anything to do with the origin of *species*? Therefore, is it not simply preposterous to so much as mention them in relation to the question touching the utility of specific characters?

Well, whether or not it is absurd and preposterous to consider climatic variations in connexion with the origin of species, will depend, and depend exclusively, on what it is that we are to understand by a species. Hitherto I have assumed, for the sake of argument, that we all know what is meant by a species. But the time has now come for showing that such is far from being the case. And as it would be clearly absurd and preposterous to conclude anything with regard to specific characters before agreeing upon what we mean by a character as specific, I will begin by giving all the logically possible definitions of a species.

1. *A group of individuals descended by way of natural generation from an originally and specially created type.*

This definition may be taken as virtually obsolete.

2. *A group of individuals which, while fully fertile* inter se, *are sterile with all other individuals—or, at any rate, do not generate fully fertile hybrids.*

This purely physiological definition is not nowadays entertained by any naturalist. Even though the physiological distinction be allowed to count for something in otherwise doubtful cases, no systematist would constitute a species on such grounds alone. Therefore we need not concern ourselves with this definition, further than to observe that it is often taken as more or less supplementary to each of the following definitions.

3. *A group of individuals which, however many characters they share with other individuals, agree in presenting one or more characters of a peculiar kind, with some certain degree of distinctness.*

In this we have the definition which is practically followed by all naturalists at the present time. But, as we shall presently see more fully, it is an extremely lax definition. For it is impossible to determine, by any fixed and general rule, what degree of distinctness on the part of peculiar characters is to be taken as a uniform standard of specific separation. So long as naturalists believed in special creation, they could feel that by following this definition (3) they were at any rate doing their best to tabulate very real distinctions in nature—viz. between types as originally produced by a supernatural cause, and as subsequently more or less modified (i.e. within the limits imposed by the test of cross-fertility) by natural causes. But evolutionists are unable to hold any belief in such real distinctions, being confessedly aware that all distinctions between species and varieties are purely artificial. So to speak, they well know that it is they themselves who create species, by determining round what degrees of differentiation their diagnostic boundaries shall be drawn. And, seeing that these degrees of differentiation so frequently shade into one another by indistinguishable stages (or, rather, that they *always* do so, unless intermediate varieties have perished), modern naturalists are well awake to the impossibility of securing any approach to a uniform standard of specific distinction. On this account many of them feel a pressing need for some firmer definition of a species than this one—which, in point of fact, scarcely deserves to be regarded as a definition at all, seeing that it does not formulate any definite criterion of specific distinctness, but leaves every man to follow his own standards of discrimination. Now, as far as I can see, there are only two definitions of a species which will yield to evolutionists the steady and uniform criterion required. These two definitions are as follows.

4. *A group of individuals which, however many characters they share with other individuals, agree in presenting one or more characters of a peculiar and hereditary kind, with some certain degree of distinctness.*

It will be observed that this definition is exactly the same as the last one, save in the addition of the words "and hereditary." But, it is needless to say, the addition of these words is of the highest importance, inasmuch as it supplies exactly that objective and rigid criterion of specific distinctness which the preceding definition lacks. It immediately gets rid of the otherwise hopeless wrangling over species as "good" and "bad," or "true" and "climatic," of which (as we have seen) Kerner's essay is such a remarkable outcome. Therefore evolutionists have more and more grown to lay stress on the hereditary character of such peculiarities as they select for diagnostic features of specific distinctness. Indeed it is not too much to say that, at the present time, evolutionists in general recognize this character as, theoretically, indispensable to the constitution of a species. But it is likewise not too much to say that, practically, no one of our systematic naturalists has hitherto concerned himself with this matter. At all events, I do not know of any who has ever taken the trouble to ascertain by experiment, with regard to any of the species which he has constituted, whether the peculiar characters on which his diagnoses have been founded are, or are not, hereditary. Doubtless the labour of constituting (or, still more, of *re*-constituting) species on such a basis of experimental inquiry would be insuperable; while, even if it could be accomplished, would prove undesirable, on account of the chaos it would produce in our specific nomenclature. But, all the same, we must remember that this nomenclature as we now have it—and, therefore, the partitioning of species as we have now made them—has no reference to the criterion of heredity. Our system of distinguishing between species and varieties is not based upon the definition which we are now considering, but upon that which we last considered—frequently coupled, to some undefinable extent, with No. 2.

5. There is, however, yet another and closer definition, which may be suggested by the ultra-Darwinian school, who maintain the doctrine of natural selection as the only possible cause of the origin of species, namely:—

A group of individuals which, however many characters they share with other individuals, agree in presenting one or more characters of a peculiar, hereditary, and adaptive kind, with some certain degree of distinctness.

Of course this definition rests upon the dogma of utility as a necessary attribute of characters *quâ* specific—i.e. the dogma against which the whole of the present discussion is directed. Therefore all I need say with reference to it is, that at any rate it cannot be adduced in any argument where the validity of its basal dogma is in question. For it would be a mere begging of this question to argue that every species must present at least one peculiar and adaptive character, because, according to definition, unless an organic type does present at least one such character, it is not a specific type. Moreover, and quite apart from this, it is to be hoped that naturalists as a body will never consent to base their diagnostic work on what at best must always be a highly speculative extension of the Darwinian theory. While, lastly, if they were to do so with any sort of consistency, the precise adaptation which each peculiar character subserves, and which because of this adaptation is constituted a character of specific distinction, would have to be determined by actual observation. For no criterion of specific distinction could be more vague and mischievous than this one, if it were to be applied on grounds of mere inference that such and such a character, because seemingly constant, must "necessarily" be either useful, vestigial, or correlated.

Such then, as far as I can see, are all the definitions of a species that are logically possible[122]. Which of them is chosen by those who maintain the necessary usefulness of all specific characters? Observe, it is for those who maintain this doctrine to choose their definition: it is not for me to do so. My contention is, that the term does not admit of any definition sufficiently close and constant to serve as a basis for the doctrine in question—and this for the simple reason that species-makers have never agreed among themselves upon any criterion of specific distinction. My opponents, on the other hand, are clearly bound to take an opposite view, because, unless they suppose that there is some such definition of a species, they would be self-convicted of the absurdity of maintaining a great generalization on a confessedly untenable basis. For example, a few years ago I was allowed to raise a debate in the Biological Section of the British Association on the question to which the present chapters are devoted. But the debate ended as I had anticipated that it must end. No one of the naturalists present could give even the vaguest definition of what was meant by a species—or, consequently, of a character as specific. On this account the debate ended in as complete a destruction as was possible of the doctrine that all the distinctive characters of every species must necessarily be useful, vestigial, or correlated. For it became unquestionable that the same generalization admitted of being made, with the same degree of effect, touching all the distinctive characters of every "snark."

Probably, however, it will be thought unfair to have thus sprung a difficult question of definition in oral debate. Therefore I allude to this fiasco at the British Association, merely for the purpose of emphasizing the necessity of agreeing upon some definition of a species, before we can conclude anything with regard to the generalization of specific characters as necessarily due to natural selection. But when a naturalist has had full time to consider this fundamental matter of definition, and to decide on what his own shall be, he cannot complain of unfairness on the part of any one else who holds him to what he thus says he means by a species. Now Mr. Wallace, in his last work, has given a matured statement of what it is that he means by a species. This, therefore, I will take as the avowed basis of his doctrine touching the necessary origin and maintenance of all specific characters by natural selection. His definition is as follows:—

> "An assemblage of individuals which have become somewhat modified in structure, form, and constitution, *so as to adapt them to slightly different conditions of life*; which can be differentiated from allied assemblages; which reproduce their like; which usually breed together; and, perhaps, when crossed with their near allies, always produce offspring which are more or less sterile *inter se*[123]."

From this definition the portion which I have italicized must be omitted in the present discussion, for the reasons already given while considering definition No. 5. What remains is a combination of Nos. 2 and 4. According to Mr. Wallace, therefore, our criterion of a species is to be the heredity of peculiar characters, combined, perhaps, with a more or less exclusive fertility of the component individuals *inter se*. This is the basis on which his generalization of the utility of specific characters as necessary and universal is reared. Here, then, we have something definite to go upon, at all events as far as Mr. Wallace is concerned. Let us see how far such a basis of definition is competent to sustain his generalization.

First of all it must be remarked that, as species have actually been constituted by systematists, the test of exclusive fertility does not apply. For my own part I think this is to be regretted, because I believe that such is the only natural—and therefore the only firm—basis on which specific distinctions can be reared. But, as previously observed, this is not the view which has been taken by our species-makers. At most they regard the physiological criterion as but lending some additional weight to their judgement upon morphological features, in cases where it is doubtful whether the latter alone are of sufficient distinctness to justify a recognition of specific value. Or, conversely, if the morphological features are clearly sufficient to justify such a recognition, yet if it happens to be known that there is full fertility between the form presenting them and other forms which do not, then the latter fact will usually prevent naturalists from constituting the well differentiated form a species on grounds of its morphological features alone—as, for instance, in the case of our domesticated varieties. In short, the physiological criterion has not been employed with sufficient closeness to admit of its being now comprised within any practical definition of the term "species"—if by this term we are to understand, not what any one may think species *ought to be*, but what species actually *are*, as they have been constituted for us by their makers.

From all this it follows that the definition of the term "species" on which Mr. Wallace relies for his deduction with respect to specific characters, is the definition No. 4. In other words, omitting his *petitio principii* and his allusion to the test of fertility, the great criterion in his view is the criterion of Heredity. And in this all other evolutionists, of whatever school, will doubtless agree with him. They will recognize that it is really the distinguishing test between "climatic varieties" and "true species," so that however widely or however constantly the former may diverge from one another in regard to their peculiar characters, they are not to be classed among the latter unless their peculiar characters are likewise hereditary characters.

Now, if we are all agreed so far, the only question that remains is whether or not this criterion of Heredity is capable of supplying a basis for the generalization, that all characters which have been ranked as of specific value must necessarily be regarded as presenting also an adaptive, or life-serving, value? I will now endeavour to show that there are certain very good reasons for answering this question in the negative.

(A.)

In the first place, even if the modifications induced by the direct action of a changed environment are not hereditary, who is to know that they are not? Assuredly not the botanist or zoologist who in a particular area finds what he is fully entitled to regard as a well-marked specific type. Only by experiments in transposition could it be proved that the modifications have been produced by local conditions; and although the researches of many experimentalists have shown how considerable and how constant such modifications may be, where is the systematic botanist who would ever think of transplanting an apparently new species from one distant area to another before he concludes that it is a new species? Or where is the systematic zoologist who would take the trouble to transport what appears to be an obviously endemic species of animal from one country to another before venturing to give it a new specific name? No doubt, both in the case of plants and animals, it is tacitly assumed that constant differences, if sufficient in amount to be regarded as specific differences are hereditary; but there is not one case in a hundred where the validity of this assumption has ever been tested by experiments in transposition. Therefore naturalists are apt to regard it as remarkable when the few experiments which have been made in this direction are found to negative their assumption—for example, that a diagnostic character in species of the genus *Hieratium* is found by transplantation not to be hereditary, or that the several named species of British trout are similarly proved to be all "local varieties" of one another. But, in point of fact, there ought to be nothing to surprise us in such results—unless, indeed, it is the unwarrantable nature of the assumption that any given differences of size, form, colour, &c., which naturalists may have regarded as of specific value, are, on this account, hereditary. Indeed, so surprising is this assumption in the face of what we know touching both the extent and the constancy of climatic variation, that it seems to me such a naturalist as Kerner, who never considers the criterion of heredity at all, is less assailable than those who profess to constitute this their chief criterion of specific distinction. For it is certain that whatever their professions may have nowadays become, systematic naturalists have never been in the habit of really following this criterion. In theory they have of late years attached more and more weight to definition No. 4; but in practice they have always adopted definition No. 3. The consequence is, that in literally numberless cases (particularly in the vegetable kingdom) "specific characters" are assumed to be hereditary characters merely because systematic naturalists have bestowed a specific name on the form which presents them. Nor is this all. For, conversely, even when it is known that constant morphological characters are unquestionably hereditary characters, if they happen to present but small degrees of divergence from those of allied forms, then the form which presents them is not ranked as a species, but as a constant variety. In other words, when definitions 3 and 4 are found to clash, it is not 4, but 3, that is followed. In short, even up to the present time, systematic naturalists play fast and loose with the criterion of Heredity to such an extent, that, as above observed, it has been rendered wellnigh worthless in fact, whatever may be thought of it in theory.

Now, unless all this can be denied, what is the use of representing that a species is distinguished from a variety—"climatic" or otherwise—by the fact that its constituent individuals "reproduce their like"? We are not here engaged on any abstract question of what might have been the best principles of specific distinction for naturalists to have adopted. We are engaged on the practical question of the principles which they actually have adopted. And of these principles the reproduction of like by like, under all circumstances of environment, has been virtually ignored.

(B.)

In the second place, supposing that the criterion of Heredity had been as universally and as rigidly employed by our systematists in their work of constructing species as it has been but occasionally and loosely employed, could it be said that even then a basis would have been furnished for the doctrine that all specific characters must necessarily be useful characters? Obviously not, and for the following reasons.

It is admitted that climatic characters are not necessarily—or even generally—useful characters. Consequently, if there be any reason for believing that climatic characters may become in time hereditary characters, the doctrine in question would collapse, even supposing that all specific types were to be re-constituted on a basis of experimental inquiry, for the purpose of ascertaining which of them conform to the test of Heredity. Now there are very good reasons for believing that climatic characters not unfrequently do become hereditary characters; and it was mainly in view of those reasons that I deemed it worth while to devote so much space in the preceding chapter to the facts of climatic variation. I will now state the reasons in question under two different lines of argument.

We are not as yet entitled to conclude definitely against the possible inheritance of acquired characters. Consequently, we are not as yet entitled to assume that climatic characters—i. e. characters acquired by converse with a new environment, continued, say, since the last glacial period—can never have become congenital characters. But, if they ever have become congenital characters, they will have become, at all events as a general rule, congenital characters that are useless; for it is conceded that, *quâ* climatic characters, they have not been due to natural selection.

Doubtless the followers of Weismann will repudiate this line of argument, if not as entirely worthless, at all events as too questionable to be of much practical worth. But even to the followers of Weismann it may be pointed out, that the Wallacean doctrine of the origin of all specific characters by means of natural selection was propounded many years before either Galton or Weismann had questioned the transmission of acquired characters. However. I allow that this line of argument has now become—for the time being at all events—a dubious line, and will therefore at once pass on to the second line, which is not open to doubt from any quarter.

Whether or not we accept Weismann's views, it will here be convenient to employ his terminology, since this will serve to convey the somewhat important distinctions which it is now my object to express.

In the foregoing paragraphs, under heading (A), we have seen that there must be "literally numberless forms" which have been ranked as true species, whose diagnostic characters are nevertheless not congenital. In the case of plants especially, we know that there must be large numbers of named species which do not conform to the criterion of Heredity, although we do not know which species they are. For present purposes, however, it is enough for us to know that there are many such named species, where some change of environment has acted directly and similarly on all the individual "somas" exposed to it, without affecting their "germ-plasms," or the material bases of their hereditary qualities. For named species of this kind we may employ the term *somatogenetic species*.

But now, if there are any cases where a change of environment does act on the germ-plasms exposed to it, the result would be what we may call *blastogenetic species*—i.e. species which conform to the criterion of Heredity, and would therefore be ranked by all naturalists as "true species." It would not signify in such a case whether the changed conditions of life first affected the soma, and then, through changed nutrition, the germ-plasm; or whether from the first it directly affected the germ-plasm itself. For in either case the result would be a "species," which would continue to reproduce its peculiar features by heredity.

Now, the supposition that changed conditions of life may thus affect the congenital endowments of germ-plasm is not a gratuitous one. The sundry facts already given in previous chapters are enough to show that the origin of a blastogenetic species by the direct action on germ-plasm of changed conditions of life is, at all events, a possibility. And a little further thought is enough to show that this possibility becomes a probability—if not a virtual certainty. Even Weismann—notwithstanding his desire to maintain, as far as he possibly can, the "stability" of germ-plasm—is obliged to allow that external conditions acting on the organism may in some cases modify the hereditary qualities of its germ-plasm, and so, as he says, "determine the phyletic development of its descendants." Again, we have seen that he is compelled to interpret the results of his own experiments on the climatic varieties of certain butterflies by saying, "I cannot explain the facts otherwise than by supposing the passive acquisition of characters produced by direct influences of climate"; by which he means that in this case the influence of climate acts directly on the hereditary qualities of germ-plasm. Lastly, and more generally, he says:—

> "But although I hold it improbable that individual variability can depend on a direct action of external influences upon the germ-cells and their contained germ-plasm, because—as follows from sundry facts—the molecular structure of the germ-plasm must be very

difficult to change, yet it is by no means to be implied that this structure may not possibly be altered by influences of the same kind continuing for a very long time. Thus it seems to me the possibility is not to be rejected, that influences continued for a long time, that is, for generations, such as temperature, kind of nourishment, &c., which may affect the germ-cells as well as any other part of the organism, may produce a change in the constitution of the germ-plasm. But such influences would not then produce individual variation, but would necessarily modify in the same way all the individuals of a species living in a certain district. It is possible, though it cannot be proved, that many climatic varieties have arisen in this manner."

So far, then, we have testimony to this point, as it were, from a reluctant witness. But if we have no theory involving the "stability of germ-plasm" to maintain, we can scarcely fail to see how susceptible the germ-plasm is likely to prove to changed conditions of life. For we know how eminently susceptible it is in this respect when gauged by the practical test of fertility; and as this is but an expression of its extraordinarily complex character, it would indeed be surprising if it were to enjoy any immunity against modification by changed conditions of life. We have seen in the foregoing chapter how frequently and how considerably somatogenetic changes are thus caused, so as to produce "somatogenetic species"—or, where we happen to know that the changes are not hereditary, "climatic varieties." But the constitution of germ-plasm is much more complex than that of any of the structures which are developed therefrom. Consequently, the only wonder is that hitherto experimentalists have not been more successful in producing "blastogenetic species" by artificial changes of environment. Or, as Ray Lankester has well stated this consideration, "It is not difficult to suggest possible ways in which the changed conditions, shown to be important by Darwin, could act through the parental body upon the nuclear matter of the egg-cell and sperm-cell, with its immensely complex and therefore unstable constitution.... The wonder is, not that [blastogenetic] variation occurs, but that it is not excessive and monstrous in every product of fertilization[124]."

If to this it should be objected that, as a matter of fact, experimentalists have not been nearly so successful in producing congenital modifications of type by changed conditions of life as they have been in thus producing merely somatic modifications; or if it should be further objected that we have no evidence at all in nature of a "blastogenetic species" having been formed by means of climatic influences alone,—if these objections were to be raised, they would admit of the following answer.

With regard to experiments, so few have thus far been made upon the subject, that objections founded on their negative results do not carry much weight—especially when we remember that these results have not been uniformly negative, but sometimes positive, as shown in Chapter VI. With regard to plants and animals in a state of nature, the objection is wholly futile, for the simple reason that in as many cases as changed conditions of life may have caused an hereditary change of specific type, there is now no means of obtaining "evidence" upon the subject. But we are not on this account entitled to conclude against the probability of such changes of specific type having been more or less frequently thus produced. And still less can we be on this account entitled to conclude against the *possibility* of such a change having ever occurred in any single instance. Yet this is what must be concluded by any one who maintains that the origin of all species—and, *a fortiori*, of all specific characters—must *necessarily* have been due to natural selection.

Now, if all this be admitted—and I do not see how it can be reasonably questioned—consider how important its bearing becomes on the issue before us. If germ-plasm (using this term for whatever it is that constitutes the material basis of heredity) is ever capable of having its congenital endowments altered by the direct action of external conditions, the resulting change of hereditary characters, whatever else it may be, need not be an adaptive change. Indeed, according to Weismann's theory of germ-plasm, the chances must be infinitely against the change being an adaptive one. On the theory of pangenesis—that is to say, on the so-called Lamarckian principles—there would be much more reason for entertaining the possibly adaptive character of hereditary change due to the direct action of the environment. Therefore we arrive at this curious result. The more that we are disposed to accept Weismann's theory of heredity, and with it the corollary that natural selection is the sole cause of adaptive modification in species the less are we entitled to assume that all specific characters must necessarily be adaptive. Seeing that in nature there are presumably many cases like those of Hoffmann's plants, Weismann's butterflies, &c., where the hereditary qualities of germ-plasm have (on his hypothesis) been modified by changed conditions of life, we are bound to believe that, in all cases where such changes do not happen to be actively deleterious, they will persist. And inasmuch as characters which are only of "specific" value must be the characters most easily—and therefore most frequently—induced by any slight changes in the constitution of germ-plasm, while, for the same reason (namely, that of their trivial nature) they are least likely to prove injurious, it follows that the less we believe in the functionally-produced adaptations of Lamarck, the more ought we to resist the assumption that all specific characters must necessarily be adaptive characters.

Upon the whole, then, and with regard to the direct action of external conditions, I conclude—not only from general considerations, but also from special facts or instances quite sufficient for the purpose—that these must certainly give rise to immense numbers of somatogenetic species on the one hand, and probably to considerable numbers of blastogenetic species on the other; that in neither case is there any reason for supposing the distinctively "specific characters" to be other than "neutral" or "indifferent"; while there are the best of reasons for concluding the contrary. So that, under this division of our subject alone (B), there appears to be ample justification for the statement that "a large proportional number of specific characters" are in reality, as they are in appearance, destitute of significance from a utilitarian point of view.

(C.)

Thus far in the present chapter we have been dealing exclusively with the case of "climatic variation," or change of specific type due to changes in the external conditions of life. But it will be remembered that, in the preceding chapter, allusion was likewise made to changes of specific type due to internal causes, or to what Darwin has called "the nature of the organism." Under this division of our subject I mentioned especially Sexual Selection, which is supposed to arise in the aesthetic taste of animals themselves; Isolation, which is supposed to originate new types by allowing the average characters of an isolated section of an old type to develop a new history of varietal change, as we shall see more fully in the ensuing part of this treatise; and the Laws of Growth, which is a general term for the operation of unknown causes of change incidental to the living processes of organisms which present the change.

Now, under none of these divisions of our subject can there be any question touching the criterion of Heredity. For if new species—or even single specific characters of new species—are ever produced by any of these causes, they must certainly all "reproduce their like." Therefore the only question which can here obtain is as to whether or not such causes ever do originate new species, or even so much as new specific characters. Mr. Wallace, though not always consistently, answers this question in the negative; but the great majority of naturalists follow Darwin by answering it in the affirmative. And this is enough to show the only point which we need at present concern ourselves with showing—viz. that the question is, at the least, an open one. For as long as this question is an open one among believers in the theory of natural selection, it must clearly be an unwarrantable deduction from that theory, that all species, and *a fortiori* all specific characters, are necessarily due to natural selection. The deduction cannot be legitimately drawn until the possibility of any other cause of specific modification has been excluded. But the bare fact of the question as just stated being still and at the least an open question, is enough to prove that this possibility has not been excluded. Therefore the deduction must be, again on this ground alone (C), unwarrantable.

Such are my several reasons—and it is to be observed that they are all *independent* reasons—for concluding that it makes no practical difference to the present discussion whether or not we entertain Heredity as a criterion of specific distinction. Seeing that our species-makers have paid so little regard to this criterion, it is neither absurd nor preposterous to have adduced, in the preceding chapter, the facts of climatic variation. On the contrary, as the definition of "species" which has been practically followed by our species-makers in No. 3, and not No. 4, these facts form part and parcel of our subject. It is perfectly certain that, in the vegetable kingdom at all events, "a large proportional number" of specifically diagnostic characters would be proved by experiment to be "somatogenetic"; while there are numerous constant characters classed as varietal, although it is well known that they are "blastogenetic." Moreover, we can scarcely doubt that many specific characters which are also hereditary characters owe their existence, not to natural selection, but to the direct action of external causes on the hereditary structure of "germ-plasm"; while, even apart from this consideration, there are at least three distinct and highly general principles of specific change, which are accepted by the great majority of Darwinists, and the only common peculiarity of which is that they produce hereditary changes of specific types without any reference to the principle of utility.

CHAPTER X
Characters as Adaptive and Specific
(*concluded*).

Our subject is not yet exhausted. For it remains to observe the consequences which arise from the dogma of utility as the only *raison d'être* of species, or of specific characters, when this dogma is applied in practice by its own promoters.

Any definition of "species"—excepting Nos. 1, 2, and 5, which may here be disregarded—must needs contain some such phrase as the one with which Nos. 3 and 4 conclude. This is, that peculiar characters, in order to be recognized as of specific value, must present neither more nor less than "some certain degree of distinctness." If they present more than this degree of distinctness, the form, or forms, in question must be ranked as generic; while if they present less than this degree of distinctness, they must be regarded as varietal—and this even if they are known to be mutually sterile. What, then, is this certain degree of distinctness? What are its upper and lower limits? This question is one that cannot be answered. From the very nature of the case it is impossible to find a uniform standard of distinction whereby to draw our boundary lines between varieties and species on the one hand, or between species and genera on the other. One or two quotations will be sufficient to satisfy the general reader upon this point.

Mr. Wallace himself alludes to "the great difficulty that is felt by botanists in determining the limits of species in many large genera," and gives as examples well-known instances where systematic botanists of the highest eminence differ hopelessly in their respective estimates of "specific characters." Thus:—

> "Mr. Baker includes under a single species, Rosa canina, no less than twenty-eight named varieties distinguished by more or less constant characters, and often confined to special localities, and to these are referred about seventy of the species of British and continental botanists. Of the genus Rubus or bramble, five British species are given in Bentham's *Handbook of British Flora*, while in the fifth edition of Babington's *Manual of British Botany*, published about the same time, no less than forty-five species are described. Of willows (Salix) the same two works enumerate fifteen and thirty-one species respectively. The

hawkweeds (Hieracium) are equally puzzling, for while Mr. Bentham admits only seven British species, Professor Babington describes no less than seventy-two, besides several named varieties[125]."

Mr. Wallace goes on to quote further instances, such as that of Draba verna, which Jordan has found to present, in the south of France alone, no less than fifty-two permanent varieties, which all "come true from seed, and thus present all the characteristics of a true species"; so that, "as the plant is very common almost all over Europe, and ranges from North America to the Himalayas, the number of similar forms over this wide area would probably have to be reckoned by hundreds, if not by thousands[126]."

One or two further quotations may be given to the same general effect, selected from the writings of specialists in their several departments.

"There is nothing that divides systematists more than what constitutes a genus. Species that resemble each other more than other species, is perhaps the best definition that can be given. This is obviously an uncertain test, much depending on individual judgement and experience; but that, in the evolution of forms, such difficulties should arise in the limitation of genera and species was inevitable. What is a generic character in one may be only a specific character in another. As an illustration of the uncertain importance of characters, I may mention the weevil genus *Centrinus* in which the leading characters in the classification of the family to which it belongs are so mixed that systematists have been content to keep the species together in a group that cannot be defined.... No advantage or disadvantage is attached, apparently, to any of the characters. There are about 200 species, all American.

The venation of the wings of insects is another example of modifications without serving any special purpose. There is no vein in certain Thripidae, and only a rudiment or a single vein in Chalcididae. There are thousands of variations more or less marked, some of the same type with comparatively trivial variation, others presenting distinct types, even in the same family, such genera, for example, as *Polyneura*, *Tettigetra*, *Huechys*, &c. in the Cicadidae.

Individual differences have often been regarded as distinctive of species; varieties also are very deceptive, and races come very near to species. A South-American beetle, *Arescus histrio*, has varieties of yellow, red, and black, or these colours variously intermixed, and, what is very unusual, longitudinal stripes in some and transverse bars in others, and all taken in the same locality. Mr. A. G. Butler, of the British Museum, is of opinion that 'what is generally understood by the term species (that is to say, a well-defined, distinct, and constant type, having no near allies) is non-existent in the Lepidoptera, and that the nearest approach to it in this order is a constant, though but slightly differing, rare or local form—that genera, in fact, consist wholly of a gradational series of such forms (Ann. Mag. Nat. Hist. 5, xix. 103)[127].'"

So much as regards entomology, and still living forms. In illustration of the same principles in connexion with palaeontological series, I may quote Würtenberger, who says:—

"With respect to these fossil forms [i.e. multitudinous forms of fossil Ammonites], it is quite immaterial whether a very short or a somewhat longer part of any branch be dignified with a separate name, and regarded as a species. The prickly Ammonites, classed under the designation of Armata, are so intimately connected that it becomes impossible to separate the accepted species sharply from one another. The same remark applies to the group of which the manifold forms are distinguished by their ribbed shells, and are called Planulata[128]."

I had here supplied a number of similar quotations from writers in various other departments of systematic work, but afterwards struck them out as superfluous. For it is not to be anticipated that any competent naturalist will nowadays dispute that the terms "variety," "species," and "genus" stand for merely conventional divisions, and that whether a given form shall be ranked under one or the other of them is often no more than a matter of individual taste. From the nature of the case there can be no objective, and therefore no common, standards of delimitation. This is true even as regards any one given department of systematic work; but when we compare the standards of delimitation which prevail in one department with those which prevail in another, it becomes evident that there is not so much as any attempt at agreeing upon a common measure of specific distinction.

But what, it may well be asked, is the use of thus insisting upon well-known facts, which nobody will dispute? Well, in the first place, we have already seen, in the last chapter, that it is incumbent on those who maintain that all species, or even all specific characters, must be due to natural selection, to tell us what they mean by a species, or by characters as specific. If I am told to believe that the definite quality A is a necessary attribute of B, and yet that B is "not a distinct entity," but an undefinable abstraction, I can only marvel that any one should expect me to be so simple. But, without recurring to this point, the use of insisting on the facts above stated is, in the second place, that otherwise I cannot suppose any general reader could believe them in view of what is to follow. For he cannot but feel that the cost of believing them is to render inexplicable the mental processes of those naturalists who, in the face of such facts, have deduced the following conclusions.

The school of naturalists against which I am contending maintains, as a generalization deduced from the theory of natural selection, that all species, or even all specific characters, must necessarily owe their origin to the principle of utility. Yet this same school does not maintain any such generalization, either with regard to varietal characters on the one hand, or to generic characters on the other. On the contrary, Professor Huxley, Mr. Wallace, and all other naturalists who agree with them in refusing to entertain so much as the abstract possibility of any cause other than natural selection having been productive of species, fully accept the fact of other causes having been largely concerned in the production of varieties, genera, families, and all higher groups, or of the characters severally distinctive of each. Indeed, Mr. Wallace does not question what appears to me the extravagant estimate of Professor Cope, that the non-adaptive characters distinctive of those higher groups are fully equal, in point of numbers, to the adaptive. But, surely, if the theory of evolution by natural selection is, as we all agree, a true theory of the origin of species, it must likewise be a true theory of the origin of genera; and if it be supposed essential to the integrity of the theory in its former aspect that all specific characters should be held to be useful, I fail to see how, in regard to its latter aspect, we are so readily to surrender the necessary usefulness of all generic characters. And exactly the same remark applies to the case of constant "varieties," where again the doctrine of utility as universal is not maintained. Yet, according to the general theory of evolution, constant varieties are what Darwin termed "incipient species," while species are what may be termed "incipient genera." Therefore, if the doctrine of utility as universal be conceded to fail in the case of varieties on the one hand and of genera on the other, where is the consistency in maintaining that it must "necessarily" hold as regards the intermediate division, species? Truly the shade of Darwin may exclaim, "Save me from my friends." And truly against logic of this description a follower of Darwin must find it difficult to argue. If one's opponents were believers in special creation, and therefore stood upon some definite ground while maintaining this difference between species and all other taxonomic divisions, there would at least be some issue to argue about. But when on the one hand it is conceded that species are merely arbitrary divisions, which differ in no respect as to the process of their evolution from either varieties or genera, while on the other hand it is affirmed that there is thus so great a difference in the result, all we can say is that our opponents are entangling themselves in the meshes of a sheer contradiction.

Or, otherwise stated, specific characters differ from varietal characters in being, as a rule, more pronounced and more constant: on this account advocates of utility as universal apply the doctrine to species, while they do not feel the "necessity" of applying it to varieties. But now, generic and all higher characters are even more constant and more pronounced than specific characters—not to say, in many cases, more generally diffused over a larger number of organisms usually occupying larger areas. Therefore, *a fortiori*, if for the reasons above stated evolutionists regard it as a necessary deduction from the theory of natural selection that all specific characters must be useful, much more ought it to be a necessary deduction from this theory that all generic, and still more all higher, characters must be useful. But, as we have seen, this is not maintained by our opponents. On the contrary, they draw the sharpest distinction between specific and all other characters in this respect, freely conceding that both those below and those above them need not—and very often do not—present any utilitarian significance.

Although it appears to me that this doctrine is self-contradictory, and on this ground alone might be summarily dismissed, as it is now held in one or other of its forms by many naturalists, I will give it a more detailed consideration in both its parts—namely, first with respect to the distinction between varieties and species, and next with respect to the distinction between species and genera.

Until it can be shown that species are something more than merely arbitrary divisions, due to the disappearance of intermediate varietal links; that in some way or another they *are* "definite entities," which admit of being delineated by the application of some uniform or general principles of definition; that, in short, species have only then been classified as such when it has been shown that the origin of each has been due to the operation of causes which have not been concerned in the production of varieties;—until these things are shown, it clearly remains a gratuitous dogma to maintain that forms which have been called species differ from forms which have been called varieties in the important respect, that they (let alone each of all their distinctive characters) must necessarily have been due to the principle of utility. Yet, as we have seen, even Mr. Wallace allows that a species is "not a distinct entity," but "an assemblage of individuals which have become somewhat modified in structure, form, and constitution"; while estimates of the kinds and degrees of modification which are to be taken as of specific value are conceded to be undefinable, fluctuating, and in not a few cases almost ludicrously divergent.

Perhaps one cannot more forcibly present the rational value of this position than by noting the following consequences of it. Mr. Gulick writes me that while studying the land-shells of the Sandwich Islands, and finding there a rich profusion of unique varieties, in cases where the intermediate varieties were rare he could himself have created a number of species by simply throwing these intermediate varieties into his fire. Now it follows from the dogma which we are considering, that, by so doing, not only would he have created new species, but at the same time he would have proved them due to natural selection, and endowed the diagnostic characters of each with a "necessarily" adaptive meaning, which previously it was not necessary that they should present. Before his destruction of these intermediate varieties, he need have felt himself under no obligation to assume that any given character at either end of the series was of utilitarian significance: but, after his destruction of the intermediate forms, he could no longer entertain any question upon the matter, under pain of being denounced as a Darwinian heretic.

Now the application is self-evident. It is a general fact, which admits of no denial, that the more our knowledge of any flora or fauna increases, the greater is the number of intermediate forms which are brought to light, either as still existing or as having once existed. Consequently, the more that such knowledge increases, the more does our catalogue of "species" diminish. As Kerner says, "bad species" are always multiplying at the expense of "good species"; or, as Oscar Schmidt (following Häckel) similarly remarks, if we could know as much about the latter as we do about the former, "all species, without any exception, would become what species-makers understand by 'bad species'[129]." Hence we see that, just as Mr. Gulick could have created good species by secretly destroying his intermediate varieties, so has Nature produced her "good species" for the delectation of systematists. And just as Mr. Gulick, by first hiding and afterwards revealing his intermediate forms, could have made the self-same characters in the first instance necessarily useful, but ever afterwards presumably useless, so has Nature caused the utility of diagnostic characters to vary with our knowledge of her intermediate forms. It belongs to the essence of our theory of descent, that in *all* cases these intermediate forms must either be now existing or have once existed; and, therefore, that the work of species-makers consists in nothing more than marking out the *lacunae* in our knowledge of them. Yet we are bound to believe that wherever these *lacunae* in our knowledge occur, there occurs also the objective necessity of causation as utilitarian—a necessity, however, which vanishes so soon as our advancing information supplies the intermediate forms in question. It may indeed appear strange that the utility or non-utility of organic structures should thus depend on the accidents of human knowledge; but this is the Darwinian faith, and he who doubts the dogma is to be anathema.

Turning next to the similar distinction which it is sought to draw between species and genera, here it will probably be urged, as I understand it to be urged by Mr. Wallace, that generic characters (and still more characters of families, orders, &c.) refer back to so remote a state of things that utility may have been present at their birth which has disappeared in their maturity. In other words, it is held that all generic characters were originally specific characters; that as such they were all originally of use; but that, after having been rendered stable by heredity, many of them may have ceased to be of service to the descendants of those species in which they originated, and whose extinction has now made it impossible to divine what that service may have been.

Now, in the first place; this is not the interpretation adopted by Darwin. For instance, he expressly contrasts such cases with those of vestigial or "rudimentary" structures, pointing out that they differ from vestigial structures in respect of their permanence. One quotation will be sufficient to establish the present point.

> "A structure which has been developed through long-continued selection, when it ceases to be of service to a species, generally becomes variable, as we see with rudimentary organs, for it will no longer be regulated by this same power of selection. But when, from the nature of the organism and of the conditions, modifications have been induced which are unimportant for the welfare of the species, they may be, and apparently often have been, transmitted in nearly the same state to numerous, otherwise modified, descendants[130]."

Here, and in the context, we have a sufficiently clear statement of Darwin's view—first, that unadaptive characters may arise in *species* as "fluctuating variations, which sooner or later become *constant* through the nature of the organism and of surrounding conditions, as well as through the intercrossing of distinct individuals, but *not* through natural selection"[131]; second, that such unadaptive characters may then be transmitted in this their stable condition to species-progeny, so as to become distinctive of genera, families, &c.; third, that, on account of such characters not being afterwards liable to diverse adaptive modifications in different branches of the species-progeny, they are of more value as indicating lines of pedigree than are characters which from the first have been useful; and, lastly, they are therefore now empirically recognized by systematists as of most value in guiding the work of classification. To me it appears that this view is not only perfectly rational in itself, but likewise fully compatible with the theory of natural selection—which, as I have previously shown, is *primarily* a theory of adaptive characters, and therefore not necessarily a theory of *all* specific characters. But to those who think otherwise, it must appear—and does appear—that there is something wrong about such a view of the case—that it was not consistent in the author of the *Origin of Species* thus to refer non-adaptive generic characters to a parentage of non-adaptive specific characters. Nevertheless, as a matter of fact, Darwin was perfectly consistent in putting forth this view, because, unlike Wallace, he was not under the sway of any antecedent dogma erroneously deduced from the theory of natural selection.

Next without reference to Darwin's authority, let us see for ourselves where the inconsistency really lies. To allow that generic characters may be useless, while denying that specific characters can ever be so (unless correlated with others that are useful), involves an appeal to the argument from ignorance touching the ancestral habits, life-conditions, &c., of a parent species now extinct. Well, even upon this assumption of utility as obsolete, there remains to be explained the "stability" of useless characters now distinctive of genera, families, orders, and the rest. We know that specific characters which have owed their origin to utility and have afterwards ceased to present utility, degenerate, become variable, inconstant, "rudimentary," and finally disappear. Why, then, should these things not happen with regard to useless generic distinctions? Still more, why should they not happen with regard to family, ordinal, and class distinctions? On the lines against which I am arguing it would appear impossible that any answer to this question can be suggested. For what explanation can be given of the contrast thus presented between the obsolescence of specific characters where previous utility is demonstrable, and the permanence of higher characters whose previous utility is assumed? As we have already seen, Mr. Wallace himself employs this consideration of permanence and constancy against the view that any cause other than natural selection can have been concerned in the origin and maintenance of *specific* characters. But he does not seem to see that the consideration cuts two ways—and much more forcibly against his views than in favour of them. For while, as already shown in the chapter before last, it is sufficiently easy to dispose of the consideration as Wallace uses it (by simply pointing out with Darwin that any causes other than natural selection which may have been concerned in the genesis of *specific* characters, must, if equally uniform in their operation, equally give rise to permanence and constancy in their results); on the other hand, it becomes impossible to explain the stability of useless *generic* characters, if, as Wallace's use of the argument requires, natural selection is the only possible cause of stability. The argument is one that cannot be played with fast and loose. Either utility is the sole condition to the stability of *any* diagnostic character (in which case it is not open to Mr. Wallace to assume that all *generic* or higher characters which are now useless have owed their origin to a past utility); or else utility is not the sole condition to stability (in which case his use of the present argument in relation to *specific* characters collapses). We have seen, indeed, in the chapter before last, that his use of the argument collapses anyhow, or quite irrespective of his inconsistent attitude towards generic characters, with which we were not then concerned. But the point now is that, as a mere matter of logic, the argument from stability as Wallace applies it to the case of specific characters, is incompatible with his argument that useless generic characters may originally have been useful specific characters. It can scarcely be questioned that the transmutation of a species into a genus must, as a rule, have allowed time enough for a newly acquired—i.e. peculiar specific-character—to show some signs of undergoing degeneration, if, as supposed, the original cause of its development and maintenance was withdrawn when the parent species began to ramify into its species-progeny. Yet, as Darwin says, "it is notorious that specific characters are more variable than generic[132]." So that, upon the whole, I do not see how on grounds of general reasoning it is logically possible to maintain Mr. Wallace's distinction between specific and generic characters in respect of necessary utility.

But now, and lastly, we shall reach the same conclusion if, discarding all consideration of general principles and formal reasoning, we fasten attention upon certain particular cases, or concrete facts. Thus, to select only two illustrations within the limits of genera, it is a diagnostic feature of the genus *Equus* that small warty callosities occur on the legs. It is impossible to suggest any useful function that is now discharged by these callosities in any of the existing species of the genus. If it be assumed that they must have been of some use to the species from which the genus originally sprang, the assumption, it seems to me, can only be saved by further assuming that in existing species of the genus these callosities are in a vestigial condition—i. e. that in the original or parent species they performed some function which is now obsolete. But against these assumptions there lies the following fact. The callosities in question are not similarly distributed through all existing species of the genus. The horse has them upon all his four legs, while other species have them only upon two. Therefore, if all specific characters are necessarily due to natural selection, it is manifest that these callosities are *not* now vestigial: on the contrary, they *must* still be—or, at best, have recently been—of so much importance to all existing species of the genus, that not only is it a matter of selection-value to all these species that they should possess these callosities; but it is even a matter of selection-value to a horse that he should possess four of them, while it is equally a matter of selection-value to the ass that he should possess only two. Here, it seems to me, we have once more the doctrine of the necessary utility of specific characters reduced to an absurdity; while at the same time we display the incoherency of the distinction between specific characters and generic characters in respect of this doctrine. For the distinction in such a case amounts to saying that a generic character, if evenly distributed among all the species, need not be an adaptive character; whereas, if any one of the species presents it in a slightly different form, the character must be, on this account, necessarily adaptive. In other words, the uniformity with which a generic character occurs among the species of the genus is taken to remove that character from the necessarily useful class, while the absence of such uniformity is taken as proof that the character must be placed within the necessarily useful class. Which is surely no less a *reductio ad absurdum* with regard to the generic character than the one just presented with regard to its variants as specific characters. And, of course, this twofold absurdity is presented in all cases where a generic character is unequally distributed among the constituent species of a genus.

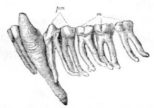

FIG. 4.—Lower Teeth of Orang (after Tomes).

But here is an illustration of another class of cases. Mr. Tomes has shown that the molar teeth of the Orang present an extraordinary and altogether superfluous amount of attachment in their sockets—the fangs being not only exceedingly long, and therefore deeply buried in the jaw-bone, but also curving round one another, so as still further to strengthen the whole[133]. In the allied genera of anthropoid apes there is no such abnormal amount of attachment. Now, the question is, of what conceivable use can it *ever* have been, either to the existing genus, or to its parent species, that such an abnormal amount of attachment should obtain? It certainly is not required to prevent dislocation of the teeth, seeing that in all allied genera, and even in man himself, the amount of attachment is already so great that teeth will break before they can be drawn by anything short of a dentist's forceps. Therefore I conclude that this peculiarity in the dentition of the genus must have arisen in its parent species by way of what Darwin calls a "fluctuating variation," without utilitarian significance. And I adduce it in the present connexion because the peculiarity is one which is equally unamenable to a utilitarian explanation, whether it happens to occur as a generic or a specific character.

Numberless similar cases might be quoted; but probably enough has now been said to prove the inconsistency of the distinction which our opponents draw between specific and all higher characters in respect of utility. In point of fact, a very little thought is enough to show that no such distinction admits of being drawn; and, therefore, that any one who maintains the doctrine of utility as universal in the case of specific characters, must in consistency hold to the same doctrine in the case of generic and all higher characters. And the fact that our opponents are unable to do this becomes a virtual confession on their part of the futility of the generalization which they have propounded[134].

On what then do Mr. Wallace and his followers rely for their great distinction between specific and all other characters in respect of utility? This is the final and fundamental question which I must leave these naturalists themselves to answer; for my whole contention is, that it is unanswerable. But although I am satisfied that they have nothing on which to base their generalization, it seems worth while to conclude by showing yet one further point. And this is, that these naturalists themselves, as soon as they quit merely abstract assertions and come to deal with actual facts, contradict their own generalization. It is worth while to show this by means of a few quotations, that we may perceive how impossible it is for them to sustain their generalization in the domain of fact.

As it is desirable to be brief, I will confine myself to quoting from Mr. Wallace.

> "Colour may be looked upon as a necessary result of the highly complex chemical constitution of animal tissues and fluids. The blood, the bile, the bones, the fat, and other tissues have characteristic, and often brilliant colours, which we cannot suppose to have been determined for any special purpose as colours, since they are usually concealed. The external organs and integuments, would, by the same general laws, naturally give rise to a greater variety of colour[135]."

Surely comment is needless. Have the colour of external organs and integuments nothing to do with the determining of specific distinctions by systematists? Or, may we not rather ask, are there any other "characters" which have had more to do with their delineation of animal species? Therefore, if "the external organs and integuments naturally give rise to a greater variety of colours," for non-utilitarian reasons, than is the case with internal organs and tissues; while even the latter present, for similarly non-utilitarian reasons, such variety and intensity of colours as they do; must it not follow that, on the ground of the "Laws of Growth" alone, Mr. Wallace has conceded the entire case as regards "a large proportional number of specific characters" being non-adaptive—"spontaneous" in their occurrence, and "meaningless" in their persistence?

Once more:—

> "The enormously lengthened plumes of the bird of paradise and of the peacock, can, however, have no such use [i.e. for purposes of defence], but must be rather injurious than beneficial in the birds' ordinary life. The fact that they have been developed to so great an extent in a few species is an indication of such perfect adaptation to the conditions of existence, such complete success in the battle for life, that there is, in the adult male at all events, a surplus of strength, vitality, and growth-power, which is able to expend itself in this way without injury. That such is the case is shown by the great abundance of most of the species which possess these wonderful superfluities of plumage.... Why, in allied species, the development of accessory plumes has taken different forms, we are unable to say, except that it may be due to that individual variability which has served as a starting-point for so much of what seems to us strange in form, or fantastic in colour, both in the animal and vegetable world[136]."

Here, again, one need only ask, How can such statements be reconciled with the great dogma, "which is indeed a necessary deduction from the theory of Natural Selection, namely, that none of the definite facts of organic nature, no special organ, no characteristic form or marking can exist, but which must now be, or once have been, *useful*"? Can it be said that the plumes of a bird of paradise present "no characteristic form," or the tail of a peacock "no characteristic marking"? Can it be held that all the "fantastic colours," which Darwin attributes to sexual selection, and all the "strange forms" in the vegetable world which present no conceivable reference to adaptation, are to be ascribed to "individual variability" without reference to utility, while at the same time it is held, "as a necessary deduction from the theory of Natural Selection," that *all* specific characters must be "*useful*"? Or must we not conclude that we have here a contradiction as direct as a contradiction can well be[137]?

Nor is it any more possible to reconcile these contradictory statements by an indefinite extension of the term "correlation," than we found it to be in the cases previously quoted. It might indeed be logically possible, howsoever biologically absurd, to attribute the tail of a peacock—with all its elaboration of structure and pattern of colour, with all the drain that its large size and weight makes upon the vital resources of the bird, with all the increased danger to which it exposes the bird by rendering it more conspicuous, more easy of capture, &c.—to correlation with some useful character peculiar to peacocks. But to say that it is due to correlation with general "vitality," is merely to discharge the doctrine of correlation of any assignable meaning. Vitality, or "perfect adaptation to the conditions of existence," is obviously a prime condition to the occurrence of a peacock's tail, as it is to the occurrence of a peacock itself; but this is quite a different thing from saying that the specific characters which are presented by a peacock's tail, although useless in themselves, are correlated with some other and useful specific characters of the same bird—as we saw in a previous chapter with reference to secondary sexual characters in general. Therefore, when Mr. Wallace comes to the obvious question why it is that even in "allied species," which must be in equally "perfect adaptation to the conditions of existence," there are no such "wonderful superfluities of plumage," he falls back—as he previously fell back—on whatever unknown *causes* it may have been which produced the peacock's tail, when the primary *condition* to their operation has been furnished by "complete success in the battle for life."

I have quoted the above passages, not so much for the sake of exposing fundamental inconsistencies on the part of an adversary, as for the sake of observing that they constitute a much truer exposition of "Darwinism" than do the contradictory views expressed in some other parts of the work bearing that title. For even if characters of so much size and elaboration as the tail of a peacock, the plumes of a bird of paradise &c., are admitted to be due to non-utilitarian causes, much more must innumerable other characters of incomparably less size and elaboration be mere "superfluities." Without being actually deleterious, "a large proportional number of specific characters," whose utility is not apparent, must *a fortiori* have been due to "individual variation," to "general laws which determine the production" of such characters—or, in short, to some causes other than natural selection. And this, I say, is a doctrine much more in harmony with "Darwinism" than is the contradictory doctrine which I am endeavouring to resist.

But once again, and still more generally, after saying of "the delicate tints of spring foliage, and the intense hues of autumn," that "as colours they are unadaptive, and appear to have no more relation to the well-being of plants themselves than do the colours of gems and minerals," Mr. Wallace proceeds thus:—

"We may also include in the same category those algae and fungi which have bright colours—the red snow of the Arctic regions, the red, green, or purple seaweeds, the brilliant scarlet, yellow, white or black agarics, and other fungi. All these colours are probably the direct results of chemical composition or molecular structure, and being thus normal products of the vegetable organism, need no special explanation from our present point of view; and the same remark will apply to the varied tints of the bark of trunks, branches and twigs, which are often of various shades of brown and green, or even vivid reds and yellows[138]."

Here, as Mr. Gulick has already observed, "Mr. Wallace seems to admit that instead of useless specific characters being unknown, they are so common and so easily explained by 'the chemical constitution of the organism' that they claim no special attention[139]." And whatever answer Mr. Wallace may make to this criticism, I do not see how he is to meet the point at present before us—namely, that, upon his own showing, there are in nature numberless instances of "characters which are useless without being hurtful," and which nevertheless present absolute "constancy." If, in order to explain the contradiction, he should fall back upon the principle of correlation, the case would not be in any way improved. For, here again, if the term correlation were extended so as to include "the chemical constitution or the molecular structure of the organism," it would thereby be extended so as to discharge all Darwinian significance from the term.

Summary.

I will conclude this discussion of the Utility question by recapitulating the main points in an order somewhat different from that in which they have been presented in the foregoing chapters. Such a variation may render their mutual connexions more apparent. But it is only to the main points that allusion will here be made, and, in order the better to show their independent character, I will separately number them.

1. The doctrine of utility as universal, whether with respect to species only or likewise with respect to specific characters, is confessedly an *a priori* doctrine, deduced by way of general reasoning from the theory of natural selection.

2. Being thus founded exclusively on grounds of deduction, the doctrine cannot be combated by any appeal to facts. For this question is not one of fact: it is a question of reasoning. The treatment of our subject matter is logical: not biological.

3. The doctrine is both universal and absolute. According to one form of it *all* species, and according to another form of it *all* specific characters, must *necessarily* be due to the principle of utility.

4. The doctrine in both its forms is deduced from a definition of the theory of natural selection as a theory, and the sole theory, of the origin of *species*; but, as Professor Huxley has already shown, it does not really follow, even from this definition, that all specific *characters* must be "necessarily useful." Hence the two forms of the doctrine, although coincident with regard to species, are at variance with one another in respect of specific characters. Thus far, of course, I agree with Professor Huxley; but if I have been successful in showing that the above definition of the theory of natural selection is logically fallacious, it follows that the doctrine in both its forms is radically erroneous. The theory of natural selection is not, accurately speaking, a theory of the origin of species: it is a theory of the origin and cumulative development of adaptations, to whatever order of taxonomic division these may happen to belong. Thus the premisses of the deduction which we are considering collapse: the principle of utility is shown not to have any other or further reference to species, or to specific characters, than it has to fixed varieties, genera, families, &c., or to the characters severally distinctive of each.

5. But, quitting all such antecedent considerations, we next proceeded to examine the doctrine *a posteriori*, taking the arguments which have been advanced in favour of the doctrine, other than those which rest upon the fallacious definition. These arguments, as presented by Mr. Wallace, are two in number.

First, it is represented that natural selection must occupy the whole field, because no other principle of change can be allowed to operate in the presence of natural selection. Now I fully agree that this statement holds as regards any principle of change which is deleterious, but I cannot agree that it does so as regards any such principle which is merely neutral. No reason has ever been shown why natural selection should interfere with "indifferent" characters—to adopt Professor Huxley's term—supposing such to have been produced by any of the agencies which we shall presently have to name. Therefore this argument—or rather assertion—goes for nothing.

Mr. Wallace's second argument is, that utility is the only principle which can endow specific characters with their characteristic stability. But this again is mere assertion. Moreover, it is assertion opposed alike to common sense and to observable fact. It is opposed to common sense, because it is obvious that any other principle would equally confer stability on characters due to it, provided that its action is constant, as Darwin expressly held. Again, this argument is opposed to fact, because we know of thousands of cases where peculiar characters are stable, which, nevertheless, cannot possibly be due to natural selection. Of such are the Porto Santo rabbits, the niata cattle, the ducks in St. James' Park, turkeys, dogs, horses, &c., and, in the case of plants, wheat, cabbage, maize, &c., as well as all the hosts of climatic varieties, both of animals and plants, in a state of nature. Indeed, on taking a wide survey of the facts, we do not find that the principle of utility is any better able to confer stability of character than are many other principles, both known and unknown. Nay, it is positively less able to do so than are some of these other principles. Darwin gives two very probable reasons for this fact; but I need not quote them a second time. It is enough to have seen that this argument from stability or constancy is no less worthless than the previous one. Yet these are the only two arguments of a corroborative kind which Mr. Wallace adduces whereby to sustain his "necessary deduction."

6. At this point, therefore, it may well seem that we need not have troubled ourselves any further with a generalization which does not appear to have anything to support it. And to this view of the case I should myself agree, were it not that many naturalists now entertain the doctrine as an essential article of their Darwinian creed. Hence, I proceeded to adduce considerations *per contra*.

Seeing that the doctrine in question can only rest on the assumption that there is no cause other than natural selection which is capable of originating any single species—if not even so much as any single specific character—I began by examining this assumption. It was shown first that, on merely antecedent grounds, the assumption is "infinitely precarious." There is absolutely no justification for the statement that in all the varied and complex processes of organic nature natural selection is the only possible cause of specific change. But, apart altogether from this *a priori* refutation of the dogma, our analysis went on to show that, in point of actual fact, there are not a few well-known causes of high generality, which, while having no connexion with the principle of utility, are demonstrably capable of originating species and specific characters—if by "species" and "specific characters" we are to understand organic types which are ranked as species, and characters which are described as diagnostic of species. Such causes I grouped under five different headings, viz. Climate, Food, Sexual Selection, Isolation, and Laws of Growth. Sexual Selection and Isolation are, indeed, repudiated by Mr. Wallace; but, in common I believe with all biologists, he accepts the other three groups of causes as fully adequate to produce such kinds and degrees of modification as are taken to constitute specific distinction. And this is amply sufficient for our present purposes. Besides, under the head of Sexual Selection, it does not signify in the present connexion whether or not we accept Darwin's theory on this subject. For, in any case, the facts of secondary sexual characters are indisputable: these characters are, for the most part, specific characters: and they cannot be explained by the principle of utility. Even Mr. Wallace does not attempt to do so; and the explanation which he does give is clearly incompatible with his doctrine touching the necessarily life-serving value of all specific characters. Lastly, the same has to be said of the Laws of Growth. For we have just seen that on the grounds of this principle likewise Mr. Wallace abandons the doctrine in question. As regards Isolation, much more remains to be said in the ensuing portion of this work, while, as regards Climatic Variation, there are literally innumerable cases where changes of specific type are known to have been caused by this means.

7. To the latter class of cases, however, it will be objected that these changes of specific type, although no doubt sufficiently "stable" so long as the changed conditions remain constant, are found by experiment not to be hereditary; and this clearly makes all the difference between a true specific change and a merely fictitious appearance of it.

Well, in the first place, this objection can have reference only to the first two of the five principles above stated. It can have no reference to the last three, because of these heredity constitutes the very foundation. This consideration ought to be borne in mind throughout. But now, in the second place, even as regards changes produced by climate and food, the reply is nugatory. And this for three reasons, as follows.

(*a*) No one is thus far entitled to conclude against the possible transmission of acquired characters; and, so long as there is even so much as a possibility of climatic (or any other admittedly non-utilitarian) variations becoming in this way hereditary, the reply before us merely begs the question.

(*b*) Even supposing, for the sake of argument, that acquired characters can never in any case become congenital, there remains the strong probability—sanctioned as such even by Weismann—that changed conditions of life may not unfrequently act upon the material of heredity itself, thus giving rise to specific changes which are from the first congenital, though not utilitarian. Indeed, there are not a few facts (Hoffmann's plants, Weismann's butterflies, &c.), which can only be explained either in this way, or as above (*a*). And in the present connexion it is immaterial which of these alternative explanations we choose to adopt, seeing that they equally refute our opponents' objection. And not only do these considerations—(*a*) and (*b*)—refute this particular objection; they overturn on new and independent grounds the whole of our opponents' generalization. For the generalization is, that the principle of utility, acting through natural selection, is "necessarily" the sole principle which can be concerned in hereditary changes of specific type. But here we perceive both a possibility (*a*) and a probability (*b*), if not indeed a certainty, that quite other principles have been largely concerned in the production of such changes.

(*c*) Altogether apart from these considerations, there remains a much more important one. For the objection that fixed—or "stable"—climatic varieties differ from true species in not being subject to heredity, raises the question—What are we to understand by a "species"? This question, which was thus far purposely left in abeyance, had now to be dealt with seriously. For it would clearly be irrational in our opponents to make this highly important generalization with regard to species and specific characters, unless they are prepared to tell us what they mean by species, and therefore by characters as specific. In as far as there is any ambiguity on this point it makes entirely for our side in the debate, because even any small degree of uncertainty with regard to it would render the generalization in question proportionally unsound. Yet it is notorious that no word in existence is more vague, or more impossible to define, than the word "species." The very same men who at one time pronounce their great generalization with regard to species, at another time asseverate that "a species is not a definite entity," but a merely abstract term, serving to denote this that and the other organic type, which this that and the other systematist regards as deserving such a title. Moreover it is acknowledged that systematists differ among themselves to a wide extent as to the kinds and degrees of peculiarity which entitle a given form to a specific rank. Even in the same department of systematic work much depends on merely individual taste, while in different departments widely different standards of delimination are in vogue. Hence, our *reductio ad absurdum* consists in this—that whether a given form is to be regarded as necessarily due to natural selection, and whether all its distinctive characters are to be regarded as necessarily utilitarian characters, will often depend on whether it has been described by naturalist A or by naturalist B. There is no one criterion—there is not even any one set of criteria—agreed upon by naturalists for the construction of specific types. In particular, as regards the principle of heredity, it is not known of one named species in twenty—probably not in a hundred—whether its diagnostic characters are hereditary characters; while, on the other hand, even in cases where experiment has proved "constant varieties" to be hereditary—and even also cross-sterile with allied varieties—it is only some three or four living botanists who for these reasons advocate the elevation of such varieties to the rank of species. In short, as we are not engaged on any abstract question touching the principles on which species ought to have been constituted by their makers, but upon the actual manner in which they have been, the criterion of heredity must needs be disregarded in the present discussion, as it has been in the work of systematists. And the result of this is, that any objection to our introducing the facts of climatic variation in the present discussion is excluded. In particular, so far as any question of heredity is concerned, all these facts are as assuredly as they are cogently relevant. It is perfectly certain that there is "a large proportional number" of named species—particularly of plants—which further investigation would resolve into climatic varieties. With the advance of knowledge, "bad species" are always increasing at the expense of "good species," so that we are now justified in concluding with Kerner, Häckel, and other naturalists best qualified to speak on this subject, that if we could know as much about the past history and present relations of the remaining good species as we do about the bad, all the former, without exception, would become resolved into the latter. In point of fact, and apart altogether from the inductive experience on which this conclusion is based, the conclusion follows "as a necessary deduction" from the general theory of descent. For this theory essentially consists in supposing either the past or the present existence of intermediate varietal forms in all cases, with the consequence that "good species" serve merely to mark *lacunae* in our knowledge of what is everywhere a finely graduated process of transmutation. Hence, if we place this unquestionably "necessary deduction" from the general theory of descent side by side with the alleged "necessary deduction" from the theory of natural selection, we cannot avoid the following absurdity—Whether or not a given form is to be regarded as necessarily due to natural selection, and all its characters necessarily utilitarian, is to be determined, and determined solely, by the mere accident of our having found, or not having found, either in a living or in a fossil state, its varietal ancestry.

8. But this leads us to consider the final and crowning incongruities which have been dealt with in the present chapter. For here we have seen, not only that our opponents thus draw a hard and fast line between "varieties" and "species" in regard to "necessary origin" and "necessary utility," but that they further draw a similar line between "species" and "genera" in the same respects. Yet, in accordance with the general theory of evolution, it is plainly as impossible to draw any such line in the one case as it is to do so in the other. Just as fixed varieties are what Darwin called "incipient species," so are species incipient genera, genera incipient families, and so on. Evolutionists must believe that the process of evolution is everywhere the same. Nevertheless, while admitting all this, the school of Huxley contradicts itself by alleging some unintelligible exception in the case of "species," while the school of Wallace presses this exception so as to embrace "specific characters." Indeed Mr. Wallace, while maintaining that all specific characters must necessarily be useful, maintains at the same time that any number of varietal characters on the one hand, and a good half of generic characters on the other, are probably useless. Thus he contradicts his argument from the "constancy of specific characters" (seeing that generic characters are still more constant), as later on we saw that he contradicts his deductive generalization touching their necessary utility, by giving a non-utilitarian explanation of whole multitudes of specific characters. I need not, however, again go over the ground so recently traversed; but will conclude by once more recurring to the only explanation which I have been able to devise of the otherwise inexplicable fact, that in regard to this subject so many naturalists still continue to entangle themselves in the meshes of absurdity and contradiction.

The only conceivable explanation is, that these naturalists have not yet wholly divested themselves of the special creation theory. Although professing to have discarded the belief that "species" are "definite entities," differing in kind from "varieties" on the one hand and from "genera" on the other, these writers are still imbued with a vague survival of that belief. They well know it to belong to the very essence of their new theory that "species" are but "pronounced varieties," or, should we prefer it, "incipient genera"; but still they cannot altogether escape the pre-Darwinian conception of species as organic units, whose single mode of origin need not extend to other taxonomic groups, and whose characters therefore present some exceptional significance to the scientific naturalist. So to speak, such divinity doth still hedge a species, that even in the very act of declaring it but an idol of their own creation, these naturalists bow before their fetish as something that is unique—differing alike in its origin and in its characters from the varieties beneath and the genera above. The consequence is that they have endeavoured to reconcile these incompatible ideas by substituting the principle of natural selection for that of supernatural creation, where the particular case of "species" is concerned. In this way, it vaguely seems to them, they are able to save the doctrine of some one mode of origin as appertaining to species, which need not "necessarily" appertain to any other taxonomic division. All other such divisions they regard, with their pre-Darwinian forefathers, as merely artificial constructions; but, likewise with these forefathers, they look upon species as natural divisions, proved to be such by a single and necessary mode of origin. Hence, Mr. Wallace expressly defines a species with reference to this single and necessary mode of origin (*see* above, p. 235), although he must be well aware that there is no better, or more frequent, proof of it in the case of species, than there is in that of somewhat less pronounced types on the one hand (fixed varieties), or of more pronounced types on the other (genera, families, &c.). Hence, also, the theory of natural selection is defined as *par excellence* a theory of the origin of species; it is taken as applying to the particular case of the origin of species in a peculiarly stringent manner, or in a manner which does not apply to the origin of any other groups. And I believe that an important accessory reason of the continuance of this view for more than thirty years after the publication of the *Origin of Species by means of Natural Selection,* is to be found in the title of that work. "Natural Selection" has thus become verbally associated with "Origin of Species," till it is thoughtlessly felt that, in some way or another, natural selection must have a peculiar reference to those artificially delineated forms which stand anywhere between a fixed variety and a so-called genus. This verbal association has no doubt had the effect of still further preserving the traditional halo of mystery which clings to the idea of a "species." Hence it comes that the title which Darwin chose—and, looking to the circumstances of the time, wisely chose—for his great work, has subsequently had the effect of fostering the very idea which it was the object of that work to dissipate, namely, that species are peculiar entities, which differ more or less in origin or kind from all other taxonomic groups. The full title of this work is—*The Origin of Species by means of Natural Selection: or the Preservation of Favoured Races in the Struggle for Life.* Now, supposing that instead of this its author had chosen some such title as the following:—*The Origin of Organic Types by means of Adaptive Evolution: or Survival of the Fittest Forms in the Struggle for Life.* Of course this would have been a bad substitute from various points of view; but could any objection have been urged against it from our present point of view? I do not see that there could. Yet, if such had been the title, I have little doubt that we should never have heard of those great generalizations with regard to species and specific characters, the futility of which it has been the object of these chapters to expose.

In conclusion, it only remains to reiterate that in thus combating what appears to me plainly erroneous deductions from the theory of natural selection, I am in no wise combating that theory itself. On the contrary, I hope that I am rendering it no unimportant service by endeavouring to relieve it of a parasitic growth—an accretion of false logic. Regarding as I do the theory of natural selection as, primarily, a theory of the origin (or cumulative development) of adaptations, I see in merely non-adaptive characters—be they "specific" or other—a comparatively insignificant class of phenomena, which may be due to a great variety of incidental causes, without any further reference to the master-principle of natural selection than that in the presence of this principle none of these non-adaptive characters can be actively deleterious. But that there may be "any number of indifferent characters" it is no part of the theory of natural selection to deny; and all attempts to foist upon it *a priori* "deductions" opposed alike to the facts of nature and to the logic of the case, can only act to the detriment of the great generalization which was expressly guarded from such fallacies by the ever-careful judgement of Darwin.

APPENDICES AND NOTES

APPENDIX I
ON PANMIXIA.

There are several points of considerable theoretical importance connected with Panmixia, which were omitted from the text, in order to avoid distracting attention from the main issue which is there under consideration. These side issues may now be appropriately presented in the form in which they were published in *Nature*, March 13, 1890[140]. After stating, in almost the same words, what has already been said in Chapter X, this paper proceeds, with the exception of a few verbal alterations, as follows.

"There is, however, one respect in which Professor Weismann's statement of the principle of panmixia differs from that which was considered by Mr. Darwin; and it is this difference of statement—which amounts to an important difference of theory—that I now wish to discuss.

"The difference in question is, that while Professor Weismann believes the cessation of selection to be capable of inducing degeneration down to the almost complete disappearance of a rudimentary organ, I have argued that, *unless assisted by some other principle*, it can at most only reduce the degenerating organ to considerably above one-half its original size—or probably not through so much as one-quarter. The ground of this argument (which is given in detail in the *Nature* articles of 1873-1874) is, that panmixia depends for its action upon fortuitous variations round an ever-diminishing average—the average thus diminishing because it is no longer *sustained* by natural selection. But although no longer sustained by *natural selection*, it does continue to be sustained by *heredity*; and therefore, as long as the force of heredity persists unimpaired, fortuitous variations alone—or variation which is no longer controlled by natural selection—cannot reduce the dwindling organ to so much as one-half of its original size; indeed, as above foreshadowed, the balance between the positive force of heredity and the negative effects of promiscuous variability will most likely be arrived at above the middle line thus indicated. Only if for any reason the force of heredity begins to fail can the average round

- 172 -

which the cessation of selection works become a progressively diminishing average. In other words, so long as the original force of heredity as regards the useless organ remains unimpaired, the mere withdrawal of selection cannot reduce the organ much below the level of efficiency above which it was previously *maintained* by the *presence* of selection. If we take this level to be 80 or 90 per cent. of the original size, cessation of selection will reduce the organ through the 10 or 20 per cent., and there leave it fluctuating about this average, unless for any reason the force of heredity begins to fail—in which case, of course, the average will progressively fall in proportion to the progressive weakening of this force.

"Now, according to my views, the force of heredity under such circumstances is always bound to fail, and this for two reasons. In the first place, it must usually happen that when an organ becomes useless, natural selection as regards that organ will not only *cease*, but become *reversed*. For the organ is now absorbing nutriment, causing weight, occupying space, and so on, *uselessly*. Hence, even if it be not also a source of actual danger, 'economy of growth' will determine a reversal of selection against an organ which is now not merely useless, but deleterious. And this degenerating influence of the reversal of selection will throughout be assisted by the cessation of selection, which will now be always acting round a continuously sinking average. Nevertheless, a point of balance will eventually be reached in this case, just as it was in the previous case where the cessation of selection was supposed to be working alone. For, where the reversal of selection has reduced the diminishing organ to so minute a size that its presence is no longer a source of detriment to the organism, the cessation of selection will carry the reduction a small degree further; and then the organ will remain as a 'rudiment.' And so it will remain permanently, unless there be some further reason why the still remaining force of heredity should be abolished. This further (or second) reason I found in the consideration that, however enduring we may suppose the force of heredity to be, we cannot suppose that it is actually everlasting; and, therefore, that we may reasonably attribute the eventual disappearance of rudimentary organs to the eventual failure of heredity itself. In support of this view there is the fact that rudimentary organs, although very persistent, are not everlasting. That they should be very persistent is what we should expect, if the hold which heredity has upon them is great in proportion to the time during which they were originally useful, and thus firmly stamped upon the organization by natural selection causing them to be strongly inherited in the first instance. For example, we might expect that it would be more difficult finally to eradicate the rudiment of a wing than the rudiment of a feather; and accordingly we find it a general rule that long-enduring rudiments are rudiments of organs distinctive of the higher taxonomic divisions—i.e. of organs which were longest in building up, and therefore longest sustained in a state of working efficiency.

"Thus, upon the whole, my view of the facts of degeneration remains the same as it was when first published in these columns seventeen years ago, and may be summarized as follows.

"The cessation of selection when working alone (as it probably does during the first centuries of its action upon structures or colours which do not entail any danger to, or perceptible drain upon, the nutritive resources of the organism) cannot cause degeneration below, probably, some 10 to 20 per cent. But if from the first the cessation of selection has been assisted by the *reversal* of selection (on account of the degenerating structure having originally been of a size sufficient to entail a perceptible drain on the nutritive resources of the organism, having now become a source of danger, and so forth), the two principles acting together will continue to reduce the ever-diminishing structure down to the point at which its presence is no longer a perceptible disadvantage to the species. When that point is reached, the reversal of selection will terminate, and the cessation of selection will not then be able of itself to reduce the organ through more than at most a very few further percentages of its original size. But, after this point has been reached, the now total absence of selection, either for or against the organ, will sooner or later entail this further and most important consequence, a failure of heredity as regards the organ. So long as the organ was of use, its efficiency was constantly *maintained* by the *presence* of selection—which is merely another way of saying that selection was constantly maintaining the force of heredity as regards that organ. But as soon as the organ ceased to be of use, selection ceased to maintain the force of heredity; and thus, sooner or later, that force began to waver or fade. Now it is this wavering or fading of the force of heredity, thus originally due to the cessation of selection, that in turn co-operates with the still continued cessation of selection in reducing the structure below the level where its reduction was left by the actual reversal of selection. So that from that level downwards the cessation of selection, and the consequent failing of heredity, act and react in their common work of causing obsolescence. In the case of newly added characters, the force of heredity will be less than in that of more anciently added characters; and thus we can understand the long endurance of 'vestiges' characteristic of the higher taxonomic divisions, as compared with those characteristic of the lower. But in all cases, if time enough be allowed under the cessation of selection, the force of heredity will eventually fall to zero, when the hitherto obsolescent structure will finally become obsolete. In cases of newly added and comparatively trivial characters, with regard to which reversal of selection is not likely to take place (e.g. slight differences of colour between allied species), cessation of selection is likely to be very soon assisted by a failure in the force of heredity; seeing that such newly added characters will not be so strongly inherited as are the more ancient characters distinctive of higher taxonomic groups.

"Let us now turn to Weismann's view of degeneration. First of all, he has omitted to perceive that 'panmixia' alone (if unassisted either by reversed selection or an inherent diminishing of the force of heredity) cannot reduce a functionless organ to the condition of a *rudiment*. Therefore he everywhere represents panmixia (or the mere *cessation* of selection) as of itself sufficient to cause degeneration, say from 100 to 5, instead of from 100 to 90 or 80, which, for the reasons above given, appeared (and still appears) to me about the most that this principle can accomplish, so long as the original force of heredity continues unimpaired. No doubt we have here what must be regarded as a mere oversight on the part of Professor Weismann; but the oversight is rendered remarkable by the fact that he *does* invoke the aid of reversed selection *in order to explain the final disappearance of a rudiment.* Yet it is self-evident that the reversal of selection must be much more active during the initial than during the final stages of degeneration, seeing that, *ex hypothesi,* the greater the degree of reduction which has been attained the less must be the detriment arising from any useless expenditure of nutrition, &c.

"And this leads me to a second oversight in Professor Weismann's statement, which is of more importance than the first. For the place at which he does invoke the assistance of reversed selection is exactly the place at which reversed selection must necessarily have ceased to act. This place, as already explained, is where an obsolescent organ has become rudimentary, or, as above supposed, reduced to 5 per cent. of its original size; and the reason why he invokes the aid of reversed selection at this place is in order to save his doctrine of 'the stability of germ-plasm.' That the force of heredity should finally become exhausted if no longer *maintained* by the *presence* of selection, is what Darwin's theory of perishable gemmules would lead us to expect, while such a fact would be fatal to Weismann's theory of an imperishable germ-plasm. Therefore he seeks to explain the eventual failure of heredity (which is certainly a fact) by supposing that after the point at which the cessation of selection alone can no longer act (and which his first oversight has placed some 80 per cent. too low), the reversal of selection will begin to act directly against the force of heredity as regards the diminishing organ, until such direct action of reversed selection will have removed the organ altogether. Or, in his own words, 'The complete disappearance of a rudimentary organ can only take place by the operation of natural selection; this principle will lead to its diminution, inasmuch as the disappearing structure takes the place and the nutriment of other useful and important organs.' That is to say, the rudimentary organ finally disappears, not because the force of heredity is finally exhausted, but because natural selection has begun to utilize this force against the continuance of the organ—always picking out those congenital variations of the organ which are of smallest size, and thus, by its now *reversed* action, *reversing* the force of heredity as regards the organ.

"Now the oversight here is in not perceiving that the smaller the disappearing structure becomes, the less hold must 'this principle' of reversed selection retain upon it. As above observed, during the earlier stages of reduction (or while co-operating with the cessation of selection) the reversal of selection will be at its *maximum* of efficiency; and, as the process of diminution continues, a point must eventually be reached at which the reversal of selection can no longer act. Take the original mass of a now obsolescent organ in relation to that of the entire organism of which it then formed a part to be represented by the ratio 1:100. For the sake of argument we may assume that the mass of the organism has throughout remained constant, and that by 'mass' in both cases is meant capacity for absorbing nutriment, causing weight, occupying space, and so forth. Now, we may further assume that when the mass of the organ stood to that of its organism in the ratio of 1:100, natural selection was strongly reversed with respect to the organ. But when this ratio fell to 1:1000, the activity of such reversal must have become enormously diminished, even if it still continued to exercise any influence at all. For we must remember, on the one hand, that the reversal of selection can only act as long as the presence of a diminishing organ continues to be so injurious that variations in its size are matters of life and death in the struggle for existence; and, on the other hand, that natural selection in the case of the diminishing organ does not have reference to the presence and the absence of the organ, but only to such variations in its mass as any given generation may supply. Now, the process of reduction does not end even at 1:1000. It goes on to 1:10,000, and eventually 1:∞. Consequently, however great our faith in natural selection may be, a point must eventually come for all of us at which we can no longer believe that the reduction of an obsolescent organ is due to reversed selection. And I cannot doubt that if Professor Weismann had sufficiently considered the matter, he would not have committed himself to the statement that 'the complete disappearance of a rudimentary organ can only take place by the operation of natural selection.'

"According to my view, the complete disappearance of a rudimentary organ can only take place by the *cessation* of natural selection, which permits the eventual exhaustion of heredity, when heredity is thus simply left to itself. During all the earlier stages of reduction, the cessation of selection was assisted in its work by the reversal of selection; but when the rudiment became too small for such assistance any longer to be supplied, the rudiment persisted in that greatly reduced condition until the force of heredity with regard to it was eventually worn out. This appears to me, as it appeared in 1873, the only reasonable conclusion that can be drawn from the facts. And it is because this conclusion is fatal to Professor Weismann's doctrine of the permanent 'stability' of germ-plasm, while quite in accordance with all theories which belong to the family of pangenesis, that I deem the facts of degeneration of great importance as tests between these rival interpretations of the facts of heredity. It is on this account that I have occupied so much space with the foregoing discussion; and I shall be glad to ascertain whether any of the followers of Professor Weismann are able to controvert these views.

"GEORGE J. ROMANES."

"P.S.—Since the above article was sent in, Professor Weismann has published in these columns (February 6) his reply to a criticism by Professor Vines (October 24, 1889). In this reply he appears to have considerably modified his views on the theory of degeneration; for while in his Essays he says (as in the passage above quoted) that 'the complete disappearance of a rudimentary organ can only take place by the operation of natural selection'—i.e. only by the *reversal* of selection,—in his reply to Professor Vines he says, 'I believe that I have proved that organs no longer in use become rudimentary, and must finally disappear, solely by 'panmixia'; not through the direct action of disuse, but because natural selection no longer sustains their standard structure'—i.e. solely by the *cessation* of selection. Obviously, there is here a flat contradiction. If Professor Weismann now believes that a rudimentary organ 'must finally disappear *solely*' through the *withdrawal* of selection, he has abandoned his previous belief that 'the complete disappearance of a rudimentary organ can *only* take place by the *operation* of selection.' And this change of belief on his part is a matter of the highest importance to his system of theories as a whole, since it betokens a surrender of his doctrine of the 'stability' of germ-plasm—or of the virtually everlasting persistence of the force of heredity, and the consequent necessity for a reversal of this force itself (by natural selection placing its premium on *minus* instead of on *plus* variations), in order that a rudimentary organ should finally disappear. In other words, it now seems he no longer believes that the force of heredity in one direction (that of sustaining a rudimentary organ) can only be abolished by the active influence of natural selection determining this force in the opposite direction (that of removing a rudimentary organ). It seems he now believes that the force of heredity, if merely left to itself by the withdrawal of natural selection altogether, will sooner or later become exhausted through the mere lapse of time. This, of course, is my own theory of the matter as originally published in these columns; but I do not see how it is to be reconciled with Professor Weismann's doctrine of so high a degree of stability on the part of germ-plasm, that we must look to the Protozoa and the Protophyta for the original source of congenital variations as now exhibited by the Metazoa and Metaphyta. Nevertheless, and so far as the philosophy of degeneration is concerned, I shall be very glad if (as it now appears) Professor Weismann's more recent contemplation has brought his principle of panmixia into exact coincidence with that of my cessation of selection."

Before passing on it may here be noted that, to any one who believes in the inheritance of acquired characters, there is open yet another hypothetical cause of degeneration, and one to which the final disappearance of vestigial organs may be attributed. Roux has shown in his work on *The Struggle for Existence between Parts of an Organism* that the principle of selection must operate in every constituent tissue, and as between every constituent cell of which an organism is composed. Now, if an organ falls into disuse, its constituent cells become worsted in their struggles with other cells in the organism. Hence, degeneration of the disused organ may progressively increase, quite independently of any struggle for existence on the part of the organism as a whole. Consequently, degeneration may proceed without any reference to the principle of "economized nutrition"; and, if it does so, and if the effects of its doing so are transmitted from generation to generation, the disused organ will finally disappear by means of Roux's principle.

The long communication above quoted led to a still longer correspondence in the pages of *Nature*. For Professor Ray Lankester wrote[141] to impugn the doctrine of panmixia, or cessation of selection, *in toto*, arguing with much insistence that "cessation of selection must be supplemented by economy of growth in order to produce the results attributed to panmixia." In other words, he denied that panmixia alone can cause degeneration in any degree at all; at most, he said, it can be but "a condition," or "a state," which occurs when an organ or part ceases to be useful, and therefore falls under the degenerating influence of active causes, such as economy of nutrition. Or, in yet other words, he refused to recognize that any degenerative process can be due to natural selection as merely withdrawn: only when, besides being *withdrawn*, natural selection is *reversed*, did he regard a degenerative process as possible. As a result of the correspondence, however, he eventually[142] agreed that, if the "birth-mean" of an organ, in respect either of size or complexity of structure, be lower than the "selection-mean" while the organ is useful (a fact which he does not dispute); then, if the organ ceases to be useful, it will degenerate by the withdrawal of selection alone. Which, of course, is merely a re-statement of the doctrine of panmixia, or cessation of selection, in somewhat varied terminology—provided that the birth-mean be taken over a number of generations, or not only over a few following the selection-mean of the structure while still in its highest state of efficiency. For the sake of brevity I will hereafter speak of these "few following" generations by the term of "first generations."

It remains to consider the views of Professor Lloyd Morgan upon the subject. In my opinion he is the shrewdest, as well as the most logical critic that we have in the field of Darwinian speculation; therefore, if possible, I should like to arrive at a full agreement with him upon this matter. His latest utterance with regard to it is as follows:—

> "To account for the diminution of organs or structures no longer of use, apart from any inherited effects of disuse, Mr. Romanes has invoked the Cessation of Selection; and Mr. Francis Galton has, in another connexion, summarized the effects of this cessation of selection in the convenient phrase 'Regression to Mediocrity.' This is the Panmixia of Professor Weismann and his followers; but the phrase regression to mediocrity through the cessation of selection appears to me preferable. It is clear that so long as any organ or structure is subject to natural selection through elimination, it is, if not actually undergoing improvement, kept at a high standard of efficiency through the elimination of all those

individuals in which the organ in question falls below the required standard. But if, from change in the environment or any other cause, the character in question ceases to be subject to selection, elimination no longer takes place, and the high standard will no longer be maintained. There will be reversion to mediocrity. The probable amount of this reversion is at present a matter under discussion[143]."

So far, then, Professor Lloyd Morgan is in complete agreement with previous writers upon the subject. He does not doubt that the cessation of selection must always be a cause of degeneration: the only question is as to the *potency* of this cause, or the *amount* of degeneration which it is capable of effecting.

Taking, first, the case of bulk or size of an organ, as distinguished from its organization or complexity, we have seen that Weismann represents the cessation of selection—even if working quite alone, or without any assistance from the reversal of selection—to be capable of reducing a fully developed organ to the state of a rudiment, or even, if we take his most recent view, of abolishing the organ *in toto*.

Professor Lloyd Morgan, on the other hand, does not think that the cessation of selection alone can cause reduction further than the level of "mediocrity" in the first generations—or, which is much the same thing, further than the difference between the "birth-mean" and the "selection-mean" of the first generations. This amount of reduction he puts at 5 per cent., as "a very liberal estimate."

Here, then, we have three estimates of the amount of degeneration which can be produced by panmixia alone, where mere size or bulk of an organ is concerned—say, 3 to 5 per cent., 10 to 20 per cent., and 95 per cent. to 0. At first sight, these differences appear simply ludicrous; but on seeking for the reasons of them, we find that they are due to different views touching the manner in which panmixia operates. The oversights which have led to Weismann's extremely high estimate have already been stated. The reason of the difference between the extremely low estimate of Professor Lloyd Morgan, as compared with my own intermediate one, is, that he supposes the power of panmixia to become exhausted as soon as the level of mediocrity of the first generations has become the general level in succeeding generations. In my view, however, the level of mediocrity is itself a sinking level in successive generations, with the result that there is no reason why the reducing power of panmixia should ever become exhausted, save that the more reduction it effects the greater is the force of heredity which remains to be overcome, as previously explained. Thus the only question between Professor Lloyd Morgan and myself is—Does the level of mediocrity fall in successive generations under the cessation of selection, or does it remain permanently where it used to be under the presence of selection? Does the "birth-mean" remain constant throughout any number of generations, notwithstanding that the sustaining influence of selection has been withdrawn; or does it progressively sink as a consequence of such withdrawal?

In order to answer this question we had better begin by considering now the case of organization of structure, as distinguished from mere size of structure. Take any case where a complex organ—such as a compound eye—has been slowly elaborated by natural selection, and is it not self-evident that, when natural selection is withdrawn, the complex structure will deteriorate? In other words, the level of mediocrity, say in the hundred thousandth generation after the sustaining influence of natural selection has been withdrawn, will not be so high as it was in the first generations. For, by hypothesis, there is now no longer any elimination of unfavourable variations, which may therefore perpetuate themselves as regards any of the parts of this highly complex mechanism; so that it is only a matter of time when the mechanism must become disintegrated. I can scarcely suppose that any one who considers the subject will question this statement, and therefore I will not say anything that might be said in the way of substantiating it. But, if the statement be assented to, it follows that there is no need to look for any cause of deterioration, further than the withdrawal of selection—or cessation of the principle which (as we are supposing) had hitherto been the sole means of maintaining efficient harmony among all the independently variable parts of the highly complex structure.

Now, I hold that the same thing is true, though in a lesser degree, as regards degeneration of size. That there is no difference *in kind* between the two cases, Professor Lloyd Morgan implicitly allows; for what he says is—

> "In any long-established character, such as wing-power in birds, brain-development, the eyes of crustacea, &c., no shortcomer in these respects would have been permitted by natural selection to transmit his shortcomings for hundreds of generations. All tendency to such shortcomings would, one would suppose, have been bred out of the race. If after this long process of selection there still remains a strong tendency to deterioration, this tendency demands an explanation[144]."

Here, then, deterioration as to size of structure (wings of birds), and deterioration as to complexity of structure (brain and eyes) are expressly put upon the same footing. Therefore, if in the latter case the "tendency to deterioration" does not "demand an explanation," beyond the fact that the hitherto maintaining influence has been withdrawn, neither is any such further explanation demanded in the former case. Which is exactly my own view of the matter. It is also Mr. Galton's view. For although, in the passage formerly quoted, Professor Lloyd Morgan appears to think that by the phrase "Regression to Mediocrity" Mr. Galton means to indicate that panmixia can cause degeneration only as far as the mediocrity level of the first generations, this, in point of fact, is not what Galton means, nor is it what he says. The phrase in question occurs "in another connexion," and, indeed, in a different publication. But where he expressly alludes to the cessation of selection, this is what he says. The italics are mine.

> "A special cause may be assigned for the effects of use in causing hereditary *atrophy* of disused parts. It has already been shown that all exceptionally developed organs tend to deteriorate: consequently, those that are not *protected* by selection will *dwindle*. The level of muscular efficiency in the wing of a strongly flying bird [curiously enough, the same case that is chosen by Professor Lloyd Morgan to illustrate his opposite view], is like the level of water in the leaky vessel of a Danaid, only secured to the race by *constant effort*, so to speak. *Let the effort be relaxed ever so little, and the level immediately falls*[145]."

I take it, then, that the burden of proof lies with Professor Lloyd Morgan to show why the withdrawal of selection is *not* sufficient to account for degeneration any further than the mediocrity-level in the former presence of selection. Why does "the strong tendency[146] to deterioration demand an explanation," further than the fact that when all variations below the average in every generation are allowed to survive, they must gradually lower the average itself through a series of generations? To answer that any such tendency "would have been bred out of the race" by the previous action of selection, is to suppose that the function of selection is at an end when once it has built up a structure to the highest point of working efficiency,—that the presence of selection is no longer required to *maintain* the structure at that point. But it is enough to ask in reply—Why, under the cessation of selection, does *complexity* of structure degenerate so much more rapidly than *size* of structure? Why is it, for instance, that "the eyes of crustacea" in dark caves have entirely disappeared, while their foot-stalks (when originally present) still remain? Can it be maintained that "for hundreds of generations" natural selection was more intent on developing the foot-stalks than the eyes which were mounted upon them—so that while the latter were left by selection with "a strong tendency to deterioration," the former have had this tendency "bred out in the race"[147]?

To sum up. There is now no question in any quarter touching the fact that panmixia, or the cessation of selection, is a true cause of degeneration. The only question is as to the amount of degeneration which it is able to effect when not assisted by the reversal of selection, or any other cause of degeneration. Moreover, even with regard to this question of amount, there is no doubt on any side that panmixia alone causes degeneration *more rapidly* where it has to do with complexity of organization, than it does where it is concerned with a mere reduction of mass.

The question as to the amount of degeneration that is caused by the cessation of selection alone is without any practical importance where species in a state of nature are concerned, because here the cessation of selection is probably always associated more or less with the reversal of it; and it is as impossible as it is immaterial to determine the relative shares which these two co-operating principles take in bringing about the observed results. But where organisms in a state of domestication are concerned, the importance of the question before us is very great. For if the cessation of selection alone is capable of reducing an organ through 10 or 12 per cent. of its original size, nearly all the direct evidence on which Darwin relied in favour of use-inheritance is destroyed. On the other hand, if reduction through 5 per cent. be deemed a "very liberal estimate" of what this principle can accomplish, the whole body of Darwin's direct evidence remains as he left it. I have now given my reasons for rejecting this lower estimate on the one band, and what seems to me the extravagant estimate of Weismann on the other. But my own intermediate estimate is enough to destroy the apparent proof of use-inheritance that was given by Darwin. Therefore it remains for those who deny Lamarckian principles, either to accept some such estimate, or else to acknowledge the incompatibility of any lower one with the opinion that there is no evidence in favour of these principles.

APPENDIX II
On Characters as Adaptive and Specific.

It is the object of this Appendix to state, more fully than in the text, the opinions with regard to this subject which have been published by the two highest authorities on the theory of natural selection—Darwin and Professor Huxley. I will take first the opinion of Professor Huxley, quoted *in extenso*, and then consider it somewhat more carefully than seemed necessary in the text.

As far as I am aware, the only occasion on which Professor Huxley has alluded to the subject in question, is in his obituary notice of Darwin in the *Proceedings of the Royal Society*, Vol. XLIV, No. 269, p. xviii. The allusion is to my paper on *Physiological Selection*, in the *Journal of the Linnæan Society*, Zool. Vol. XIX, pp. 337-411. But it will be observed that the criticism has no reference to the theory which it is the object of that paper to set forth. It refers only to my definition of the theory of natural selection as primarily a theory of the origin, or cumulative development, of adaptations. This criticism, together with my answer thereto at the time, is conveyed in the following words.

> "Every variety which is selected into a species is favoured and preserved in consequence of being, in some one or more respects, better adapted to its surroundings than its rivals. In other words, every species which exists, exists in virtue of adaptation, and whatever accounts for that adaptation accounts for the existence of the species. To say that Darwin has put forward a theory of the adaptation of species, but not of their origin, is therefore to misunderstand the first principles of the theory. For, as has been pointed out, it is a necessary consequence of the theory of selection that every species must have some one or more structural or functional peculiarities, in virtue of the advantage conferred by which it has fought through the crowd of its competitors, and achieved a certain duration. In this sense, it is true that every species has been 'originated' by selection."

> Now, in the first place, I have nowhere said that "Darwin has put forward a theory of the adaptation of species, but not of their origin." I said, and continue to say, that he has put forward a theory of *adaptations in*

general, and that where such adaptations appertain to species only (i.e. are peculiar to particular species), the theory becomes "*also* a theory of the origin of the species which present them." The only possible misunderstanding, therefore, which can here be alleged against me is, that I fail to perceive it as a "necessary consequence of the theory of selection that *every* species *must* have some one or more structural or functional *peculiarities*" of an adaptive or utilitarian kind. Now, if this is a misunderstanding, I must confess to not having had it removed by Mr. Huxley's exposition.

The whole criticism is tersely conveyed in the form of two sequent propositions—namely, "Every species which exists, exists in virtue of adaptation; and whatever accounts for that adaptation accounts for the existence of the species." My answer is likewise two-fold. First, I do not accept the premiss; and next, even if I did, I can show that the resulting conclusion would not overturn my definition. Let us consider these two points separately, beginning with the latter, as the one which may be most briefly disposed of.

I. Provisionally conceding that "every species which exists, exists in virtue of adaptation," I maintain that my definition of the theory of natural selection still holds good. For even on the basis of this concession, or on the ground of this assumption, the theory of natural selection is not shown to be "*primarily*" a theory of the origin of species. It follows, indeed, from the assumption—is, in fact, part and parcel of the assumption—that all species have been originated by natural selection; but why? *Only because natural selection has originated those particular adaptive features in virtue of which (by the hypothesis) species exist as species.* It is only in virtue of having created these features that natural selection has created the species presenting them—just as it has created genera, families, orders, &c., in virtue of *other* adaptive features extending through progressively wider areas of taxonomic division. Everywhere and equally this principle has been "primarily" engaged in the evolution of adaptations, and if one result of its work has been that of enabling the systematist to trace lines of genetic descent under his divisions of species, genera, and the rest, such a result is but "secondary" or "incidental."

In short, it is "*primarily*" a theory of adaptations *wherever these occur*, and only becomes "*also*" or "*incidentally*" a theory of species in cases where adaptations happen to be restricted in their occurrence to organic types of a certain order of taxonomic division.

II. Hitherto, for the sake of argument, I have conceded that, in the words of my critic, "it is a necessary consequence of the theory of selection that every species must have some one or more structural or functional peculiarities" of an adaptive kind. But now I will endeavour to show that this statement does not "follow as a necessary consequence" from "the theory of selection."

Most obviously "it follows" from the theory of selection that "every variety which is selected into a species is favoured and preserved in consequence of being, in some one or more respects, better adapted to its surroundings than its rivals." This, in fact, is no more than a re-statement of the theory itself. But it does *not* follow that "every species which exists, exists in virtue of adaptation" *peculiar to that species*; i.e. that every species which exists, exists *in virtue of having been* "*selected*." This may or may not be true as a matter of fact: as a matter of logic, the inference is not deducible from the selection theory. Every variety which is "*selected into*" a species must, indeed, present some such peculiar advantage; but this is by no means equivalent to saying, "in other words," that every variety which *becomes* a species must do so. For the latter statement imports a completely new assumption—namely, that every variety which *becomes* a species must do so because it has been "*selected into*" a species. In short, what we are here told is, that if we believe the selection principle to have given origin to some species, we must further believe, "as a necessary consequence," that it has given origin to all species.

The above reply, which is here quoted *verbatim* from *Nature*, Vol. 38, p. 616-18, proceeded to show that it does not belong to "the first principles of the theory of natural selection" to deny that no other cause than natural selection can possibly be concerned in the origin of species; and facts were given to prove that such unquestionably has been the case as regards the origin of "local" or "permanent" *varieties*. Yet such varieties are what Darwin correctly terms "incipient" species, or species in process of taking *origin*. Therefore, if Professor Huxley's criticism is to stand at all, we must accept it "as a necessary consequence of the theory of selection," that every such *variety* "which exists, exists in virtue of adaptation"—a statement which is *proved* to be untrue by the particular cases forthwith cited. But as this point has been dealt with much more fully in the text of the present treatise, I shall sum up the main points in a few words.

The criticism is all embodied in two propositions—namely, (*a*) that the theory of natural selection carries with it, as a "necessary consequence," the doctrine that survival of the fittest has been the cause of the origin of *all* species; and (*b*) that therefore it amounts to one and the same thing whether we define the theory as a theory of species or as a theory of adaptations. Now, as a mere matter of logical statement, it appears to me that both these propositions are unsound. As regards the first, if we hold with Darwin that other causes have co-operated with natural selection in the origination of some (i. e. many) species, it is clearly no part of the theory of natural selection to assume that none of these causes can ever have acted independently. In point of fact, as we have seen in the foregoing chapters, such has probably and frequently been the case under the influences of isolation, climate, food, sexual selection, and laws of growth; but I may here adduce some further remarks with regard to yet another possible cause. If the Lamarckian principles are valid at all, no reason can be shown why in some cases they may not have been competent *of themselves* to induce morphological changes of type by successive increments, until a transmutation of species is effected by their action alone—as, indeed, Weismann believes to have been the case with all the species of Protozoa[148]. That such actually has often been the case also with numberless species of Metozoa, is the belief of the neo-Lamarckians; and whether they are right or wrong in holding this belief, it is equally certain that, *as a matter of logical reasoning*, they are not compelled by it to profess any *disbelief* in the agency of natural selection. They may be mistaken as to the facts, as Darwin in a lesser degree may have been similarly mistaken; but just as Darwin has nowhere committed himself to the statement that *all* species must *necessarily* have been originated by natural selection, so these neo-Lamarckians are perfectly logical in holding that *some* species may have been wholly caused by the inheritance of acquired characters, as *other* species may have been wholly caused by the natural selection of congenital characters. In short, unless we begin by assuming (with Wallace and against Darwin) that there *can be no other cause* of the origin of species than that which is furnished by natural selection, we have no basis for Professor Huxley's statement "that every species has been originated by selection"; while, if we do set out with this assumption, we end in a mere tautology.

What ought to be done is to prove the validity of this assumption; but, as Professor Huxley makes no attempt to do this, his criticism amounts to mere begging of the question.

And now, as regards the second point (*b*), even if we grant the assumption that natural selection is the only possible cause of the origin of species—or, which is the same thing, that every species has been originated by natural selection,—is it likewise the same thing whether we define the theory of natural selection as a theory of species or as a theory of adaptations? Professor Huxley's criticism endeavours to show that it is; but a little consideration is enough to show that it is not. What does follow from the assumption is, that, *so far as specific characters are concerned*, it is one and the same thing to say that the theory is a theory of species, and to say that it is a theory of adaptations. But specific characters are not conterminous with adaptive characters; for innumerable adaptive characters are not distinctive of species, but of genera, families, orders, classes, and sub-kingdoms. Therefore, if it is believed (as, of course, Professor Huxley believes) that the theory in question explains the evolution of all adaptive characters, obviously it is not one and the same thing to define it indifferently as a theory of species or as a theory of adaptations.

Now, all this is not merely a matter of logic chopping. On the contrary, the question whether we are to accept or to reject the deduction that all species must necessarily have owed their origin to natural selection, is a question of no small importance to the general theory of evolution. And our answer to this question must be determined by that which we give to the ulterior question—Is the theory of natural selection to be defined as a theory of species, or as a theory of adaptations?

We now pass on to our consideration of Darwin's opinion touching the question, as stated by himself,—"The doctrine of utility, how far true?" As I cannot ascertain that Darwin has anywhere expressed an opinion as to whether natural selection has been necessarily concerned in the origin of all *species*, the issue here is as to whether he held this with regard to all *specific characters*. It will be remembered that while opposing this doctrine as erroneous both in logic and in fact, I have represented that it is not a doctrine which Darwin sanctioned; but, on the contrary, that it is one which he expressly failed to sanction, by recognizing the frequent inutility of specific characters. Mr. Wallace, on the other hand, alleges that Darwin did believe in the universal—as distinguished from the general—utility of such characters. And he adds that he has "looked in vain in Mr. Darwin's works" for any justification of my statements to the contrary[149]. Therefore I will endeavour to show that Mr. Wallace's search has not been a very careful one.

We must remember, however, that it was not until the appearance of my paper on *Physiological Selection*, four years after Darwin's death, that the question now in debate was raised. Consequently, he never had occasion to deal expressly with this particular question—viz. whether "the doctrine of utility" has any *peculiar* reference to *specific* characters—as he surely would have done had he entertained the important distinction between specific and all other characters which Mr. Wallace now alleges that he did entertain. But, be this as it may, we cannot expect to find in Darwin's writings any express allusion to a question which had not been raised until 1886. The most we can expect to find are scattered sentences which prove that the distinction in question was never so much as present to his mind,—i. e. never occurred to him as even a possible distinction.

I will first take the passages which Mr. Wallace himself supplies from among those which I had previously indicated.

> "But when, from the nature of the organism and of the conditions, modifications have been induced which are unimportant for the welfare of the *species*, they may be, and apparently often have been, transmitted in nearly the same state to numerous, otherwise modified, descendants[150]."

On this passage Mr. Wallace remarks that the last five words "clearly show that such characters are usually not 'specific,' in the sense that they are such as distinguish species from one another, but are found in numerous allied species." But I cannot see that the passage shows anything of the sort. What to my mind it does show is, (*a*) that Mr. Darwin repudiated Mr. Wallace's doctrine touching the *necessary* utility of *all* specific characters: (*b*) that he takes for granted the contrary doctrine touching the inutility of *some* specific characters: (*c*) that without in this place alluding to the proportional number of useless specific characters, he refers their origin in some cases to "the nature of the organism" (i.e. "spontaneous variability" due to internal causes), and in other cases to "the conditions" (i.e. variability induced by external causes): (*d*) that when established as a specific character by heredity, such a useless character was held by him not to tend to become obsolete by the influence of natural selection or any other cause; but, on the contrary, to be "transmitted in nearly the same state to numerous, otherwise modified, descendants"—or progeny of the species in genera, families, &c.: (*e*) and, therefore, that useless characters which are now distinctive of genera, families, &c., were held by him frequently, if not usually, to point to uselessness of origin, when first they arose as merely specific characters. Even the meaning which Mr. Wallace reads into this passage must imply every one of these points; and therefore I do not see that he gains much by apparently seeking to add this further meaning—viz. that in Darwin's opinion there must have been some unassignable reason preventing the occurrence of useless specific characters in cases where species are *not* destined to become the parents of genera.

Moreover, any such meaning is out of accordance with the context from which the passage is taken. For, after a long consideration of the question of utility, Darwin sums up,—"We thus see that with plants many morphological changes may be attributed to the laws of growth and the interaction of parts, *independently of natural selection.*" And then he adds,— "From the fact of the above characters being *unimportant for the welfare of the species,* any slight variations which occurred in them *would not have been augmented through natural selection.*" Again, still within the same passage, he says, while alluding to the causes other than natural selection which lead to changes of specific characters,—"If the *unknown cause* were to act almost uniformly for a length of time, we may infer that the result would be almost uniform; and in this case *all* the individuals of the *species* would be modified in the same manner." For my own part I do not understand how Mr. Wallace can have overlooked these various references to *species*, all of which occur on the very page from which he is quoting. The whole argument is to show that "many morphological changes may be attributed to the laws of growth and the inter-action of parts [*plus* external conditions of life], independently of natural selection"; that such non-adaptive changes, when they occur as "specific characters," may, if the species should afterwards give rise to genera, families, &c., become distinctive of these higher divisions. But there is nothing here, or in any other part of Darwin's writings, to countenance the inconsistent notion which Mr. Wallace appears to entertain,—viz. that species which present useless characters are more apt to give rise to genera, families, &c., than are species which do not present such characters.

The next passage which Mr. Wallace quotes, with his comments thereon, is as follows. The italics are his.

> "'Thus a large yet undefined extension may safely be given to the direct and indirect results of natural selection; but I now admit, after reading the essay of Nägeli on plants, and the remarks by various authors with respect to animals, more especially those recently made by Professor Broca, that in the earlier editions of my Origin of Species I perhaps attributed too much to the action of natural selection, or the survival of the fittest. I have altered the fifth edition of the Origin so as to confine my remarks to adaptive changes of structure; *but I am convinced, from the light gained during even the last few years, that very many structures which now appear to be useless, will hereafter be proved to be useful, and will therefore come within the range of natural selection.*

Nevertheless I did not formerly consider sufficiently the existence of structures which, as far as we can at present judge, are neither beneficial nor injurious; and this I believe to be one of the greatest oversights as yet detected in my work.'

Now it is to be remarked that neither in these passages nor in any of the other less distinct expressions of opinion on this question, does Darwin ever admit that "specific characters"—that is, the particular characters which serve to distinguish one species from another—are ever useless, much less that "a large proportion of them" are so, as Mr. Romanes makes him "freely acknowledge." On the other hand, in the passage which I have italicised he strongly expresses his view that much of what we suppose to be useless is due to our ignorance; and as I hold myself that, as regards many of the supposed useless characters, this is the true explanation, it may be well to give a brief sketch of the progress of knowledge in transferring characters from the one category to the other[151]."

It is needless to continue this quotation, because of course no one is disputing that an enormous number of specific characters whose utility is unknown are nevertheless useful, and therefore due to natural selection. In other words, the question is not—Are there not many useful specific characters whose utility is unknown? but—Does it follow from the theory of natural selection that all specific characters must necessarily be useful? Well, it appears to me that without going further than the above passage, which Mr. Wallace has quoted, we can see clearly enough what was Darwin's opinion upon the subject. He did not believe that it followed *deductively* from his theory that all specific characters must necessarily be useful; and therefore he regarded it as a question of *fact*—to be determined by induction as distinguished from deduction—in what proportional number of cases they are so. Moreover he gives it as his more matured opinion, that, "as far as we can at present judge" (i.e. from the present state of observation upon the subject: if, with Mr. Wallace, his judgement were *a priori*, why this qualification?), he had not previously sufficiently considered the existence of non-adaptive characters—and this he ended by believing was one of the greatest oversights as yet detected in his work. To me it has always seemed that this passage is one of the greatest exhibitions of candour, combined with solidity of judgement, that is to be met with even in the writings of Darwin. There is no talk about any deductive "necessity"; but a perfect readiness to allow that causes other than natural selection may have been at work in evoking non-adaptive characters, so that the fifth edition of the *Origin of Species* was altered in order to confine the theory of natural selection to "adaptive changes"—i.e. to constitute it, as I have said in other words, "a theory of the origin, or cumulative development, of *adaptations*."

If to this it be said that in the above passage there is no special mention of *species*, the quibble would admit of a three-fold reply. In the first place, the quibble in question had never been raised. As already stated, it is only since the appearance of my own paper on *Physiological Selection* that anybody ever thought of drawing a distinction between species and genera, such that while all specific characters must be held necessarily useful, no such necessity extends to generic characters. In the second place, that Darwin must have had specific characters (as well as generic) in his mind when writing the above passage, is rendered unquestionable by the fact that many of the instances of inutility adduced by Nägeli and Broca have reference to specific characters. Lastly, as shown in the passages previously quoted from the sixth edition of the *Origin of Species*, Darwin attributed the origin of useless generic characters to useless specific characters; so that Mr. Wallace really gains nothing by his remark that specific characters are not specially mentioned in the present passage.

Once more:—

> "Darwin's latest expression of opinion on this question is interesting, since it shows he was inclined to return to his earlier view of the general, or universal, utility of specific characters[152]."

This "latest expression of opinion," as I shall immediately prove, shows nothing of the kind—being, in fact, a mere re-statement of the opinion everywhere and at all times expressed by Darwin, touching the caution that must be observed in deciding, *with respect to individual cases*, whether an apparently useless specific character is to be regarded as really useless. Moreover, at no time and in no place did Darwin entertain any "view of the general, or universal, utility of specific characters." But the point now is, that if (as was the case) Darwin "inclined" to depart more and more from his earlier view of the highly *general* utility of specific characters; and if (as was not the case) he ended by showing an inclination "*to return*" to this earlier view; what becomes of the whole of Mr. Wallace's contention against which this Appendix is directed, namely, *that Darwin never entertained any other view than that of the "general, or universal, utility of specific characters"*?

The "latest expression of opinion" which Mr. Wallace quotes, occurs in a letter written to Professor Semper in 1878. It is as follows:—

"As our knowledge advances, very slight differences, considered by systematists as of no importance in structure, are continually found to be functionally important; and I have been especially struck with this fact in the case of plants, to which my observations have of late years been confined. Therefore it seems to me rather rash to consider the slight differences between representative species, for instance those inhabiting the different islands of the same archipelago, as of no functional importance, and as not in any way due to natural selection[153]."

Now, with regard to this passage it is to be observed, as already remarked, that it refers to the formation of final judgements touching *particular cases*: there is nothing to show that the writer is contemplating *general principles*, or advocating on deductive grounds the dogma that specific characters must be necessarily and universally adaptive characters. Therefore, what he here says is neither more nor less than I have said. For I have always held that it would be "rather rash" to conclude that any given cases of apparent inutility are certainly cases of real inutility, *merely on the ground that utility is not perceived*. But this is clearly quite a distinct matter from resisting the *a priori* generalization that all cases of apparent inutility must certainly be cases of real utility. And, I maintain, in every part of his writings, without any exception, where Darwin alludes to this matter of general principle, it is in terms which directly contradict the deduction in question. As the whole of this Appendix has been directed to proving that such is the case, it will now, I think, be sufficient to supply but one further quotation, in order to show that the above "latest expression of opinion," far from indicating that in his later years Darwin "inclined" to Mr. Wallace's views upon this matter, is quite compatible with a distinct "expression of opinion" to the contrary, in a letter written less than six years before his death.

"In my opinion *the greatest error which I have committed*, has been not allowing sufficient weight to the direct action of the environment, i.e. food, climate, &c., *independently of natural selection*. Modifications thus caused, *which are neither of advantage nor disadvantage to the modified organisms*, would be especially favoured, as I can now see chiefly through your observations, *by isolation in a small area, where only a few individuals lived under nearly uniform conditions*[154]."

I will now proceed to quote further passages from Darwin's works, which appear to have escaped the notice of Mr. Wallace, inasmuch as they admit of no doubt regarding the allusions being to *specific* characters.

"We may easily err in attributing importance to characters, and in believing that they have been developed through natural selection. We must by no means overlook the effects of the definite action of changed conditions of life,—of so-called spontaneous variations, which seem to depend in a quite subordinate degree on the nature of the conditions,—of the tendency to reversion to long-lost characters,—of the complex laws of growth, such as of correlation[155], compensation, of pressure of one part on another, &c., and finally of sexual selection, by which characters of use to one sex are often gained and then transmitted more or less perfectly to the other sex, though of no use to this sex. But structures thus indirectly gained, *although at first of no advantage to a species,* may subsequently have been taken advantage of by its modified descendants, under new conditions of life and newly acquired habits[156]."

It appeared—and still appears—to me, that where so many causes are expressly assigned as producing useless *specific* characters, and that some of them (such as climatic influences and independent variability) must be highly general in their action, I was justified in representing it as Darwin's opinion that "a large proportional number of specific characters" are useless to the *species* presenting them, although afterwards they may sometimes become of use to genera, families, &c. Moreover, this passage goes on to point out that specific characters which at first sight appear to be obviously useful, are sometimes found by fuller knowledge to be really useless—a consideration which is the exact inverse of the argument from ignorance as used by Mr. Wallace, and serves still further to show that in Darwin's opinion utility is by no means an invariable, still less a "necessary," mark of specific character. The following are some of the instances which he gives.

"The sutures in the skulls of young mammals have been advanced as a beautiful adaptation for aiding parturition, and no doubt they may facilitate, or be indispensable for this act; but as sutures occur in the skulls of young birds and reptiles, which have only to escape from a broken egg, we may infer that this structure has *arisen from the laws of growth,* and has been taken advantage of in the parturition of the higher animals[157]."

"The naked skin on the head of a vulture is generally considered as a direct adaptation for wallowing in putridity; and so it may be, *or it may possibly be due to the direct action of the putrid matter,* but we should be very cautious in drawing any such inference [i.e. as to utility] when we see the skin on the head of the clean-feeding male Turkey is likewise naked[158]."

Similarly, in the *Descent of Man* it is said:—

"Variations of the same *general* nature have *often been taken advantage of* and accumulated through sexual selection in relation to the propagation of the species, and through natural selection in relation to the general purposes of life. Hence, *secondary sexual characters, when equally transmitted to both sexes, can be distinguished from ordinary specific characters, only by the light of analogy.* The modifications acquired through sexual selection are often so strongly pronounced that the two sexes have frequently been ranked as distinct species, or even as distinct genera[159]."

As Mr. Wallace does not recognize sexual selection, he incurs the burden of proving utility (in the life-preserving sense) in all these "frequently" occurring cases where there are such "strongly pronounced modifications," and we have already seen in the text his manner of dealing with this burden. But the point here is, that whether or not we accept the theory of sexual selection, we must accept it as Darwin's opinion—first, that in their beginnings, as *specific* characters, these sexual modifications were often of a merely "*general nature*" (or without reference to utility even in the life-embellishing sense), and only *afterwards* "have often been taken advantage of and accumulated through *sexual* selection": and, secondly, that "we know they have been acquired in some instances *at the cost not only of inconvenience, but of exposure to actual dangers*[160]."

We may now pass on to some further, and even stronger, expressions of opinion with regard to the frequent inutility of *specific* characters.

"I have made these remarks only to show that, if we are unable to account for the characteristic differences of our several domestic breeds, which nevertheless are generally admitted to have arisen through ordinary generation from one or a few parent stocks, we ought not to lay too much stress on our ignorance of the precise cause [i.e. whether natural selection or some other cause] of the slight analogous differences between true *species*.... I fully admit that *many* structures are now of no use to their possessors, and may never have been of any use to their progenitors; but this does not prove that they were formed solely for beauty or variety. No doubt the definite action of changed conditions, and the various causes of modification, lately specified, have all produced an effect, *probably a great effect, independently of any advantage thus gained....* It is scarcely possible to decide how much allowance ought to be made for such causes of change, as the definite action of external conditions, so-called spontaneous variations, and the complex laws of growth; but, *with these important exceptions,* we may conclude that the structure of every living creature either now is, or formerly was, of some direct or indirect use to its possessor[161]."

Here again, if we remember how "important" these "exceptions" are, I cannot understand any one doubting Darwin's opinion to have been that a large proportional number of specific characters are useless. For that it is "species" which he here has mainly in his mind is evident from what he says when again alluding to the subject in his "Summary of the Chapter"— namely, "In *many* other cases [i.e. in cases where natural selection has not been concerned] modifications are probably the direct result of the laws of variation or of growth, independently of any good having been thus gained." Now, not only do these "laws" apply as much to species as they do to genera; "but," the passage goes on to say, "even such structures have often, we may feel assured, been subsequently taken advantage of, and still further modified, for the good of *species* under new conditions of life." Obviously, therefore, the inutility in such cases is taken to have been prior to any utility subsequently acquired; and genera are not historically prior to the species in which they originate.

Here is another quotation:—

"Thus, as I am inclined to believe, morphological differences, which we consider as important—such as the arrangement of the leaves, the divisions of the flower or of the ovarium, the position of the ovules, &c.—*first* appeared in *many* cases as *fluctuating variations,* which sooner or later became constant through the nature of the organism and of the surrounding conditions, as well as through the intercrossing of distinct individuals, *but not through natural selection;* for as these morphological characters do not affect the welfare of the *species,* any slight deviations in them could not have been governed or accumulated through this latter agency. It is a strange result which we thus arrive at, namely, that characters of slight vital importance to the *species,* are the most important to the systematist; but, as we shall hereafter see when we treat of the genetic principle of classification, this is by no means so paradoxical as it may at first appear[162]."

Clearly the view here expressed is that characters which are now distinctive of higher taxonomic divisions "first appeared" in the parent species of such divisions; for not only would it be unreasonable to attribute the rise and preservation of useless characters to "fluctuating variations" affecting a number of species or genera similarly and simultaneously; but it would be impossible that, if such were the case, they could be rendered "constant through the nature of the organism and of the surrounding conditions, as well as through the intercrossing of distinct individuals[163]."

Here is another passage to the same general effect. In alluding to the objection from inutility as advanced by Bronn, Broca, and Nägeli, Mr. Darwin says:—"There is much force in the above objection"; and, after again pointing out the important possibility in any particular cases of hidden or former use, and the action of the laws of growth, he goes on to say,—"In the third place, we have to allow for the direct and definite action of changed conditions of life, and for so-called spontaneous variations, in which the nature of the conditions plays quite a subordinate part[164]." Elsewhere he says,—"It appears that I formerly underrated the frequency and value of these latter forms of variation as leading to permanent modifications of structure *independently of natural selection*[165]." The "forms of variation" to which he here alludes are "variations which seem to us in our ignorance to arise spontaneously"; and it is evident that such variations cannot well "arise" in two or more species of a genus similarly and simultaneously, so as independently to lead "to permanent modifications of structure" in two or more parallel lines. It is further evident that by "spontaneous variations" Darwin alludes to extreme cases of spontaneous departure from the general average of specific characters; and therefore that lesser or more ordinary departures must be of still greater "frequency."

Again, speaking of the principles of classification, Darwin writes:—

"We care not how trifling a character may be—let it be the mere inflection of the angle of the jaw, the manner in which an insect's wing is folded, whether the skin be covered by hair or feathers—if it prevail throughout many and different species, especially those having very different habits of life, it assumes high value [i.e. for purposes of classification]; for we can account for its presence in so many forms with such *different habits*, only by inheritance from a common parent. We may err in this respect in regard to single points of structure, but when several characters, let them be ever so trifling, concur throughout a large group of beings *having different habits*, we may feel almost sure, on the theory of descent, that these characters have been inherited from a common ancestor; and we know that such aggregated characters have especial value in classification[166]."

Now it is evident that this argument for the general theory of evolution would be destroyed, if Wallace's assumption of utility of specific characters as universal were to be entertained. And the fact of apparently "trifling" characters occurring throughout a large group of beings "having different habits" is proof that they are really trifling, or without utilitarian significance.

It is needless to multiply these quotations, for it appears to me that the above are amply sufficient to establish the only point with which we are here concerned, namely, that Darwin's opinion on the subject of utility in relation to specific characters was substantially identical with my own. And this is established, not merely by the literal meaning of the sundry passages here gathered together from different parts of his writings; but likewise, and perhaps still more, from the tone of thought which pervades these writings as a whole. It requires no words of mine to show that the literal meaning of the above quotations is entirely opposed to Mr. Wallace's view touching the *necessary* utility of *all* specific characters; but upon the other point—or the general tone of Mr. Darwin's thought regarding such topics—it may be well to add two remarks.

In the first place, it must be evident that so soon as we cease to be bound by any *a priori* deduction as to natural selection being "the exclusive means of modifications," it ceases to be a matter of much concern to the theory of natural selection in what proportion other means of modification have been at work—especially when non-adaptive modifications are concerned, and where these have reference to merely "specific characters," or modifications of the most incipient kind, least generally diffused among organic types, and representing the incidence of causes of less importance than any others in the process of organic evolution considered as a whole. Consequently, in the second place, we find that Darwin nowhere displays any solicitude touching the proportional number of specific characters that may eventually prove to be due to causes other than natural selection. He takes a much wider and deeper view of organic evolution, and, having entirely emancipated himself from the former conception of species as the organic units, sees virtually no significance in specific characters, except in so far as they are also adaptive characters.

Such, at all events, appears to me the obvious interpretation of his writings when these are carefully read with a view to ascertaining his ideas upon "Utilitarian doctrine: how far true." And I make these remarks because it has been laid to my charge, that in quoting such passages as the above I have been putting "a strained interpretation" upon Darwin's utterances: "such admissions," it is said, "Mr. Romanes appears to me to treat as if wrung from a hostile witness[167]." But, from what has gone before, it ought to be apparent that I take precisely the opposite view to that here imputed. Far from deeming these and similar passages as "admissions wrung from a hostile witness," and far from seeking to put any "strained interpretation" upon them, I believe that they are but the plain and unequivocal expressions of an opinion which I have always understood that Darwin held. And if any one has been led to think otherwise, I throw back this charge of "strained interpretation," by challenging such a person to adduce a single quotation from any part of Darwin's works, which can possibly be held to indicate that he regarded passages like those above quoted as in any way out of conformity with his theory of natural selection—or as put forward merely to "admit the possibility of explanations, to which really, however, he did not attach much importance." To the best of my judgement it is only some bias in favour of Mr. Wallace's views that can lead a naturalist to view in this way the clear and consistent expression of Darwin's.

That Mr. Wallace himself should be biassed in this matter might, perhaps, be expected. After rendering the following very unequivocal passage from the *Origin of Species* (p. 72)—"There can be little doubt that the tendency to vary in the same manner has often been so strong, *that all individuals of the same species have been similarly modified without the aid of any form of selection*"—Mr. Wallace says, "But no proof whatever is offered of this statement, and it is so entirely opposed to all we know of the facts of variation as given by Darwin himself, that the important word 'all' is probably an oversight." But, if Mr. Wallace had read the very next sentence he would have seen that here the important word "all" could not *possibly* have been "an oversight." For the passage continues,—"Or only a third, fifth, or tenth part of the individuals may have been thus affected, of which fact several instances could be given. Thus Graba estimates that about one-fifth of the guillemots in the Faroe Islands consist of a variety so well marked, that it was formerly ranked as a distinct species under the name of Uria lacrymans." And even if this passage had not been thus specially concerned with the question of the *proportion* in which "*individuals of the same species have been similarly modified without the aid of any form of selection*" the oversight with respect to "the important word 'all'" would still have remained an oversight of a recurrent character, as the following additional quotations from other parts of Darwin's writings may perhaps render apparent.

> "There must be some efficient cause for each slight individual difference, as well as for more strongly marked variations which occasionally arise; and if the unknown cause were to act persistently, it is almost certain that *all* the individuals of the *species* would be similarly modified[168]."

> "The acquisition of a useless part can hardly be said to raise an organism in the natural scale.... We are so ignorant of the exciting cause of the above specified modifications; but if the unknown cause were to act almost uniformly for a length of time, we may infer that the result would be almost uniform; and in this case *all* the individuals of the *species* would be modified in the same manner[169]."

Moreover, when dealing even with such comparatively slight changes as occur between our domesticated varieties—and which, *a fortiori*, are less likely to become "stable" through the uniform operation of causes other than selection, seeing that they are not only smaller in amount than occurs among natural species, but also have had but a comparatively short time in which to accumulate—Darwin is emphatic in his assertion of the same principles. For instance, in the twenty-third chapter of the *Variation of Plants and Animals under Domestication*, he repeatedly uses the term "definite action of external conditions," and begins the chapter by explaining his use of the term thus:—

> "By the term definite action, as used in this chapter, I mean an action of such a nature that, when many individuals of the same variety are exposed during several generations to any change in their physical conditions of life, *all*, or *nearly all*, the individuals are modified in the same manner. A new *sub-variety* would thus be produced *without the aid of selection*[170]."

As an example of the special instances that he gives, I may quote the following from the same work:—

> "Each of the endless variations which we see in the plumage of our fowls must have had some efficient cause; and if the same cause were to act uniformly during a long series of generations on many individuals, *all* probably would be modified in the same manner."

And, as instances of his more general statements in Chapter XXIII, these may suffice:—

> "The direct action of the conditions of life, whether leading to definite or indefinite results, *is a totally distinct consideration from the effects of natural selection*.... The direct and definite action of changed conditions, in contradistinction to the accumulation of indefinite variations, *seems to me so important* that I will give a large additional body of miscellaneous facts[171]."

Then, after giving these facts, and showing how in the case of species in a state of nature it is often impossible to decide how much we are to attribute to natural selection and how much to the definite action of changed conditions, he begins his general summary of the chapter thus:—

> "There can be no doubt, from the facts given in the early part of this chapter, that extremely slight changes in the conditions of life sometimes act in a definite manner on our already variable domesticated productions [productions, therefore, with regard to which uniformity and 'stability' of modification are least likely to arise]; and, as the action Of changed conditions in causing general or indefinite variability is accumulative, so it may be with their definite action. Hence it is possible that *great* and *definite* modifications of structure may result from altered conditions acting during a long series of generations. In some few instances a marked effect has been produced quickly on *all*, or *nearly all*, the individuals which have been exposed to some considerable change of climate, food, or other circumstance[172]."

Once more, in order to show that he retained these views to the end of his life, I may quote a passage from the second edition of the *Descent of Man*, which is the latest expression of his opinion upon these points:—

> "Each of the endless diversities in plumage, which we see in our domesticated birds, is, of course, the result of some definite cause; and under natural and more uniform conditions, some one tint, *assuming that it was in no way injurious, would almost certainly sooner or later prevail*. The free-intercrossing of the many individuals belonging to the same species would ultimately tend to make any change of colour thus induced *uniform in character*.... Can we believe that the very slight differences in tints and markings between, for instance, the female black-grouse and red-

grouse serve as a protection? Are partridges as they are now coloured, better protected than if they had resembled quails? Do the slight differences between the females of the common pheasant, the Japan and golden pheasants, serve as a protection, or might not their plumage have been interchanged with impunity? From what Mr. Wallace has observed of the habits of certain gallinaceous birds in the East, he thinks that such slight differences are beneficial. For myself, I will only say, I am not convinced[173]."

Yet "convinced" he certainly must have been on merely *a priori* grounds, had he countenanced Mr. Wallace's reasoning from the general theory of natural selection; and the fact that he here fails to be convinced even by "what Mr. Wallace has observed of the habits of certain gallinaceous birds," appears to indicate that he had considered the question of utility with special reference to Mr. Wallace's opinion. That opinion was then, as now, the avowed result of a theoretical prepossession; and this prepossession, as the above quotations sufficiently show, was expressly repudiated by Darwin.

Lastly, this is not the only occasion on which Darwin expressly repudiates Mr. Wallace's opinion on the point in question. For it is notorious that these co-authors of the theory of natural selection have expressed divergent opinions concerning the origin by natural selection of the most general of all specific characters—cross-sterility. Although allowing that cross-sterility between allied species may be of adaptive value in "keeping incipient species from blending," Darwin persistently refused to be influenced by Wallace's belief that it is due to natural selection; i.e. the belief on which alone can be founded the "necessary deduction" with which we have been throughout concerned.

NOTE A TO PAGE 57.

I think it is desirable here to adduce one or two concrete illustrations of these abstract principles, in order to show how, as a matter of fact, the structure of Weismann's theory is such as to preclude the possibility of its assumptions being disproved—and this even supposing that the theory is false.

At first sight nothing could seem more conclusive on the side of Darwinian or Lamarckian principles than are the facts of hereditary disease, in cases where the disease has unquestionably been acquired by the parents. Take, for example, the case of gout. Here there is no suspicion of any microbe being concerned, nor is there any question about the fact of the disease being one which is frequently acquired by certain habits of life. Now, suppose the case of a man who in middle age acquires the gout by these habits of life—such as insufficient exercise, over-sufficient food, and free indulgence in wine. His son inherits the gouty diathesis, and even though the boy may have the fear of gout before his eyes, and consequently avoid over-eating and alcoholic drinking, &c., the disease may overtake him also. Well, the natural explanation of all this is, that the sins of the fathers descend upon the children; that gout acquired may become in the next generation gout transmitted. But, on the other hand, the school of Weismann will maintain that the reason why the parent contracted the gout was because he had a congenital, or "blastogenetic," tendency towards that disease—a tendency which may, indeed, have been intensified by his habits of life, but which, in so far as thus intensified, was not transmitted to his offspring. All that was so transmitted was the congenital tendency; and all that is proved by such cases as those above supposed, where the offspring of gouty parents become gouty notwithstanding their abstemious habits, is that in such offspring the congenital tendency is even more pronounced than it was in their parents, and therefore did not require so much inducement in the way of unguarded living to bring it out. Now, here again, without waiting to consider the relative probabilities of these two opposing explanations, it is enough for the purposes of the illustration to remark that it is obviously impossible to disprove either by means of the other, or by any class of facts to which they may severally appeal.

I will give only one further example to show the elusiveness of Weismann's theory, and the consequent impossibility of finding any cases in nature which will satisfy the conditions of proof which the theory imposes. In one of his papers Weismann says that if there be any truth in the Lamarckian doctrine of the transmission of acquired characters, it ought to follow that the human infant should speak by instinct. For, ever since man became human he has presumably been a talking animal: at any rate it is certain that he has been so for an innumerable number of generations. Therefore, by this time the faculty of language ought to have been so deeply impressed upon the psychology of the species, that there ought to be no need to teach the young child its use of language; and the fact that there is such need is taken by Weismann to constitute good evidence in proof of the non-transmissibility of individually acquired characters. Or, to quote his own words, "it has never yet been found that a child could read of itself, although its parents had throughout their whole lives practised this art. Not even are our children able to talk of their own accord; yet not only have their parents, but, more than that, an infinitely long line of ancestors have never ceased to drill their brains and to perfect their organs of speech.... From this alone we may be disposed to doubt whether acquired capabilities in the true sense can ever be transmitted." Well, in answer to this particular case, we have first of all to remark that the construction of even the simplest language is, psychologically considered, a matter of such enormous complexity, that there is no real analogy between it and the phenomena of instinct: therefore the fact that Lamarckian principles cannot be applied to the case of language is no evidence that they do not hold good as regards instinct. Secondly, not only the construction, but still more the use of language is quite out of analogy with all the phenomena of instinct; for, in order to use, or speak, a language, the mind must already be that of a thinking agent; and therefore to expect that language should be instinctive is tantamount to expecting that the thought of which it is the vehicle should be instinctive—i.e. that human parents should transmit the whole organization of their own intellectual experiences to their unborn children. Thirdly, even neglecting these considerations, we have to remember that language has been itself the product of an immensely long course of evolution; so that even if it were reasonable to expect that a child should speak by instinct without instruction, it would be necessary further to expect that the child should begin by speaking in some score or two of unknown tongues before it arrived at the one which alone its parents could understand. Probably these considerations are enough to show how absurd is the suggestion that Darwinians ought to expect children to speak by instinct. But, now, although it is for these reasons preposterous under any theory of evolution to expect that children should be able to use a fully developed language without instruction, it is by no means so preposterous to expect that, if all languages present any one simple set of features in common, these features might by this time have grown to be instinctive; for these simple features, being common to all languages, must have been constantly and forcibly impressed upon the structure of human psychology throughout an innumerable number of sequent generations. Now, there is only one set of features common to all languages; and this comprises the combinations of vowel and consonantal sounds, which go to constitute what we know as articulate syllables. And, is it not the case that these particular features, thus common to all languages, as a matter of fact actually *are* instinctive? Long before a young child is able to understand the meanings of any words, it begins to babble articulate syllables; and I do not know that a more striking fact can be adduced at the present stage of the Weismann controversy than is this fact which he has thus himself unconsciously suggested, namely, that the young of the only talking animal should be alone in presenting—and in unmistakably presenting—the instinct of articulation. Well, such being the state of matters as regards this particular case, in the course of a debate which was held at the Newcastle meeting of the British Association upon the heredity question, I presented this case as I present it now. And subsequently I was met, as I expected to be met, by its being said that after all the faculty of making articulate sounds might have been of congenital origin. Seeing of how much importance this faculty must always have been to the human species, it may very well have been a faculty which early fell under the sway of natural selection, and so it may have become congenital. Now, be it remembered, I am only adducing this case in illustration of the elusiveness of Weismann's theory. First of all he selects the faculty of articulate speech to argue that it is a faculty which ought to be instinctive if acquired characters ever do become instinctive; and so good does he deem it as a test case between the two theories, that he says *from it alone* we should be prepared to accept the doctrine that acquired characters can never become congenital. Then, when it is shown that the only element in articulate speech which possibly could have become congenital, actually has become congenital, the answer we receive is a direct contradiction of the previous argument: the faculty originally selected as representative of an acquired character is now taken as representative of a congenital one. By thus playing fast and loose with whatever facts the followers of Darwin may adduce, the followers of Weismann bring their own position simply to this:—All characters which can be shown to be inherited we assume to be congenital, or as we term it, "blastogenetic," while all characters which can be shown not to be inherited, we assume to be acquired, or as we term it, "somatogenetic"—and this merely on the ground that they have been shown to be inherited or not inherited as the case may be. Now, there need be no objection to such assumptions, provided they are recognized as assumptions; but so long as the very question in debate has reference to their validity as assumptions, it is closely illogical to adduce them as arguments. And this is the only point with which we are at present concerned.

NOTE B TO PAGE 89.

In answer to this illustration as previously adduced by me, Mr. Poulton has objected that the benefit arising from the peculiar mode of stinging in question is a benefit conferred, not on the insect which stings, but upon its progeny. The point of the illustration however has no reference to the maternal instinct (which here, as elsewhere, I doubt not is due to natural selection); it has reference only to the particular instinct of selective stinging, which here ministers to the purposes of the other and more general instinct of rearing progeny. Given then the maternal instinct of stinging prey for the use of progeny, the question is—What first determined the ancestors of the Sphex to sting their prey only in nine particular points? Darwin's answer to this question is as follows:—

"I have been thinking about Pompilius and its allies. Please take the trouble to read on perforation of the corolla by Bees, p. 425 of my 'Cross-fertilization,' to end of chapter. Bees show so much intelligence in their acts, that it seems not improbable to me that the progenitors of Pompilius originally stung caterpillars and spiders, &c., in any part of their bodies, and then observed by their intelligence that if they stung them in one particular place, as between certain segments on the lower side, their prey was at once paralyzed. It does, not seem to me at all incredible that this action should then become instinctive, i.e. memory transmitted from one generation to another. It does not seem necessary to suppose that when Pompilius stung its prey in the ganglion it intended or knew that their prey would keep long alive. The development of the larvae may have been subsequently modified in relation to their half-dead, instead of wholly dead prey; supposing that the prey was at first quite killed, which would have required much stinging. Turn this over in your mind," &c.

Weismann, on the other hand, can only suppose that this intensely specialized instinct had its origin in fortuitous variations in the psychology of the species. But, neglecting the consideration that, in order to become fixed as an instinct by natural selection, the particular variation required must have occurred in many different individuals, not only in the first, but also in the sequent generations, the chances against its occurring only once, or in but one single individual case, are many thousands if not millions to one.

FOOTNOTES

[1] Part I, pp. 253-256.

[2] *Contributions to the Theory of Natural Selection*, p. 47.

[3] So far as we shall be concerned with them throughout this treatise, the "Lamarckian factors" consist in the supposed transmission of acquired characters, whether the latter be due to the direct influence of external conditions of life on the one hand, or to the inherited effects of use and disuse on the other. For the phrase "inherited effects of use and disuse," I shall frequently employ the term "use-inheritance," which has been coined by Mr. Platt Ball as a more convenient expression.

[4] *Origin of Species*, 6th ed. p. 8.

[5] *Variation* &c. 2nd ed. ii. p. 280.

[6] *Variation* &c. ii. p. 367.

[7] *Origin of Species*, p. 176.

[8] This, to the best of my judgement, is the fairest extract that I can give of Mr. Wallace's most recently published opinions on the points in question. [In particular as regards (*a*) see *Darwinism* pp. 435-6.] But with regard to some of them, his expression of opinion is not always consistent, as we shall find in detail later on. Besides, I am here taking Mr. Wallace as representative of the Neo-Darwinian school, one or other prominent member of which has given emphatic expression to each of the above propositions.

[9] *Life and Letters*, vol. iii. pp. 72 and 75.

[10] Take, for example, the following, which is a fair epitome of the whole:—"I believe that this is the simplest mode of stating and explaining the law of variation; that some forms acquire something which their parents did not possess; and that those which acquire something additional have to pass through more numerous stages than their ancestors; and those which lose something pass through fewer stages than their ancestors; and these processes are expressed by the terms 'acceleration' and 'retardation'" (*Origin of the Fittest*, pp. 125, 226, and 297). Even if this be "the simplest mode of *stating* the law of variation," it obviously does nothing in the way of *explaining* the law.

[11] *Floral Structures* (Internat. Sc. Ser. lxiv. 1888): *The Making of Flowers* (Romance of Science Ser. 1891); and Linn. Soc. Papers 1893-4.

[12] "The law of correlation," and the "laws of growth," he does recognize; and shows that they furnish an explanation of the origin of many characters, which cannot be brought under "the law of utility."

[13] *Natural Selection and Tropical Nature*, p. 205; 1891.

[14] *Ibid.* pp. 197-8.

[15] For an excellent discussion on the ontogeny of the child in this connexion, see *Some Laws of Heredity*, by Mr. S. S. Buckman, pp. 290, *et seq.* (Proc. Cotteswold Nat. Field Club, vol. x. p. 3, 1892).

[16] *loc. cit.* p. 198.

[17] For a discussion of this remarkable case, see *Mental Evolution in Animals*, pp. 222-3. It appears to me that if Mr. Wallace's argument from the "latent capacities of the voice of Man" is good for anything, *a fortiori* it must be taken to prove that, in the case of the Parrot, "the organ has been prepared in anticipation" of the amusement which the cultivation of its latent capacities arouses in "civilized man."

[18] *Descent of Man*, 1st Ed. ch. xx. (Trans. Dev. Assoc. for Science, 1890).

[19] The late Prof. Moseley informed me that, during his voyage on the *Challenger*, he had seen many men whose backs were well covered with hair.—For an excellent discussion of the whole question, chiefly in the light of embryology, see the paper by Buckman already alluded to, pp. 280-289. Also, for an account of an extraordinary hairy race of men, see *Alone with the Hairy Ainu*, by A. H. Savage Landor, 1893.

[20] E.g. "The special faculties we have been discussing clearly point to the existence in man of something which he has not derived from his animal progenitors—something which we may best refer to as being of a spiritual essence or nature, capable of progressive development under favourable conditions. On the hypothesis of this spiritual nature, superadded to the animal nature of man, we are able to understand much that is otherwise mysterious or unintelligible in regard to him, especially the enormous influence of ideas, principles, and beliefs over his whole life and action. Thus alone can we understand the constancy of the martyr, the unselfishness of the philanthropist, the devotion of the patriot, the enthusiasm of the artist, and the resolute and persevering search of the scientific worker after nature's secrets. Thus we may perceive that the love of truth, the delight in beauty, the passion for justice, and the thrill of exultation with which we hear of any act of courageous self-sacrifice, are the workings within us of a higher nature which has not been developed by means of the struggle for material existence." (*Darwinism*, p. 474.) I have quoted this whole paragraph, because it is so inconsistent with the rest of

Mr. Wallace's system that a mere epitome of it might well have been suspected of error. Given an intellectual being, howsoever produced, and what is there "mysterious or unintelligible" in "the enormous influence of ideas, principles, and beliefs over his whole life and action"? Or again, if he be also a social being, what is the relevancy of adducing "the constancy of the martyr," "the unselfishness of the philanthropist," "the devotion of the patriot," "the love of truth," "the passion for justice," "the thrill of exultation when we hear of any act of courageous self-sacrifice," in evidence *against* the law of *utility*, or in order to prove that a "nature" thus endowed has "*not* been developed by means of the struggle for existence," when once this struggle has been transferred from individuals to communities? The whole passage reads like an ironical satire in favour of "Darwinism," rather than a serious argument against it.

[21] See *Proc. Zool. Soc.* June 4, 1889, for an account of the performances in this respect of the Chimpanzee "Sally." Also, for some remarks on the psychology of the subject, in *Mental Evolution in Man*, p. 215. I should like to take this opportunity of stating that, after the two publications above referred to, this animal's instruction was continued, and that, before her death, her "counting" extended as far as ten. That is to say, any number of straws asked for from one to ten would always be correctly given.

[22] In Prof. Lloyd Morgan's *Animal Life and Intelligence* there is an admirable discussion on this subject, which has been published since the above was written. The same has to be said of Weismann's Essay on Music, where much that I have here said is anticipated. With the views and arguments which Mr. Mivart has forcibly set forth I have already dealt to the best of my ability in a work on *Mental Evolution in Man*.

[23] *American Naturalist*, xxii. pp. 201-207.

[24] It is almost needless to say that besides the works mentioned in this chapter, many others have been added to the literature of Darwinism since Darwin's death. But as none of these profess to contain much that is original, I have not thought it necessary to consider any of them in this merely general review of the period in question. In subsequent chapters, however, allusions will be made to those among them which I deem of most importance.

[Since this note was written and printed the following works have been published to which it does not apply: *Animal Life and Intelligence*, by Professor Lloyd Morgan; *The Colours of Animals*, by Professor Poulton; and *Materials for the Study of Variation*, by Mr. Bateson. All these works are of high value and importance. Special reference should also be made to Professor Weismann's Essays.]

[25] Originally, Weismann's further assumption as to the perpetual stability of germ-plasm, "since the first origin of sexual reproduction," was another very important point of difference, but this has now been withdrawn.

[26] I say "*mainly* formed anew," and "*for the most part* interrupted," because even Darwin's theory does not, as is generally supposed, exclude the doctrine of Continuity *in toto*.

[27] *Theory of Heredity* (Journ. Anthrop. Inst. 1875, p. 346).

[28] Mr. Platt Ball has, indeed, argued that "use-inheritance would often be an evil," since, for example, "the condyle of the human jaw would become larger than the body of the jaw, because as the fulcrum of the lever it receives more pressure"; and similarly as regards many other hypothetical cases which he mentions. (*The Effects of Use and Disuse*, pp. 128-9 *et seq.*) But it is evident that this argument proves too much. For if the effects of use and disuse as transmitted to progeny would be an evil, it could only be because these effects as they occur in the parents are an evil—and this they most certainly are not, being, on the contrary and as a general rule, of a high order of adaptive value. Moreover, in the race, there is a superadded agency always at work, which must effectually prevent any undue accumulation of these effects—namely, natural selection, which every Darwinist accepts as a controlling principle of all or any other principles of change. Therefore, if, as first produced in the life-time of individuals, the effects of use and disuse are not injurious, much less can they become so if transmitted through the life-time of species. Again, Mr. Wallace argues that, even supposing use-inheritance to occur, its adapting work in the individual can never extend to the race, seeing that the natural selection of fortuitous variations in the directions required must always produce the adaptations *more quickly* than would be possible by use-inheritance. This argument, being one of more weight, will be dealt with in a future chapter.

[29] *Variation under Domestication*, ii. 392.

[30] In subsequent chapters, especially devoted to the question (i.e. Section II), the validity of this assumption will be considered on its own merits.

[31] I say "the followers of Weismann," because Weismann himself, with his clear perception of the requirements of experimental research, expressly states the above considerations, with the conclusions to which they lead. Nevertheless, he is not consistent in his utterances upon this matter; for he frequently expresses himself to the effect, "that the *onus probandi* rests with my opponents, and therefore they ought to bring forward actual proofs" (*Essays*, i. p. 390). But, as above shown, the *onus* rests as much with him as with his opponents; while, even if his opponents are right, he elsewhere

recognizes that they can bring "actual proofs" of the fact only as a result of experiments which must take many years to perform.

[32] Note A.

[33] For a fair and careful statement of the present balance of authoritative opinion upon the question, see H. F. Osborn, *American Naturalist*, 1892, pp. 537-67.

[34] [The above paragraph is allowed to remain exactly as Mr. Romanes left it. Chapters V and VI were however not completed. *See* note appended to Preface. C. Ll. M.

[35] See, especially, his excellent remarks on this point, *Contemp. Rev.* Sept. 1893.

[36] There is now an extensive literature within this region. The principal writers are Cope, Scott and Osborn. Unfortunately, however, the facts adduced are not crucial as test-cases between the rival theories—nearly all of them, in fact, being equally susceptible of explanation by either.

[37] For another and better illustration more recently published by Mr. Spencer, see *The Inadequacy of Natural Selection*, p. 22.

[38] *Essays on Heredity*, vol. i. p. 389.

[For further treatment of the subject under discussion *see* Weismann, *The All-sufficiency of Natural Selection* (Contemp. Rev. Sept. and Oct. 1893), and *The Effect of External Influences upon Development.* "Romanes Lecture" 1894, and Spencer, *Weismannism once more* (Cont. Rev. Oct. 1894). C. Ll. M.]

[39] *Variation*, &c., vol. ii. p. 206.

[40] E. g. *Origin of Species*, p. 178.

[41] *Darwinism*, p. 418.

[42] *Nature*, vol. xliii. pp. 410, 557; vol. xliv. pp. 7, 29. I say "adopted," because I had objected to his quoting the analogy of artificial selection, and stated, as above, that the only way to meet Mr. Spencer's "difficulty" was to deny the fact of co-adaptation as ever occurring in any case. It then appeared that Professor Meldola agreed with me as to this. But I do not yet understand why, if such were his view, he began by endorsing Mr. Wallace's analogy from artificial selection—i. e. confusing the case of co-adaptation with that of the blending of adaptations. If any one denies the fact of co-adaptation, he cannot assist his denial by arguing the totally different fact that adaptations may be blended by free intercrossing; for this latter fact has never been questioned, and has nothing to do with the one which he engaged in disputing.

[43] It may be said, with regard to this particular reflex, that it may perhaps be, so to speak, a mechanical accident, arising from the contiguity of the sensory and motor roots in the cord. But as this suggestion cannot apply to other reflexes presently to be adduced, it need not be considered.

[44] Of course it will be observed that the question is not with regard to the development of all the nerves and muscles concerned in this particular process. It is as to the development of the co-ordinating centres, which thus so delicately respond to the special stimuli furnished by variations of angle to the horizon. And it is as inconceivable in this case of reflex action, as it is in almost every other case of reflex action, that the highly specialized machinery required for performing the adaptive function can ever have had its origin in the performance of any other function. Indeed, a noticeable peculiarity of reflex mechanisms as a class is the highly specialized character of the functions which their highly organized structures subserve.

[45] We meet with a closely analogous reflex mechanism in brainless vertebrata of other kinds; but these do not furnish such good test cases, because the possibility of natural selection cannot be so efficiently attenuated. The perching of brainless birds, for instance, at once refers us to the roosting of sleeping birds, where the reflex mechanism concerned is clearly of high adaptive value. Therefore such a case is not available as a test, although the probability is that birds have inherited their balancing mechanisms from their sauropsidian ancestors, where it would have been of no such adaptive importance.

[46] *Pflüger's Archiv*, Bd. xx. s. 23 (1879).

[47] *Brain*, part xlviii, pp. 516-19 (1889).—There is still better proof of this in the case of certain rodents. For instance, observing that rats and mice are under the necessity of very frequently scratching themselves with their hind-feet, I tried the experiment of removing the latter from newly-born individuals—i.e. before the animals were able to co-ordinate their movements, and therefore before they had ever even attempted to scratch themselves. Notwithstanding that they were thus destitute of individual experience with regard to the benefit of scratching, they began their scratching movements with their stumps as soon as they were capable of executing co-ordinated movements, and afterwards continued to do so till the end of their lives with as much vigour and frequency as unmutilated animals. Although the stumps could not reach the seats of irritation which were bent towards them, they used to move rapidly in the air for a time sufficient to have given the itching part a good scratch, had the feet been present—after which the animals would resume their sundry other avocations with apparent satisfaction. These facts showed the hereditary response to irritation by parasites to be so strong, that even a whole life-

time's experience of its futility made no difference in the frequency or the vigour thereof.

[48] For details of his explanation of this particular case, for which I particularly inquired, see *Mental Evolution in Animals*, pp. 301-2.

[49] Note B.

[50] For fuller treatment see *Mental Evolution in Animals*, pp. 274-285, 378-379, 381-383.

[51] For an excellent essay on the deleterious character of early forms of religion from a biological point of view, see the Hon. Lady Welby, *An Apparent Paradox in Mental Evolution* (Journ. Anthrop. Inst. May 1891).

[52] *Essays*, i. p. 93.

[53] See *Mental Evolution in Animals*, pp. 377-8.

[54] [See H. Spencer, *The Inadequacy of Natural Selection, A Rejoinder to Professor Weismann*, Contemp. Rev. 1893; and *Weismannism once more*, Ibid. Oct. 1894; Weismann, *The All-sufficiency of Natural Selection*, Ibid. 1893; and *The Effect of External Influences upon Development*, "Romanes Lecture" 1894: also *Neuter Insects and Lamarckism*, W. Platt Ball, Natural Science, Feb. 1894, and *Neuter Insects and Darwinism*, J. T. Cunningham, Ibid. April 1894. C. Ll. M.]

[55] *Variation of Plants and Animals*, vol. ii. p. 289.

[56] *Ibid.* p. 346.

[57] *Essays*, i. p. 90.

[58] *Nature*, vol. ix. pp. 361-2, 440-1; and vol. x. p. 164.

[59] Appendix I.

[60] For a fuller statement of Mr. Galton's theory of Heredity, and its relation to Weismann's, see *An Examination of Weismannism*.

[61] For a fuller explanation of the important difference between the mere cessation and the actual reversal of selection, see Appendix I.

[62] *Animal Life*, International Scientific Series, vol. xxxi.

[63] The experiments of Galton and Weismann upon this subject are nugatory, as will be shown later on. But since the above was written an important research has been published by Mr. Cunningham, of the Marine Biological Association. For a full account I must refer the reader to his forthcoming paper in the *Philosophical Transactions*. The following is his own statement of the principal results:—

"A case which I have myself recently investigated experimentally seems to me to support very strongly the theory of the inheritance of acquired characters, I have shown that in normal flat-fishes, if the lower side be artificially exposed to light for a long time, pigmentation is developed on that side; but when the exposure is commenced while the specimens are still in process of metamorphosis, when pigment-cells are still present on the lower side, the action of light does not prevent the disappearance of these pigment-cells. They disappear as in individuals living under normal conditions, but after prolonged exposure pigment-cells reappear. The first fact proves that the disappearance of the pigment-cells from the lower side in the metamorphosis is an hereditary character, and not a change produced in each individual by the withdrawal of the lower side from the action of light. On the other hand, the experiments show that the absence of pigment-cells from the lower side throughout life is due to the fact that light does not act upon that side, for, when it is allowed to act, pigment-cells appear. It seems to me the only reasonable conclusion from these facts is, that the disappearance of pigment-cells was originally due to the absence of light, and that this change has now become hereditary. The pigment-cells produced by the action of light on the lower side are in all respects similar to those normally present on the upper side of the fish. If the disappearance of the pigment-cells were due entirely to a variation of the germ-plasm, no external influence could cause them to reappear, and, on the other hand, if there were no hereditary tendency, the colouration of the lower side of the flat-fish when exposed would be rapid and complete."—*Natural Science*, Oct. 1893.

[64] For Professor Weismann's statement of and discussion of these results see *Essays*, vol. i. p. 313.

[65] *Oesterreichische medicinische Jahrbücher*, 1875, 179.

[66] *Loc. cit.*

[67] *Essays*, vol. i. p. 315.

[68] *Les fonctions du Cerveau*, p. 102.

[69] *Essays*, vol. i. p. 82.

[70] As Weismann gives an excellent abstract of all the alleged facts up to date (*Essays*, vol. i. pp. 319-324), it is needless for me to supply another, further than that which I have already made from Brown-Séquard.

[71] *Examination of Weismannism*, p. 83.

[72] *Examination of Wiesmannism*, p. 93.

[73] *Ibid.* p. 153.

[74] *Origine des Plantes Domestiques, démontrée par la culture du Radis Sauvage* (Paris, 1869).

[75] *Journl. Agric. Soc.* 1848.

[76] *Rev. Gén. de Bot.* tom. ii. p. 64.

[77] I am indebted to the Rev. G. Henslow for the references to these cases. This and the passages which follow are quoted from his letters to me.

[78] *Gardener's Chronicle,* May 31, 1890, p. 677.

[79] Since the above was written Professor Weismann has advanced, in *The Germ-plasm,* a suggestion very similar to this. It is sufficient here to remark, that nearly all the facts and considerations which ensue in the present chapter are applicable to his suggestion, the essence of which is anticipated in the above paragraph.

[80] It also serves to show that Weismann's newer doctrine of similar "determinants" occurring both in the germ and in the somatic tissues is a doctrine which cannot be applied to rebut this evidence of the transmission of acquired characters in plants. Therefore even its hypothetical validity as applied by him to explain the seasonal variation of butterflies is rendered in a high degree dubious.

[81] [*See* note appended to Preface. C. Ll. M.]

[82] *Proc. R. S. 1871.*

[83] *Proc. R. S. 1890,* vol. xlviii. p. 457. It should be stated that the authors do not here concern themselves with any theory of heredity.

[84] *See* note appended to Preface. C. Ll. M.

[85] E.g. "The supposed transmission of this artificially produced disease (epilepsy) is the only definite instance which has been brought forward in support of the transmission of acquired characters."—*Essays,* p. 328.

[86] For a full treatment of Professor Huxley's views upon this subject, see Appendix II.

[87] Professor Huxley's views upon this matter are quoted *in extenso* in Appendix II.

[88] *Geographical Distribution of the Family Charadriidae,* p. 19.

[89] *Contributions to the Theory of Natural Selection,* p. 47 (1870); republished in 1892.

[90] *Origin of Species,* p. 70: italics mine.

[91] *Darwinism*, p. 137: italics mine.

[92] *Origin of Species*, p. 72: Mr. Wallace himself quotes this passage (*Darwinism*, p. 141); but says with regard to it "the important word 'all' is probably an oversight." In the Appendix (II), on Darwin's views touching the doctrine of utility I adduce a number of precisely equivalent passages, derived from all his different works on evolution, and *every one of them* presenting "the important word 'all.'"

[93] See Introductory Chapter, p. 20.

[94] *Darwinism*, p. 138.

[95] *Origin of Species*, p. 176: italics mine, as also in the following.

[96] *Var.* vol. ii. p. 250.

[97] *Variation*, &c. vol. i. pp. 78-79.

[98] *Darwinism*, pp. 139-40.

[99] Mr. Wallace deems the concluding words "rather confident." I was not, however, before aware that he extended his *a priori* views on utility to domesticated varieties which are bred for the slaughter-house. If he now means to indicate that these appendages are possibly due to natural selection, he is surely going very far to save his *a priori* dogma; and in the case next adduced will have to go further still.

[100] *Origin of Species*, pp. 122-3.

[101] *Darwinism*, p. 140.

[102] In the next paragraph Mr. Wallace says that the appendages in question "are apparently of the same nature as the 'sports' that arise in our domesticated productions, but which, as Mr. Darwin says, without the aid of selection would soon disappear." But I cannot find that Mr. Darwin has made any such statement: what he does say is, that whether or not a useless peculiarity will soon disappear without the aid of selection depends upon the nature of the causes which produce it. If these causes are of a merely transitory nature, the peculiarity will also be transitory; but if the causes be constant, so will be the result. Again, the point to be noticed about this "sport" is, that, unlike what is usually understood by a "sport," it affects a whole race or breed, is transmitted by sexual propagation, and has already attained so definite a size and structure, that it can only be reasonably accounted for by supposing the continued operation of *some constant* cause. This cause can scarcely be correlation of growth, since closely similar appendages are often seen in so different an animal as a goat. Here, also, they run in breeds or strains, are strongly inherited, and more "constant,"

as well as more "symmetrical" than they are in pigs. This, at all events, is the account I have received of them from goat-breeders in Switzerland.

[103] Darwin, *Variation*, &c., vol. i. pp. 92-4.

[104] *Ibid.* p. 94.

[105] Darwin, *Variation*, &c. vol. i. p. 94.

[106] Should it be objected that useless characters, according to my own view of the Cessation of Selection, ought to disappear, and therefore cannot be constant, the answer is evident. For, by hypothesis, it is only those useless characters which were at one time useful that disappear under this principle. Selection cannot cease unless it was previously present—i.e. save in cases where the now useless character was originally due to selection. Hence, in all cases where it was due to any other cause, the useless character will persist at least as long as its originating cause continues to operate. And even after the latter (whatever it may be) has ceased to operate, the useless character will but slowly degenerate, until the eventual failure of heredity causes it to disappear *in toto*—long before which time it may very well have become a genetic, or some higher, character.

[107] *Variation*, &c. vol. i. p. 340.

[108] *Variation*, &c. vol. ii. p. 271.

[109] Since the above paragraphs have been in type, the Rev. G. Henslow has published his Linnaean Society papers which are mentioned in the introductory chapter, and which deal in more detail with this subject, especially as regards the facies of desert floras.

[110] *Trans. Entom. Soc.* 1889, part i. p. 79 *et seq.*

[111] *Variation*, &c. vol. i. p. 40.

[112] *Variation*, &c. vol. i. p. 40.

[113] *Variation*, &c. vol. i. p. 120.

[114] See especially, Koch, *Die Raupen und Schmetterling der Wetterau*, and *Die Schmetterling des Südwestlichen Deutschlands*, whose very remarkable results of numerous and varied experiments are epitomized by Eimer, *Organic Evolution*, Eng. Trans. pp. 147-153; also Poulton, *Trans. Entom. Soc.* 1893.

[115] Mivart, *On Truth*, p. 378.

[116] Cockerell, *Nature*, vol. xli. p. 393.

[117] *Darwinism*, pp.[typo: period missing in scan] 296-7: italics mine.

[118] *Nature*, vol. xxxiii. p. 100.

[119] *Divergent Evolution through Cumulative Segregation*, Linn. Journ. Zoology, vol. xx. p. 215.

[120] *Habit and Intelligence*, p. 241.

[121] Allusion may here again be made to the case of the niata cattle. For here is a case where a very extreme variety is certainly not unstable, nor produced in varying proportions from the parent form. Moreover, as we have seen in the preceding chapter, this almost monstrous variety most probably originated as an individual sport—being afterwards maintained and multiplied for a time by artificial selection. Now, whether or not this was the case, we can very well see that it may have been. Hence it will serve to illustrate another possibility touching the origin and maintenance of useless specific characters. For what is to prevent an individual congenital variation of any kind (provided it be not harmful) from perpetuating itself as a "varietal," and eventually, should offspring become sufficiently numerous, a "specific character"? There is nothing to prevent this, save panmixia, or the presence of free intercrossing. But, as we shall see in the next division of this treatise, there are in nature many forms of isolation. Hence, as often as a small number of individuals may have experienced isolation in any of its forms, opportunity for perpetuation will have been given to any congenital variations which may happen to arise. Should any of these be pronounced variations, it would afterwards be ranked as a specific character. I do not myself think that this is the way in which indifferent specific characters *usually* originate. On the contrary, I believe that their origin is most frequently due to the influence of isolation on the average characters of the whole population, as briefly stated in the text. But here it seems worth while to notice this possibility of their occasionally arising as merely individual variations, afterwards perpetuated by any of the numerous isolating conditions which occur in nature. For, if this can be the case with a varietal form so extreme as to border on the monstrous, much more can it be so with such minute differences as frequently go to constitute specific distinctions. It is the business of species-makers to search out such distinctions, no matter how trivial, and to record them as "specific characters." Consequently, wherever in nature a congenital variation happens to arise, and to be perpetuated by the force of heredity alone under any of the numerous forms of isolation which occur in nature, there will be a case analogous to that of the niata cattle.

[122] It is almost needless to say that by a definition as "logical" is meant one which, while including all the differentiae of the thing defined, excludes any qualities which that thing may share in common with any other thing. But by definitions as "logically possible" I mean the number of separate definitions which admit of being correctly given of the same thing from different points of view. Thus, for instance, in the present case, since

the above has been in type the late M. Quatrefages' posthumous work on *Darwin et ses Précurseurs Français* has been published, and gives a long list of definitions of the term "species" which from time to time have been enunciated by as many naturalists of the highest standing as such (pp. 186-187). But while none of these twenty or more definitions is logical in the sense just defined, they all present one or other of the differentiae given by those in the text.

[123] Darwinism, p. 167.

[124] *Nature*, Dec. 12, 1889, p. 129.

[125] *Darwinism*, p. 77.

[126] *Darwinism*, p. 77.

[127] Pascoe, *The Darwinian Theory of the Origin of Species*, 1891, pp. 31-33, and 46.

[128] *Neuer Beitrag zum geologischen Beweis der Darwinischen Theorie*, 1873.

[129] *The Doctrine of Descent and Darwinism*, Eng. Trans. p. 102.

[130] *Origin of Species*, p. 175.

[131] *Ibid.* p. 176: italics mine.

[132] *Origin of Species*, p. 122.

[133] *A Manual of Dental Anatomy*, p. 455.

[134] It may be observed that this distinction was not propounded by Mr. Wallace—nor, so far as I am aware, by anybody else—until he joined issue with me on the subject of specific characters. Whether he has always held this important distinction between specific and generic characters, I know not; but, as originally enunciated, his doctrine of utility as universal was subject to no such limitation: it was stated unconditionally, as applying to all taxonomic divisions indifferently. The words have already been quoted on page 180; and, if the reader will turn to them, he may further observe that, prior to our discussion, Mr. Wallace made no allowance for the principle of correlation, which, as we have seen, furnishes so convenient a loop-hole of escape in cases where even the argument from our ignorance of possible utility appears absurd. In his latest work, however, he is much less sweeping in his statements. He limits his doctrine to the case of "specific characters" alone, and even with regard to them makes unlimited drafts upon the principle of correlation.

[135] *Darwinism*, p. 297.

[136] *Darwinism*, pp. 292-3.

[137] Since the above was written both Mr. Gulick and Professor Lloyd Morgan have independently noticed the contradiction.

[138] *Darwinism*, p. 302.

[139] *American Journal of Science*, Vol. XL. art. I. on *The Inconsistencies of Utilitarianism as the Exclusive Theory of Organic Evolution.*

[140] Vol. xli. p. 438.

[141] *Nature*, vol. xli. p. 486.

[142] *Ibid.* vol. xlii. p. 52.

[143] *Presidential Address to the Bristol Naturalists' Society*, 1891.

[144] *Presidential Address to the Bristol Naturalists' Society*, 1891.

[145] *A Theory of Heredity*, Journal of Anthropological Institute, 1875. Vol. v. p. 345.

[146] No one has supposed that the tendency need be "strong": it has only to be persistent.

[147] Of course it must be observed that degeneration of complexity involves also degeneration of size, so that a more correct statement of the case would be—Why, under the cessation of selection, does an organ of extreme complexity degenerate much more rapidly than one of much less complexity? For example, under domestication the brains of rabbits and ducks appear to have been reduced in some cases by as much as 50 per cent. (Darwin, and Sir J. Crichton Browne.) But if it is possible to attribute this effect—or part of it—to an artificial selection of stupid animals, I give in the text an example occurring under nature. Many other cases, however, might be given to show the general rule, that under cessation of selection complexity of structure degenerates more rapidly—and also more thoroughly—than size of it. This, of course, is what Mr. Galton and I should expect, seeing that the more complex a structure the greater are the number of points for deterioration to invade when the structure is no longer "protected by selection." (On the other hand, of course, this fact is opposed to the view that degeneration of useless structures below the "birth-mean" of the first generations, is exclusively due to the reversal of selection; for economy of growth, deleterious effect of weight, and so forth, ought to affect size of structure *much more* than complexity of it.) But I choose the above case, partly because Professor Lloyd Morgan has himself alluded to "the eyes of crustacea," and partly because Professor Ray Lankester has maintained that the loss of these eyes in dark caves is due to the reversal of selection, as distinguished from the cessation of it. In view of the above parenthesis it will be seen that the point is not of much

importance in the present connexion; but it appears to me that cessation of selection must here have had at least the larger share in the process of atrophy. For while the economy of nutrition ought to have removed the relatively large *foot-stalks* as rapidly as the *eyes*, I cannot see that there is any advantage, other than the economy of nutrition, to be gained by the rapid loss of hard-coated *eyes*, even though they have ceased to be of use.

[148] Since the above was written Professor Weismann has transferred this doctrine from the Protozoa to their ancestors.

[149] *Darwinism*, p. 131. He says:—"I have looked in vain in Mr. Darwin's works for any such acknowledgement" (i.e. "that a large proportion of specific distinctions must be conceded useless to the species presenting them").

[150] *Origin of Species*, p. 175. Italics mine.

[151] *Darwinism*, p. 132.

[152] *Darwinism*, p. 142.

[153] *Life and Letters*, vol. iii. p. 161.

[154] *Life and Letters*, vol. iii. p. 158.

[155] It must be observed that Darwin uses this word, not as Mr. Wallace always uses it (viz. as if correlation can only be with regard to adaptive characters), but in the wider sense that any change in one part of an organism—whether or not it happens to be an adaptive change—is apt to induce changes in other parts.

[156] *Origin of Species*, pp. 157-8.

[157] *Ibid.*

[158] *Origin of Species*, pp. 157-8.

[159] *Descent of Man*, p. 615.

[160] *Ibid.*

[161] *Descent of Man*, pp. 159-60.

[162] *Descent of Man*, p. 176.

[163] The passage to which these remarks apply is likewise quoted, in the same connexion as above, in my paper on *Physiological Selection*. In criticising that paper in *Nature* (vol. xxxix. p. 127), Mr. Thiselton Dyer says of my interpretation of this passage, "the obvious drift of this does not relate to specific differences, but to those which are characteristic of family." But in

making this remark Mr. Dyer could not have read the passage with sufficient care to note the points which I have now explained.

[164] *Origin of Species*, p. 171.

[165] *Ibid.* p. 421.

[166] *Origin of Species*, pp. 372-373.

[167] Mr. Thiselton Dyer in *Nature, loc. cit.*

[168] *Origin of Species*, p. 171.

[169] *Ibid.* p. 175.

[170] *Variation*, &c., vol. ii. p. 260.

[171] *Ibid.* vol. ii. p. 261.

[172] *Variation*, &c., vol. ii. p. 280.

[173] *Descent of Man*, pp. 473-4.